Newspapers and the Making

of Modern America

Newspapers and the Making of Modern America

A History

AURORA WALLACE

Greenwood Press
Westport, Connecticut · London

Library of Congress Cataloging-in-Publication Data

Wallace, Aurora.
  Newspapers and the making of modern America : a history / Aurora Wallace.
    p. cm.
  Includes bibliographical references and index.
  ISBN 0-313-32320-8 (alk. paper)
  1. American newspapers—History—20th century. 2. Journalism—Social
aspects—United States—History—20th century. I. Title.
  PN4867.W34 2005
  071'.3'0904—dc22   2005006712

British Library Cataloguing in Publication Data is available.

Library of Congress Catalog Card Number: 2005006712
ISBN: 0-313-32320-8

First published in 2005

Greenwood Press, 88 Post Road West, Westport CT 06881
An imprint of Greenwood Publishing Group, Inc.
www.greenwood.com

Printed in the United States of America

∞™

The paper used in this book complies with the
Permanent Paper Standard issued by the National
Information Standards Organization (Z39.48-1984).

10 9 8 7 6 5 4 3 2 1

Contents

Acknowledgments

The newspaper in the twentieth century is an elusive entity. Pages seem to overflow at newsstands every morning, and by the next day, tracking down a particular page can seem nearly impossible. Attempting to capture a century of such pages can be daunting indeed.

I am most grateful to those scholars whose labors in local libraries took place in time to commit this history to our public record, so that we have a sense of what is no longer available to us. This survey of American newspapers owes a great debt to the journalists, newspaper historians and urban scholars who provided its raw material. For omissions and oversights I take singular responsibility, but where detail illuminates or brings to life the daily workings of a paper perhaps long-forgotten, credit goes to my researchers, Jeremy Fenn-Smith, Devon Powers and Melissa Aronczyk. The students in the senior seminar "Newspapers and Twentieth Century America," which I taught at New York University in 2002 and 2003, took on projects that brought some fantastic newspaper stories to my attention. I am grateful also to the university for providing special funds for research and a semester of course-relief that enabled me to finish this project. Thanks go to the anonymous reviewer whose comments and challenges forced me to separate myth from fact. Eternal gratitude goes to my parents, from whom I got my love of newspapers in the first place.

Introduction

NEWSPAPERS AND THEIR CITIES, TOWNS, AND VILLAGES

The development of the press in America is a crucial part of the story of nation building, in which newspapers are cast as an indispensable tool of and for democracy. Over the nineteenth and twentieth centuries, newspapers have also become prosperous businesses in their own right as vehicles for entertainment, gossip, and commercial appeals and purveyors of sensationalized reports of the seamier side of human nature. Histories of American journalism have for the most part evaluated the degree to which newspapers have fulfilled the first function and judged the extent of the damage wrought by the second.

Theories of the press have held up contrasting metaphors of news either as reflective (or distorted) mirrors of world events or as biased agenda-setters engaged in a process of selection, editing, and shading. *Newspapers and the Making of Modern America* sees newspapers not only in relation to the world of reportable events, but also in the context of their built environments. While "media influence" is normally measured by the degree to which people are harmed by dangerous content, here this influence is shown determining and shaping the course of events in the process of place making. By investigating specific cases of newspapers in their communities, we can view the newspaper as a change agent in the construction and maintenance of community and as a prime mover in enacting policy, supporting development, building neighborhoods, and generally modifying the physical and built environment.

There is little news in the story that newspapers help to build community. Alexis de Tocqueville's observations of early newspapers in America found the press to be providing a forum for debate that facilitated the strengthening of bonds among community members and their many groups and associations, and this remains a useful lens through which to view the operations of local newspapers today.[1] Local newspapers are institutions that operate in order to support and maintain all other local organizations. And yet for all of their influence, their role has been described in these somewhat abstract terms, and has as a result remained invisible to the casual observer. We may notice a new hospital or school, better roads, railroads, airports, or bridges or the general improvement of a neighborhood without seeing a newspaper behind the change. The newspaper appears merely to report (or not) on a change instead of seeming a central actor. But when we view change through the lens of a newspaper and its owners, we can see that in the history of a place, there are central figures making decisions about how to go forward, and often those central figures are newspaper people. Newspapers often affect place directly through real estate and the manipulation of landscapes, but they also do it through less obvious efforts on behalf of community. The building of a hospital can be pointed to; the development of pride of place often cannot. Newspaper owners as citizens tend to play a greater role in making change. They are by definition more involved in activities in their communities, and they are often born joiners. They sit on chambers of commerce, hospital boards, and other community organizations. Over the twentieth century, newspaper owners have often run for public office. As a result of the efforts of newspapers, many local towns still follow the fortunes of local sports teams, beauty pageants, spelling bees, and educational scholarships. Campaigns to raise funds for local charities, disaster relief, and crime prevention are undertaken by newspapers, but their initiatives are often even more profound than this. Using the newspaper as a window into the twentieth century, we see how newspapers promoted the building of America's first postwar suburb; constructed a town where none had existed before; promoted development and new industry; built community awareness, cohesion and preservation; moved populations from one place to another; participated in campaigns both for and against slum clearance; and carved out communities within communities.

These efforts have not always been undertaken for the noblest of reasons. As often as not, it has been much in the newspaper's own interest, or more specifically in the interest of its owners, to follow such development plans. We may owe the shape of present day Miami, Long Island, or Los Angeles to former newspaper tycoons, but they did not escape profit or influence as a result. All newspapers have politics, and there are no politics without power and influence. Sometimes, the motivation was a combination of both power and support, as William Randolph Hearst once said: "I want our powerful newspapers to cooperate with other powers whenever that cooperation means most for the benefit of the community."[2] Nevertheless, newspapers have frequently campaigned on behalf of the less fortunate. This is seen no more strongly than in the black press and the alternative press, but a newspaper that does not support the growth of its local community cannot remain powerful for very long.

The story of American newspapers in the twentieth century is also one of decline, and as a result one of diminishing influence. In the 1920s, household newspaper penetration in the United States was higher than it would ever be again in the century. In the twentieth century Americans went from being a nation in which every household received an average of at least one newspaper to a nation where only half of all households did.[3] This decrease has taken place alongside many other changes in the industry, the results of which have continued to threaten the continued viability of the press as a primary source of information, to say nothing of its role as a community force. At the beginning of the century, before radio, cities like New York, teeming with new immigrants, produced more newspapers than anyone could read. Daily newspapers often had several editions per day, and it was common to read two or three different titles in one day. Newspapers survived the threat from radio by providing more comprehensive and analytical information, and by being transportable and—to use a modern term—hypertextual. Readers could pick up and leave off stories at their will, jump from page to page, and read stories out of order. Radio demanded more concentrated attention at set times and according to prearranged schedules.

Television may not have sounded the death knell of the newspaper either, but factors coincident with television certainly did. Greater mobility around the nation after World War II transplanted populations away from their hometowns and their hometown news. The automobile and mass transit made the move to the suburbs easier, leaving less time in the morning for commuters to read the newspaper. Newly congested highways made afternoon delivery to outlying areas difficult, and production schedules had to be pushed back so far that the resulting news could never hope to be current. In cities, high-rise buildings made delivery more challenging, as adult carriers tried to coordinate key access to many different buildings along their route. The competition from television also prompted newspapers to change their style; to be more like television with shorter, faster-paced, and more colorful news. These changes have been partly to blame for the loss of authority that newspapers have experienced over the century.

In an effort to survive all of these threats, newspapers began their retreat. Businesses that had been family owned, sometimes for over a century, began to sell out to increasingly large chains. Large newspaper groups were able to achieve economies of scale by buying many newspapers at a time, sharing content, clustering newspapers geographically, and closing down those that seemed redundant. In the process, the model of community leadership that had characterized newspapers in the first half of the century began to erode substantially in the second. When many newspaper companies went public in the 1960s and became beholden to shareholders rather than residents for their performance, profit margins increased and local coverage started to lose its power and influence.

This history of American newspapers tells the story of how newspapers from metropolitan dailies to rural weeklies have been influential in constructing the places where they operate. In so doing, this book traces the shift from newspapers that functioned as straightforward town boosters in support of local business at any cost to the more contemporary state of print journalism which champions the local in the abstract as it commits fewer and fewer resources to its service.

In this brief survey, we can see examples of newspapers and their relationship to their states (the *Des Moines Register*), their counties (the *Long Island Newsday*), their regions (the *Miami Herald* and the *Los Angeles Times*), their cities (the *New York Daily News*, the *New York Mirror*, and the *New York Daily Graphic*), their communities (the *Baltimore Afro-American*, the *Pittsburgh Courier*, and the *Chicago Defender*), their towns (the *Emporia Gazette,* the *Anniston Star*), their villages (the *Village Voice*, the *East Village Other*), and their nation (the *New York Times*, the *Wall Street Journal*, the *Washington Post*, and *USA Today*).

Chapter 1 begins with the urban tabloid in the 1920s, a loud, brash newcomer in the newspaper field, filled with photos, gossip, and scandal. The city that emerges out of New York's *Daily News*, *Daily Mirror,* and *Evening Graphic* is one of endless possibility, unpredictability, and opportunity. In the tabloid, the newspaper and the city show their common cause: they both seek to contain and display the endless variety of people, culture, and business.[4] They arrange chaos into meaningful sections and help the resident navigate it more easily. They provide a space for the best and the worst of humanity and celebrate the old while heralding the new. Through its crusades, scandalmongering, and over-reporting of crime, the urban tabloid kept new citizens of the city sated with dramatic details as it taught them the ways and means of their new environment. In building up urban culture, the tabloids created larger-than-life characters of the new milieu: the gangster, the reporter, the celebrity, the millionaire, the sports star, the hero, and, best of all, those famous for being famous. The tabloids of the 1920s taught a new lifestyle and a new language, filled with fast-paced slang that mirrored the rhythm of the new sounds of jazz.[5] They turned the city into a twenty-four-hour playground for some and a dangerous underworld for others, but for tab readers, it was the city itself that was first and foremost the news.

Chapter 2 retreats from the city at a time when many Americans had begun to suspect that city values were not the ones they chose to live by. During the 1930s, it seemed as though penance had to be paid for the heady excesses of the tabloid twenties, even for those who had never enjoyed it themselves. Following the stock market crash, droughts, and crop devastation, the country's farmers had their own agenda to put forward. In the pages of small-town papers like the *Emporia Gazette* in Kansas, this meant a reinvention of what it meant to be a good American: wholesome, family centered, and community oriented. Crime was downplayed, and the virtuous behavior of citizens was lauded. Errant citizens could expect to be chastised by seeing their name and address in print. Newspapers campaigned for the Good Roads Movement, farm relief, land conservation, and most of all for jobs. The small-town weekly of the 1930s was a morale booster, its pages filled with help, instruction, and advice for surviving the challenges of the decade.

In chapter 3, the mobilization for war at home and abroad is detailed through the black press. Through the efforts of a handful of industrious owners, we see a population that is moved north, mobilized, and assimilated. Again the newspapers act as a guide to initiate changes in language usage and the appropriation and invention of new symbols for freedom, democracy, and justice. Newspapers fought particularly hard on behalf of black soldiers in the military, crusading for more equitable treatment and advancement opportunities. These efforts culminated most notably in the Double V campaign that was supported by most in the black press, arguing for a second victory at home, an end to systematic racism as a reward for having served the nation in wartime. Through papers like the *Baltimore Afro-American*, the *Chicago Defender*, and the *Pittsburgh Courier*, a relentless campaign for housing, employment, and basic civic rights reshapes the landscape of northern industrial cities. Real social and economic change was brought about through the forceful efforts of the Clean Block and "don't buy where you can't work" campaigns, reallocating resources to where they were most needed and helping to make local economies self-sufficient. Nowhere do we see stronger advocates for rich cultural life, access to resources, and fairness of opportunity than in the pages of the black press.

At the other end of the spectrum were newspapers that campaigned to change the landscape, not only on behalf of their readers, but also on behalf of their owners. The *Los Angeles Times*, owned by the Chandler family, presents a case study of influence used to support the owners' other investments. Were the Chandlers not so diversified in their holdings—in land, oil, rubber, and marine and air technology—we might today have a very different Los Angeles. Certainly the sprawling city connected by freeways from end to end rather than by public transportation is a legacy of their own preferences for development. If newspapers and real estate are two sides of the same coin, it was never shown more clearly than in the *Los Angeles Times*, which developed one of America's first fully-fledged real estate sections in order to sell the many tracts of land that the Chandlers owned throughout the state.

On the East Coast, a similar remapping took place on Long Island, New York. When Alicia Patterson and Harry Guggenheim started *Newsday* in 1940, they did so in the hope that returning veterans would someday populate their county enough to provide a solid base of readers. Rather than wait for the exodus from the city to occur naturally, however, Patterson helped to build a place for them to live herself by promoting and supporting the development of America's first mass suburb in Levittown, New York. Thousands of young families flocked to Nassau County and became grateful and loyal readers of the newspaper. Helping set local council agendas, *Newsday* fought for new community colleges, better roads, and beachfront preservation.

In chapter 5, Floridian newspapers are shown to be a combination of big city tabloids via Chicago and small-town avoidance of bad news. Dependent on the fickle tourist economy, Florida has been vulnerable to wild land speculation and naturally disastrous weather. Daily newspapers in Miami and Tampa have done their parts to promote the former while doing their best to minimize the latter. Newspapers in Florida have been owned by some of the country's most enterprising entrepreneurs, place builders who left their mark not only with railroads and hotels but also with permanent additions to the landscape like man-made islands and shorelines. The rampant buying and selling of land, of both the valuable and swamp varieties, helped Florida newspapers achieve some of the highest numbers of advertising pages ever recorded.

Chapter 6 looks at the community newspaper, beginning with the *Village Voice*, from its early incarnation in New York as the "alternative" to the mainstream press. Such small and small-budget newspapers, which included such titles as the *East Village Other* and Chicago's *Seed*, helped to build communities within communities, forging new boundaries within already established cities. They helped to usher in a new language and new traditions. They were practical, instructional, and provided the necessary information for taking part in a new bohemian lifestyle. They were also participatory; writers were involved in new social movements and they reported on them as insiders. The separation between journalist and news was nonexistent, and the community that these papers constructed through their coverage was their own. This chapter follows what happens to the notion of the community newspaper when it is taken over by large chains of community newspapers, as happened in the 1990s with the company Community Newspaper Holdings Incorporated (CNHI). With little commitment to the local and funded through an Alabama state pension fund, CNHI is a startling bellwether for the future of newspapers in America.

In the final chapter, the nation as a whole is considered through the pages of what are now America's four national newspapers. Among them the oldest three, the *New York Times*, the *Wall Street Journal*, and the Washington *Post*, have done much to alter not only the physical landscape of their cities and the nation but the media landscape as well. By participating in precedent-setting cases for freedom of the press, the *Post* and the *Times* have changed the way that newspapers operate. The *Wall Street Journal*, long considered a specialist publication for the business reader, has proven its perspicacity in money issues, predicting what would become in the 1970s and 1980s the most important new focus of news at other papers. In the 1980s, the *Wall Street Journal* was responsible for setting the new economic agenda for the Reagan era by gradually showing greater support in its editorials for something that came to be known as supply-side economics. All of these papers have also led the shift toward lifestyle advertising: attracting affluent readers to luxury-goods advertising and defining an audience demographic that is neither local nor geographically determined. This shift is evident in new sections of the *New York Times* that have been designed to attract national advertisers of high-end brands: "Circuits," "Escapes," "House and Home," "Dining In/Out."

These trends are best illustrated in the youngest newspaper under consideration *USA Today*. Born out of one of the largest newspaper chains in the nation, Gannett's *USA Today* is the product of intense market research designed to attract a new category of reader. It is a daily almanac of news bites and snapshots from around the nation presented colorfully and graphically in the style of television and targeted to a broad demographic of readers on the go. At home in airports and hotel rooms around the world, the paper relentlessly constructs a singular nation, through polling, maps and charts. Now the largest circulation newspaper in the United States, *USA Today* is for all places and no place at the same time.

The selection of newspapers in this volume is not meant to be comprehensive. There are thousands of significant papers that operated in the twentieth century in America which each in their own way shaped the communities in which they operated. The papers presented here were chosen because they are particularly emblematic of their place and time, though they no doubt represent countless others that are not mentioned. The selection is also governed by the challenges faced by all modern newspaper historians: the disappearance of newspapers themselves. The daily and weekly chronicling of events that began with the regular publication of news in the 17th century has left us with more paper than can be adequately housed in existing archives. Fifty years ago, as Nicholson Baker reminds us, bound volumes of all the major newspapers in America were kept in libraries.[6] When they were deemed to be taking up too much space, libraries began to copy these pages onto microfilm and "pulp" (ie. throw away) the papers. In the process, we permanently lost the color, clarity and comprehensiveness of the originals. Now, as microfilm reels pile up, their future storage is in question. Archivists race against time with limited resources to decide what to save and what to throw away. For some papers this is more easily determined than for others. The *New York Times* has digitized its entire collection from 1851 onward, providing an invaluable resource and record of the last 150 years. Other lesser-known papers have not been as fortunate. When papers go out of business or are purchased by another company, the fate of their morgue is often uncertain. Several private companies have emerged to sell newspaper pages and reprints online as novelty items—to celebrate birthdays or help find ancestors—but these collections are incomplete and often expensive to access, making them too limited for scholarly use. The loss of the material newspaper page is a startlingly literal manifestation of the disappearance of the newspaper over the twentieth century. Not only are there fewer newspapers in existence than there were at the beginning of the century, those that have survived also face an ever declining readership. As content continues to be accessed online at increasing rates,[7] it is not difficult to imagine a future in which few people experience the thrill of opening up the pages of their local paper in the morning and seeing their community unfold before them.

Notes

1. Alexis de Tocqueville, *Democracy in America* (London: G. Dearborn & Co., 1838).

2. David Nasaw, *The Chief: The Life of William Randolph Hearst.* (New York: Houghton Mifflin, 2001), 318.

3. Philip Meyer, "The Influence Model and Newspaper Business," *Newspaper Research Journal* 25, no. 1 (2004): 66.

4. Gunther Barth, *City People: The Rise of Modern City Culture in Nineteenth Century America* (London: Oxford University Press, 1980).

5. Simon Michael Bessie, *Jazz Journalism: The Story of the Tabloid Newspapers* (New York: E.P. Dutton & Co. Inc., 1938).

6. Nicholson Baker, *Double Fold: Libraries and the Assault on Paper* (New York: Random House, 2001), 13.

7. David Asher, "Newspaper Executives Present to Wall Street," *Presstime* July/August (2004): 12.

1

TABLOIDS AND THE CITY

The *New York Daily News*, the *New York Daily Mirror*, and the *New York Evening Graphic*

The U.S. census of 1920 confirmed what many Americans had already begun to suspect in cities across the country: for the first time ever, there were more people living in cities than in rural areas. This shift toward urbanization was the central focus of an emerging new form of media, the big-city tabloid. The tabloid was the keen observer of a new society of sensational scandals, popular culture crazes, organized crime, spectator sports, skyscraper buildings, new immigration, and debates about sexual morality. In covering all of this, the tabloid not only reflected the new American city, it helped to construct it.

The *New York Daily News*

The first official tabloid in the United States was the *Illustrated Daily News*, which was started in New York in 1919 by Robert McCormick and Joseph Medill Patterson, two Chicago cousins who became intrigued with the idea of the tabloid format while in Europe during the war. The family had profited from their grandfather's contribution to the industrial revolution: the McCormick reaper, a labor-saving technology that aided in the harvesting process. The grandsons would reap the rewards of the revolution taking place in urbanity and the massive cultural shifts brought about by shorter working hours, public transportation, and improved image reproduction, all of which would influence the success of the tabloid format immensely.

McCormick and Patterson were consummate newspapermen, having been born into the newspaper family that had already achieved great success and notoriety at the *Chicago Tribune*. The cousins were also involved in many other pursuits aimed at improving the city.

McCormick worked as the president of the Sanitary District Board in the early part of the century, where he fought for better sewage systems and electric street lighting. At the age of twenty-four, Patterson was elected to the Illinois legislature, and he later became the Commissioner of Public Works, fighting against municipal corruption.[1] These early aspirations toward urban reform were part of the platform on which the new urban tabloid was based, and a deep concern for the changing shape of the city guided both of the cousins.

Increased literacy rates and a growing population of new immigrants in the twentieth century made for a fertile population of newspaper readers, but the turn toward the tabloid emphasized a different kind of reader experience. Though there were dozens of competing newspapers in New York, and Boston, Philadelphia, and Chicago all had their versions, the need for papers to differentiate themselves from older newspaper styles led to bold new experiments in content and form. The smaller size of the tabloid required less paper and was thus more economical for publishers, and from the readers' perspective it was well suited to being read on the buses, streetcars, and subways that many city inhabitants had begun taking to work. More than the size, however, it was the content of these new papers that set them apart from their broadsheet precursors. The dense columns of text found in the popular broadsheets like the *New York Times* were done away with in favor of large headlines and many, many pictures. Speedier delivery was easily accommodated by new presses, and transportation distribution systems were facilitated by new subway lines, trucks, and bridges. Now news could go from the street to the page in record time, and the pace of news production was stepped up significantly. The newspaper was becoming a more synchronized catalogue of city life, rather than an outdated report of past events.

After the tawdry and scandalous experiments in newsmaking that were the legacy of the yellow press barons Joseph Pulitzer and William Randolph Hearst, the leap to the tabloid was not so great as one might imagine. In fact, as a New Year's Day experiment in January 1901, Pulitzer's *World* was published as a tabloid with the help of tabloid entrepreneur Alfred Harmsworth (later Lord Northcliffe) from London.[2] The issue was shrugged off as a novelty, and Pulitzer himself was skeptical about an over-reliance on photographs in the newspaper, but the format would soon resurface and reinvigorate the industry. The first photograph to be reproduced in an American newspaper was actually a halftone of a shantytown printed in the *Daily Graphic* in 1880, but photographs were costly and inefficient for the presses of the day to accommodate. For the yellow press, scandals, entertainment, and celebrity journalism helped boost circulation[3] and close competition encouraged increasingly outrageous stunts of one-upmanship, but without the graphic capabilities of efficient and cost-effective photo reproduction, the sensationalism of the turn-of-the-century yellow press was largely limited to its purple prose and line drawings.

Appeals to journalistic objectivity did not have nearly the impact on circulation that stories about murder, lust, and scandal did, and the tabloids took full advantage of the seedier side of city life for story material. Even relatively innocuous cases were mined for their sensational potential, as happened during the Snyder-Gray case of 1927, a story that was given unprecedented attention on the front pages of the tabloids. On March 19, 1927, a Queens magazine editor named Albert Snyder was murdered in a plot by his wife, Ruth, and her lover Judd Gray. The case riveted readers as each step along the ill-conceived plan was recounted for the public. The clumsy efforts of the pair to get rid of the husband, including news of the "double indemnity" insurance policy Ruth had taken out on her husband's behalf, kept audiences glued to their newspapers. On January 12, 1928, Ruth Snyder was the first woman to be sent to death by electric chair. Although photographers were not allowed in to witness the execution, the *New York Daily News* coyly hired out-of-town photographer Tom Howard from the *Chicago Tribune* to attend the proceedings. With a camera hidden in his pant-leg, rigged with a shutter switch in his pocket, he surreptitiously snapped a photo right at the moment when the charge was sent through her body. An off-center, blurry, and tilted photo was later cropped and enlarged to produce perhaps the most famous front-page photograph ever published. The one-word headline accompanying the picture simply read, "DEAD"—in letters large enough to span the page. So lurid and captivating was the photo that it was reprinted by the *News* for several days after, despite calls from citizens that it was immoral and in bad taste. The *News* obeyed street sales rather than public outrage in solving the dilemma, however, noting that the first issue sold more than one million copies, breaking all previous circulation records. This one event helped to solidify the paper's reputation as "New York's Picture Paper."

The *Daily News* was as packed with photographs as the city was with people, so much so that the word *illustrated*, originally included in its title, was immediately redundant and dropped by 1920. A typical picture caption from the *News* details what many readers had themselves experienced: "Seven steamships carrying 7,000 people, including these steerage passengers aboard the *Conte Rosso*, arrive at Ellis Island after a race in fog and rain to be the first to land passengers on July 1, 1922, the start of a second fiscal year of sharply reduced immigration quotas." The city was teeming with new immigrants from all over the world, the majority of whom were not native English speakers. The newspaper was such an important tool in assimilating new

Americans to this country that the ability to read one was used as a test for citizenship. While the ethnic press was a significant force in this process, the English language tabloids made the new city considerably easier to navigate by the presence of so many pictures.

At its peak, the *News* had a small army of photographers on staff, including Arthur (Usher) Fellig, better known by his nickname Weegee, a freelancer with Acme Newspictures (later absorbed by the United Press International), who helped to define the paper's look with sharp black and white pictures of crime scenes, gangsters, and police detectives. The new German camera the Leica, developed in 1924, soon replaced the Speed Graphic as the camera of choice for tabloid photographers. The Leica was easier to use and could make use of available atmospheric light, resulting in haunting images with deep shadows of nighttime crime scenes. With this new technology, photographers like Fred Morgan, Pat Candido, Osmund Leviness, Ed Giorgrandino, Ken Korotkin, Robert Wyer, John Tresilian, Simon Nathan, Al Amy, and Bob Costello worked tirelessly to document the daily, but more often the nightly, events of the city. By 1930 these photographs accounted for 23 percent of the content of the *Daily News*.[4] In addition to the staff photographers, an increasing number of photo agencies emerged to service tabloids across the country, including Bain News Service and the National Photo Company. The country was becoming the most photographed in the world, and soon images of events, rather than written descriptions, would be the determining factor of newsworthiness.

News photographers listened to police scanners and often arrived at crime scenes before the police. By the 1930s photographers like Weegee were scouring the city in *Daily News* radio cars, chronicling the twenty-four-hour life cycle of the city. There were no bounds that they would not cross, often photographing suicide victims, bloody corpses, bodies in the morgue, and grief-stricken bystanders. The photographers had an understanding and symbiotic relationship with the city's police force, who helped, rather than hindered, the story getting to press. The police, reporters, and photographers often had similar backgrounds and had grown up in the same neighborhoods. Working together, they shared information and tips, and both groups seemed to share equally in the humbling of big-name gangsters and the social elite. It was the attention paid to regular people who became famous, or infamous, that attracted many of the *Daily News* readers.

The *Daily News* helped to elevate the common criminal to the level of celebrity, and was one of the first big city tabloids to participate in the construction of "public enemies."[5] As photographer Weegee wrote in his autobiography, *Weegee by Weegee*: "No racketeer on the FBI's list of the top 10 public enemies made the grade until he had been photographed by Weegee."[6] Previously anonymous hoodlums gained exposure and fame through tabloid photography and gripping stories of their exploits. The criminal was an important figure for the *Daily News*, which represented a certain level of class mobility among readers who were largely from the working class. In much of the *Daily News* photojournalism, criminals, gangsters, and police were pictured in or around large automobiles, a significant factor in the crime waves of the 1920s and 1930s, in which the getaway and the car chase were important elements. Automobile ownership in the 1920s was multiplying incrementally with the development of new affordable models from Ford, where by 1925 a new car was coming off the assembly line every ten seconds, and by the end of the decade one in five Americans owned a car and used it increasingly for vacationing and leisure pursuits.[7]

The United States experienced unprecedented growth and prosperity following the First World War. Production shifted to a surplus economy of consumer goods, and the market was inundated with new things to spend money on. As labor movements won important battles to regulate the number of hours per week that people spent on the job and the salaries in many industries improved, there was a dramatic shift in how people spent their time. With evenings and weekends free and more money to spend, new forms of entertainment and culture emerged, especially in big cities, to cater to this new leisure class.

The *News* chronicled an era of fame and luxury that many of its readers were unable to participate in, but this did not stop them from being enthralled with the glamour of the time. The benchmarks in design of the 1920s, art nouveau, art deco, and the fascination with all things Egyptian after the discovery of Tutankhamen's tomb, formed part of the aesthetic of the news. Young women were often photographed displaying Cleopatra haircuts, thick gold jewelry, and heavy makeup, and as a fashion register, the *News* kept pace with the look of the city and its inhabitants. Following the Art Deco Fair in Paris in July 1923, New Yorkers became enthralled with these new styles in furniture, architecture, and fashion. The new postwar luxury meant detailed depictions of wealth filled the pages to the delight of even less fortunate readers. Advertisers were now presenting the high-end goods of the new economy: automobiles, jewelry, perfumes, and crystal, each displayed with the greater realism that came with better image reproduction. Such wealth also promoted wider world travel, as citizens became not just socially but geographically mobile. Not only by car or by train, but increasingly airline travel was becoming more accessible to the general population, and stories of exotic locales encouraged more and more people to seek out new destinations.

Perhaps no story captured this new worldview as much as Charles Lindbergh's journey. His death-defying solo flight from New York to Paris in 1927 was heralded in all of the American papers, but it was the picture papers that brought his triumph to life. Though many were attempting the feat, and his claim to be first was contested, the Lone Eagle was made into an instant hero and was known around the world for his thirty-three-hour flight, helping to popularize the new age of aviation. It was a time for breaking records, and the flight had lucrative prize money attached to it, luring many such attempts. But Lindbergh's Scandinavian handsomeness, midwestern wholesomeness, and hearty athleticism made him a perfect poster boy to a nation looking for heroes. In a plane of his own design, the *Spirit of St. Louis*, Lindbergh was greeted in Paris by adoring crowds already well aware of his journey, and when he returned home, the former airmail pilot was greeted with enormous ticker-tape parades.

As with contemporary celebrities, Lindbergh's fame and assumed wealth later made him the target of blackmail schemes and the highly publicized kidnapping of his baby. Abducted from the family's home in rural New Jersey in 1932, Charley Lindbergh's kidnapping was quickly heralded as the "crime of the century." The kidnapper sent several ransom notes to the family, all from the New York area, demanding $50,000 for the infant's safe return. A date was set to collect the ransom at a location in the Bronx cemetery, but the baby was never returned. His remains were later found near the family's home, badly decomposed. Although no photographs of the body were ever published in the newspaper, they did circulate on the black market. The newspaper frenzy that ensued around the Lindbergh family home was widely assumed to have destroyed valuable crime scene evidence, and it was not until two years later that Bruno Hauptmann was brought to trial for the kidnapping and murder.

In the intervening period, newspapers became obsessed with the story, menacing the Lindbergh family and their friends for salacious details of the crime. More than two hundred journalists descended on the small town of Flemington, New Jersey, for the trial that began on January 2, 1935. Although the jury was ordered not to have any contact with the media, they could not help but pass by the enormous public gatherings around the courthouse each day, where they would see and hear newsboys shouting the headlines from each day's newspapers. Newsreels captured most of the trial, and footage of the testimonies showed in major theaters across the country. Radio reports kept the country up to date on every detail, and news journalists and photographers swarmed the courtroom. The jury returned the verdict that sent Hauptmann to the electric chair, and he was executed on April 3, 1936, without ever confessing to the crime. As a result of the mayhem

The press covering the Bruno Hauptmann case. April 1, 1936. Bettman/
CORBIS.

of this trial, reporters were banned from federal courts for the next
forty years.

Bruno Hauptmann was caught after having tried to use money
traced to the ransom exchange, and although all newspapers followed
the case closely, it was wealthy newspaper magnate William Randolph Hearst who engaged with the story directly by paying the legal
fees for Hauptmann's defense in exchange for exclusive rights to the
suspect's wife's story. The convention of "true crime" stories written
by victims, suspects, perpetrators, and bystanders had become one of
the central features of New York's competing tabloids.

Hearst's *Daily Mirror*

In an effort to capture some of the readership of the *Daily News*,
veteran newspaper owner William Randolph Hearst began a new tabloid in New York alongside his already successful *Morning American* and

Evening Journal. Hearst was late in giving in to the tabloid craze, and only started his own after efforts to buy out the *Daily News* had failed. By the early 1920s Hearst's newspaper empire was already sizable, with papers in Baltimore, San Francisco, and Seattle. In New York, however, competition was much stiffer. By the time his *Daily Mirror* was launched in 1924, most New Yorkers were already loyal followers of the *Daily News,* which had reached a daily circulation of 750,000.

Hearst had been in the newspaper business since 1887 when, at the age of 23, he took over his father's troubled *San Francisco Examiner,* the paper that would become the flagship of the influential Hearst chain. Hearst, like any serious newspaperman, wanted influence in New York, and in 1895 he bought the *New York Morning American,* adding an evening edition, *The Journal,* the following year. It was from these increasingly influential papers that Hearst would make his name engineering some of the nineteenth century's most notorious campaigns, foremost among which was his coverage leading up to the Spanish American War. Through inventive use of hyperbole and manufactured stories, Hearst helped to rally support for U.S. intervention into the conflicts in Cuba, though he did not, as is often claimed, incite the war.

As a newspaper owner, Hearst initiated many such campaigns, often putting himself and his papers at the center of the stories he covered. As he wrote to Arthur Brisbane, "If we don't improve the schools in New York we don't deserve to publish successful papers there. There is nothing in just getting circulation if we don't do anything with it."[8] Hearst also sought other forms of influence beyond running a newspaper, and was elected to Congress as a Democrat in New York in 1903 and 1905. In the intervening year, he ran an unsuccessful campaign for President, followed by an unsuccessful run for governor of New York State. Having failed as a democratically elected politician, Hearst concentrated his efforts in the media, and continued the expansion of his empire of influence.

Although he was generally contemptuous of tabloids for not allowing enough space for news and editorials, his papers were losing circulation to the *Daily News.* Hearst experimented with the tabloid format in Boston, where he owned the *Boston American,* the *Daily Advertiser,* and the *Afternoon Record.* He would soon become one of the fathers of media convergence, buying or starting operations in magazines, including *Cosmopolitan, Good Housekeeping,* and *Harper's Bazaar,* along with radio stations, newsreel companies, and the International News Service, one of the three major wire services of the time along with Associated Press and United Press International. By 1922 nearly three million American homes had radio receivers tuned to musical programs, dramas, and sports reporting.[9] In the early 1930s, recognizing the power of radio and the threat that the medium posed to news-papers for timely reporting of events, Hearst bought the radio station owned by Gimbel's Department Store, WGBS, in New York. The station was renamed WINS after Hearst's International News Service. Radio was used in conjunction with newspapers, with many papers buying their own stations, and with others merely buying airtime as sponsors. Newspapers would print the schedules of radio shows, and the radio would be used to broadcast news from the papers. Hearst was eager to use radio to promote his newspapers, although he was more successful in this endeavor on the West Coast than in New York. Sports broad-casting was one of the ways that the two forms of media worked to cross-promote each other, ensuring a solid base of male readers, and the abundance of department store advertising surrounded by advice for the lovelorn was successful in attracting female readers.

From 1926 to 1928, a battle for headlines and circulation escalated among the tabloids, and for this reason, 1927 stands out as a year of unprecedented activity of a distinctly tabloid nature. The Lindbergh flight, the Snyder-Gray scandal, and the otherwise innocuous Hall-Mills case all generated disproportionate coverage and kept city readers sated with juicy details. The September 1922 double murder of a local church minister, Reverend Edward Wheeler Hall, and the church choir's leader, Mrs. James Mills in New Brunswick, New Jersey, did not lead to an indictment when it first went to the grand jury in 1922. The case could have easily ended there, had it not been for the efforts of the *Daily Mirror*'s managing editor Phillip Payne, who re-opened the case after a long search for new evidence to resuscitate the story for news copy. The trial was covered by, among others, noted Hearst sports writer Damon Runyon, who chronicled each day's courtroom proceedings with an eye to the comedy of characters.

The trial began in November 1926, in Somerville, New Jersey, as *The People v. Mrs. Frances Stevens Hall, William Stevens, and Henry Stevens*, the wife of the Reverend Hall and two of her brothers. A cousin of hers was charged separately later, on the theory that the group of Stevenses shot the rector and his assumed lover, the choir leader. The crucial testimony was given by Mrs. Jane Gibson, known to newspaper readers as "the pig woman," presumably named for her occupation as a pig farmer, who was allegedly present the night of the murder "while riding her mule in search of corn thieves."[10] Gibson achieved infamy for having been "on her death bed" in the hospital at the time of the trial, requiring that she be wheeled in on a metal stretcher to testify. The defense tried to keep her out of the courtroom by pleading her frail condition, and the court deliberated at great length about moving the judge and jury to the hospital. Her testi-mony, along with that of many others who played minor parts in the drama, was ultimately unsuccessful in convincing the jury of the guilt of the Stevens clan, and no one was ever convicted.

The lengthy trial was covered by reporters and laypeople alike, including the husband of one of the deceased—Mr. James Mills. Journalists filed more than five million words of copy from Somerville in the first eleven days of proceedings.[11] Damon Runyon, whose column "The Brighter Side" was syndicated throughout the Hearst newspaper chain by King Features and the International News Service, had gained a following by reporting on the Snyder-Gray trial and on major sporting events. Trials and sporting events, two of the main preoccupations of the 1920s, had much in common, according to Runyon. As spectator events, they each contained the same kind of frenzied drama, speculation, wagering, and a loyal fan base.[12] At the Hall-Mills trial, he noted that the "telegraph switchboard used for the Dempsey-Tunney fight ha[d] been installed in the court house and forty-seven telegraph instruments ha[d] been hooked up. An enterprising radio outfit w[ould] unofficially broadcast the proceedings, play by play."[13] For him, the job of reporting sports and murder trials was essentially the same: "the trial is a sort of game, the players on the side of the attorneys for the defense, and on the other the attorneys for the State. The defendant figures mainly as the prize. The instrument of play is the law—it is the ball, so to speak."[14] This casual attitude toward the spectatorship of both events was evidently shared by his readers, who were likely to find asides about murder cases in his sports columns and vice versa. It was clear that baseball was not the only great American pastime of the 1920s, nor even boxing. As Runyon himself noted, "there are about as many newspapermen at a big murder trial as ever covered a heavyweight championship fight or a world's series—perhaps four hundred of them, counting the telegraph operators."[15]

The masthead touted the *Daily Mirror* as "New York's Best Picture Newspaper," and headers on each page reminded readers: "DOLLARS for PICTURES, TIPS—Phone Beekman 56000." While some of the content of the news was derived from readers, an even larger share came from news events that were masterminded by Hearst himself. One of the early proponents of "checkbook journalism," Hearst paid for stories of varying types. He paid to publish the inside stories of Rudolph Valentino, Jack Dempsey, Gene Tunney, and others. He published letters by politicians and heads of state, and he offered money to famous people from all walks of life to write for his newspapers, including, among others, Adolf Hitler and Benito Mussolini.[16]

Having unlimited funds to pay news subjects for their stories was a distinct advantage for Hearst, notably during one of the other biggest tabloid stories of 1927, the "Daddy and Peaches" saga. Edward West

Browning (Daddy) was a 52-year-old millionaire with a penchant for young girls. Advertising his predilection in the local papers led him first to a young woman who later turned out to be too old for him, at age 21. He was soon matched up with 15-year-old Frances Belle Heenan (Peaches), whose mother was eager to cash in on Browning's millions. After a quick engagement and marriage, Peaches was offered the chance to report on her daily married life with Daddy in Hearst's paper, and so began the daily soap opera of their lives together that kept readers returning to newsstands for each installment.

After a short-lived marriage, Peaches maintained her fame by suing Daddy for separation, citing mental anguish from his sexually perverse behavior. The trial in White Plains, New York, was a circus of suits and countersuits, with a colorful supporting cast that included "the Sheik," a young Valentino look-alike paid by Browning to claim that Frances had not been "pure" at the time of the engagement. The *Mirror* re-baptized Daddy "Bozo Bunny Browning," and illustrated stories about the court-room drama with photos of a bunny sporting hand drawn human features. They also gave him the moniker "Gander," running pictures of a goose—the result of a tabloid stunt in which he was given a real goose to carry around with him. The bunny and the goose were pictured on the front page of the *Mirror* frequently, as on February 3, 1927, when a rabbit, a goose, and a can of peaches took up the entire page under the cartoon headline: "Bunny's Tale." The caption below the images read: "Bozo bunny tries to can his peaches in story on stand," which started a comic strip by Walt Desmond called "IMA GANDER"—just one of the many ways the tabloids were able to extend the life of a story throughout its pages.

Once the trial was over, and the judge ruled in Browning's favor, without an alimony settlement, Peaches was subjected to constant lampoonery. Her character was continually maligned in characteristically tabloid vitriol. A typical *Mirror* story read:

> All the mud pies in the Peaches Bunny menu are not being baked in New York. Columbus, Ohio, hometown of the Heenan peach that turned out to be a lemon after Daddy Browning plucked it, has started a mud pie orgy all its own.[17]

When Peaches sought refuge on a cruise ship with her mother, newspapermen trailed her on the journey and reported on an illicit affair with a sailor that took place on-board the ship. Even off the coast of America, the teenager continued to be a source of interest throughout the year. The decision to send a reporter on such a journey was a common one at this time, and such dispatches made the separation between news and publicity stunts difficult to see, as did the number of "news" photographs of Peaches taken in the offices of the *Daily Mirror*.

Another of Hearst's publicity stunts that year aimed to capitalize on the public's fascination with air travel that had begun with Lindbergh. A nonstop flight from New York to Rome by the *Mirror's* managing editor Phillip Payne was to promote Hearst's papers and his airplane, "Old Glory." At the last minute Hearst became concerned that the stunt might be too risky, and warned Payne against it. True to Hearst's intuition, the plane crashed in September 1927 off the coast of Newfoundland, Canada, and no bodies were ever recovered. Hearst, embarrassed by the hubris of the stunt, published his warnings to Payne in the *Mirror*.[18]

In 1933, Hearst sent around a memo that would direct the editorial policy for his newspapers. It captured the essence of urban tabloid journalism:

1. Make a paper for the nicest kind of people for the great middle class. Don't print a lot of dull stuff that people are supposed to like and don't.
2. Omit things that will offend nice people. Avoid coarseness and a low tone. The most sensational news can be told if told properly.
3. Make your headlines clear and concise statements of interesting acts. They should answer the question: What is the news? Don't allow copyreaders to write headlines that are too smart or clever to be intelligible.
4. The front page is your forum. Put important items and personal news about well-known people there. Sometimes condense a big story to go on the first page rather than run it longer inside the paper.
5. Nothing is more wearisome than mere words. Have our people tell stories briefly and pointedly. Let people get the facts easily. Don't make them work at it.
6. Please instruct copyreaders to rewrite long sentences into several short ones. And please try to educate the reporters to write short sentences in the first place.
7. Photographs of interesting events with explanatory diagrams are valuable. Make every picture worth its space.
8. If you cannot show conclusively your own paper's superiority, you may be sure the public will never discover it.[19]

This policy notwithstanding, the Hearst chain was more successful as a result of its sheer size than for the quality of its writing. Hearst was always in a powerful position to force papers to sell to him by threatening to start a competitor, arranging advertiser boycotts, and other tactics of monopolization. During the Daddy and Peaches saga, *Mirror* deliverymen hijacked batches of the *Evening Graphic* and threw them into the East River.[20] In the tabloid arena, however, the *Mirror* was often bested by the higher-quality *Daily News*, and out-scandalized by the *Evening Graphic*.

Macfadden's *Evening Graphic*

On September 15, 1924, the most outrageous and perhaps consequently the shortest-lived tabloid in New York emerged. Bernarr Macfadden, a former bodybuilder and promoter of physical culture, started the *New York Evening Graphic*. As the publisher of *Physical Culture, True Confessions,* and *True Story* magazines, the millionaire Macfadden already had an inside track on the kind of celebrity gossip and Hollywood scandalmongering that was keeping other tabloids afloat. Macfadden vowed to publish "the truth," and indeed the words "Nothing But the Truth" were emblazoned on the front page of the *Graphic* every day. For him, the truth was akin to the naked truth, and through liberal use of photographs Macfadden intended to reveal, if not the naked truth of the city, then certainly that of some of its inhabitants.

Like Hearst, Macfadden was a one-man media empire, fusing interests in magazines, movies, radio, and all manner of popular culture, particularly those which celebrated the human form, like beauty pageants. He espoused transformation and social mobility through careful attention to self-presentation, a philosophy well suited to an increasingly image-based society. It was a time ideally suited to Macfadden's message; the nation was obsessed with the surface glamour of celebrities and believed that personality, charm, and good looks would triumph over strength of character on the road to success. Fan magazines contained beauty secrets of the stars and held out the promise of discovery that might pluck anyone from obscurity. In the absence of community bonds and traditional social networks, personal appearance was paramount, and advertising capitalized on the desire to remake oneself into something new. Advertisers concocted new product solutions to newly invented problems, and held out the promise of social mobility and success through proper consumption. The rhetoric of prosperity convinced people that looking rich was the same as being rich. For those unable to participate fully in the culture of luxury goods, the installment plan allowed people to "buy now and pay later" for lifestyles they could not afford.

Writing on the many factors that influenced consumption in the early decades of the twentieth century, Charles Wyand found color and illustration, along with novelty, to be of primary importance, a strategy employed unsparingly in the city's tabloids:

> The effectiveness of illustration in gaining and holding attention is every day apparent in the tremendous sale of tabloid newspapers. Word pictures are not nearly so vivid nor so readily transmitted as are those graphically presented. Moreover a dozen complex concepts can be presented pictorially in the time it takes to verbally outline one. This is an important advantage where attention must be fixed and the appeal made in the shortest time possible.[21]

Newspaper entrepreneurs, with their command of graphics and with willing advertisers at their mercy, were in a good position to capitalize on this new economy of consumption. Macfadden hired Emile Gauvreau from the *Hartford Courant* to be his editor in chief, hoping perhaps that the *Courant*'s respectability could be achieved at the *Graphic*. It was not to be, however, and the *Graphic* was made even more marginal by its excesses, at least to Gauvreau, who left the *Graphic* to work at Hearst's *Mirror* after Phillip Payne was killed in his publicity stunt plane crash.[22]

As ill reputed as the *Graphic* was to those in the newspaper industry, it was the launching pad for the careers of many seeking fame in entertainment. The *Graphic* gave Ed Sullivan his first newspaper job and was where the vaudevillian Walter Winchell first appeared. Winchell's column, "Your Broadway and Mine," was a cornerstone of 1920s popular culture. He wrote using his own insider jargon about the rarified world of the stage to a fashionable in-crowd who understood his new "slanguage," made up of phrases coined to describe the new condition of urban life. New couples were "that way" about each other, and expectant parents were "blessed." Prohibition spawned new disguise words for drinks and drinking, and in Winchell's words, flappers downed "giggle-water" in "hush-houses," or speakeasies.[23] Winchell's mix of folk gossip and fast-paced nightclub drama made the big city seem both smaller and more strange at the same time, but it was central in helping to convey the mores of urban cosmopolitanism to a loyal following of readers.[24] Being "in the know" by the standards set by Winchell's column was one of the ways in which city people were able to distinguish themselves from outsiders.

News copy at the *Graphic* often consisted of first person tell-alls written by staff reporters who ghostwrote the inner thoughts, dreams, and desires of well-known people, and signed their names at the end. These fictionalized accounts, attributed to real people in the news, were of a most sensational nature, with the kind of headlines now common

Walter Winchell next to the Daily Mirror Radio Car. Winchell was a columnist with the *New York Daily Mirror* from 1929–1963. Bettman/CORBIS.

in supermarket tabloids: "I Know Who Killed My Brother," "He Beat Me—I Love Him," and "For 36 Hours I Lived Another Woman's Love Life." The word "love" was used as a prefix whenever possible to form "love-nest," "love-pact," "love-child," "love-cheat," "love-sick," "love-crazy," "love-thief."[25] McFadden enlisted readers in the production of the news by promising them the opportunity to write stories. Like the *Daily News*, which solicited tips and photos, the picture tabloids created a sense that the inhabitants of the city were not just the subjects of the paper, but also its authors. This involvement went a great distance to bridge the gap between the news and its readers and was aided by the constant barrage of contests that filled the pages of tabloids. The *Graphic* asked readers to compete in celebrity look-alike contests and offered cash prizes and film screen tryouts for features such as "Embarrassing Moments," "Stingiest Persons," and "Cutest Sayings."[26]

Whereas the *Daily News* and the *Daily Mirror* worked to outpace and scoop each other in the news departments, the strategy of the *Graphic* went well beyond the usual limits of tabloid journalism. Macfadden

borrowed from the production techniques of his magazines in illustrat-
ing, manufacturing, and coloring the news for his paper. While Winchell
bent the language to serve his ends, the art department was similarly
inventive. The paper became famous for the "composograph," in which
two photographs were blended together to make two people appear together, or even to morph two people into one. Through photographic
trickery, Macfadden could illustrate impossible and implausible scenar-
ios, including operating room scenes, behind-closed-doors episodes, and
entirely fabricated situations. News photographs were often staged in
a studio for a feature called "Graphic Photo Drama from Life."[27] Com-
posographs showed Daddy and Peaches in their boudoir, and on St.
Patrick's Day in 1927 the *Graphic*'s art department designed a mock-up of
Rudolph Valentino and Enrico Caruso, both dead, meeting in the af-
terlife.[28] Using similar methods of art and photographic manipulation,
Graphic readers had already been given a glimpse into Valentino's body
cavity during surgery.

Macfadden's obsession with the body showed itself in numerous ways
throughout his newspaper. There were, indeed, many graphic treatments, but news copy most often exalted the virtues of healthy living.
Macfadden was strictly anti-drug, anti-medicine, and anti-doctor, preferring to expound on healthy diets instead. He was ahead of his time in
denouncing cigarettes and tobacco as dangerous, and he showed the ill
effects of too much sugar. Alongside his newspapers and magazines, he
published book titles such as *The Truth About Tobacco, The Miracle of Milk,*
and *Home Health Manual.*[29] Another of his personal issues that became
common fodder for the paper was his stance against corporal punish-
ment. He was constantly in search of photos that documented execu-
tions, and when none were forthcoming he would stage his own,
sometimes using his own staff in faked hangings. One photo of an
execution carried the unappetizing headline "Roasted Alive."

Women were photographed to the full extent of nudity allowable,
with common contrivances supplied for their compromising positions,
including bubble baths, bathing suit pageants, or dresses torn as the
result of some victimization. The *Graphic* did not yet exist when the first
"bathing beauty pageant" was held in 1921 in Atlantic City, but it would
be instrumental in detailing this event when it became known as the
Miss America Pageant. The swimsuit craze of the 1920s, orchestrated by
the introduction of the Jantzen company's one-piece bathing suit, and
the new pastime of recreational swimming, normalized the appearance
of women's bodies in form-fitting elastic costumes.

In 1925 the *Graphic* illustrated the courtroom scene of the Rhinelander annulment suit, in which a husband sued his wife for mis-
representing her race before getting married, with a faked photo of the
bride nearly nude in front of the judge and jury.[30] Such stunts earned

the paper the nickname "the *Pornographic*" and even "the *Fornographic*" by critics. Macfadden was not only indulging his own beliefs about the worship of the human form, but also testing the bounds of a new sexual morality that accompanied a perceived shift in women's roles from the guardians of public morality to the harbingers of sexual misconduct. Shorter hemlines, bootlegged alcohol and the culture of speakeasies, and the popularization of Freudian psychology freed sexuality from the confines of marital procreation and ushered in an era of debates and panic about urban sexuality that made for tantalizing tabloid headlines.

All of this resulted in what Oswald Garrison Villard called "gutter journalism." New York publicist Aben Kandel complained the new media reduced "the highest ideals of the newspaper to the process of fastening a camera lens to every boudoir keyhole."[31] Journalist Samuel T. Moore, writing in the *Independent* in 1926, said that "in some cities these publications are edited with decency and constitute merely an interesting experiment in American journalism. In Manhattan they are an unholy blot on the fourth estate—bawdy, inane and contemptible."[32]

This contempt was felt most strongly for the *Graphic*, whose circulation reached six hundred thousand but which was never attractive to mainstream advertisers, who feared that the content would alienate potential customers. The *Graphic* was left to be supported by fringe health, diet, and beauty aids, those industries that McFadden himself supported, and which all promised fast and easy methods of transforming bodies into perfect specimens of physical culture. While some claimed that this freedom from mainstream advertisers gave the paper greater editorial control, others saw it as finding virtue in circumstance. The *Evening Graphic* folded, after losing millions, in 1932, and leaves behind little trace, as no library in its day or after would carry it.

If the *Evening Graphic* leaves little legacy, this is not so for tabloids in general. Cumulatively, the picture papers were as responsible for constructing the cities they were in as they were for documenting it. People came to see urban America in a whole new way as a result of their efforts. The heyday of the twenties came alive through these pages, through epic court battles both silly and serious, and through the dramatic victories and rigors of the leading sports figures of the day, like Babe Ruth, Shoeless Joe Jackson, Gene Tunney, and Jack Dempsey. For the first time news reporters themselves became public figures too: Runyon, Winchell, and others were men about town, and they were as much participants of the new culture as they were its documenters. In jazz journalism the new rhythm of the city was encapsulated, and it was faster, more upbeat, and more exciting than what had gone before. The high-flying escapades of Lindbergh were matched by the low-down, dirty crime waves that accompanied Prohibition, speakeasies, bathtub gin, and gangsters with automatic weapons and getaway cars.

If we have a mental picture of this time in our heads, it is largely due to the efforts of the big-city tabloids, which chronicled the heady action in a blitz of photographs and then went on to influence its main competitor in the visual image industry, motion pictures. So overlapping were these two realms that their boundaries became difficult to distinguish, as increasing numbers of journalists brought their stories and experiences to the big screen. Not only did the crime news of the day make for intriguing screenplays, as happened when the Ruth Snyder story was used as inspiration for the plot of the 1944 Billy Wilder film *Double Indemnity*, but reporters and photographers were themselves often wooed by Hollywood to add to their facts to the fiction industry. Louis Weitzenkorn left the *Evening Graphic* to make crime films in Hollywood and wrote about his newspaper days in *Five Star Final*, a play that was later adapted for film. This play would not receive nearly the acclaim of *The Front Page*. Written by Chicago newspapermen Ben Hecht and Charles MacArthur, *The Front Page* was remade as a film several times, including as *His Girl Friday* in 1940. Sam Fuller, a crime reporter at the *Graphic*, would also become better known for his crime films, *Pick-Up on South Street* (1953), *The Crimson Kimono* (1959), *Underworld U.S.A.* (1961), and *The Naked Kiss* (1964), and for his account of the Hearst-Pulitzer rivalry, *Park Row* (1952).

Veteran photographer Weegee also turned his attention to Hollywood, both appearing in and producing several films. His tabloid style brought him to the film *Naked City* as a consultant in 1947–1948. Damon Runyon became a producer and writer in Hollywood at RKO and Twentieth Century Fox, where many of his newspaper and magazine stories were turned into films such as *Little Miss Marker* (1934), *The Big Street* (1942), and *Guys and Dolls* (1955). Borrowing from each other, the tabloid and the burgeoning film industry provided a gritty visual image of the city that was often even darker and more dangerous than the cities they were representing. During the height of film noir, filmmakers conspired with the newspaper to create a vision of modern times in which stories went from the newsstand to the screen, and stories "torn from the headlines" were the rage.

With these industries working in concert, and with the developing magazine and advertising industries alongside, it is hard to overestimate the significance of the tabloid in shaping our perception of the 1920s and the city. But not everyone was in favor of this approach to news coverage, most notably those living outside the city, the dwindling but nevertheless substantial minority of the population still living in rural areas. Perhaps in response to the Great Depression or as a backlash to the corruption and crime found in big cities, the 1930s were marked by an important shift in influence and importance of the small-town, country newspaper.

Notes

1. John Chapman, *Tell It to Sweeney: The Informal History of the* New York Daily News (Garden City, NY: Doubleday, 1961), 28–34.

2. Denis Brian, *Pulitzer: A Life* (New York: John Wiley and Sons, 2001), 266.

3. See John D. Stevens, *Sensationalism and the New York Press* (New York: Columbia University Press, 1991).

4. William Hannigan, *New York Noir* (New York: Rizzoli, 1999).

5. See David E. Ruth, *Inventing the Public Enemy: The Gangster in American Culture, 1918–1934* (Chicago and London: University of Chicago Press, 1996).

6. Arthur Fellig, *Weegee by Weegee: An Autobiography* (New York: Ziff-Davis, 1961).

7. William E. Leuchtenburg, *The Perils of Prosperity, 1914–1932*, 2d ed. (Chicago and London: University of Chicago Press, 1993), 179.

8. David Nasaw, *The Chief: The Life of William Randolph Hearst* (Boston and New York: Houghton Mifflin, 2001), 322.

9. Leuchtenburg, *Perils of Prosperity*, 196.

10. Damon Runyon, *Trials and Tribulations* (London: Xanadu Publications, 1946), 12.

11. Frederick Lewis Allen, *Only Yesterday: An Informal History of the 1920s* (New York: Perennial Classics, 2000), 186.

12. Runyon, *Trials and Tribulations*, 282.

13. Runyon, *Trials and Tribulations*, 12.

14. Runyon, *Trials and Tribulations*, 283.

15. Runyon, *Trials and Tribulations*, 283.

16. Nasaw, *The Chief*, 323.

17. *New York Daily Mirror,* February 4, 1927.

18. Nasaw, *The Chief*, 380.

19. Rob Leicester Wagner, *Red Ink, White Lies: The Rise and Fall of Los Angeles Newspapers, 1920–1962.* (Upland, CA: Dragonflyer Press, 2000).

20. Mel Heimer, *The Long Count: The Legendary Battle for the Heavyweight Championship* (New York: Atheneum, 1969).

21. Charles Wyand, *The Economics of Consumption* (New York: Macmillan Company, 1937), 158. See also James Guimond, *American Photography and the American Dream* (Chapel Hill: University of North Carolina Press, 1991).

22. Emile Gauvreau's experiences working for tabloids were told in his novel, *The Scandal Monger* (New York: Macaulay, 1932).

23. Neal Gabler, *Walter Winchell: Gossip, Power and the Culture of Celebrity* (New York: Alfred A. Knopf, 1994), 87–88.

24. Gabler, *Winchell*, 87–88.

25. Samuel T. Moore, "Those Terrible Tabloids," *The Independent*, 6 March 1926, 264.

26. Moore, "Tabloids," 264.

27. Moore, "Tabloids," 264.

28. The image of Valentino and Caruso was reprinted on the cover of Silas Bent's 1927 book *Ballyhoo*, about the rise of entertainment newspapers, celebrity journalism, public relations, and commercialism in the 1920s.

29. S. L. Harrison, *Cavalcade of Journalists, 1900–2000* (Miami: Wolf Den Books, 2002), 53.

30. Moore, "Tabloids," 264.

31. Aben Kandel, "A Tabloid a Day," *Forum 77*, no. 3 (1927): 384. Quoted in Simon Bessie, *Jazz Journalism: The Story of the Tabloid Newspapers* (New York: E.P. Dutton & Co. Inc., 1938), 19.

32. Moore, "Tabloids," 264.

2

SMALL-TOWN REFORM NEWSPAPERS

The *Des Moines Register,* the *Emporia Gazette,* and the *Anniston Star*

The 1928 presidential election was not the victory for urbanity that some had anticipated. Governor Al Smith from New York, the grandson of an Irish immigrant family living on the Lower East Side of New York City, may have been representative of the growing population in New York, but he symbolized all that rural Americans feared. Smith was seen by many Americans to be entangled with eastern big business, an alignment that could not have been less appealing for those in the Midwest and the South. Even though Smith campaigned on aid to farmers, labor issues, and governmental reform, as a "wet" and a Catholic from the big city, he could not compete with the much more down-to-earth Herbert Hoover from Iowa. As Walter Lippmann wrote, in "the derby-hatted, cigar-smoking eastern urbanite, the fear assumed a force and poignancy inspired by the feeling that the clamorous life of the city should not be acknowledged as the American ideal."[1]

It was not only on the issue of the presidency that rural Americans were setting the agenda, but also on prohibition, foreign policy, and other areas of governmental reform. Despite the fact that the country's population had tipped in favor of the cities, rural areas still had a disproportionate amount of influence over national politics and had a self-appointed role and belief in their duty as the moral guardians of the real America. The presumed erosion of traditional values was hotly contested by people living in the American heartland, and one of their primary vehicles for debate was their local newspaper.

While the big cities had their scandals, trials, and tribulations, lavishly illustrated in the large metropolitan tabloids, the big story of the 1930s was a rural one. With their constant focus on the local and particularly on issues relevant to farmers during the Depression, smaller-market papers became some of the most important venues in the interwar period. It is this orientation that helps to explain the prominence of several small-town and rural weeklies during this era, including the *Des Moines Register*, the *Emporia Gazette,* and the *Anniston Star.*

The *Des Moines Register*: Real Iowa News

The *Des Moines Register* is a unique paper in its focus. Since its earliest years it has taken the state, rather than the city, as its subject. Owned and operated for seven generations by the Cowles family of Iowa, the *Register* is a quintessential twentieth-century American newspaper, following the patterns and vicissitudes of fortune that make it a microcosm of the industry as a whole. The Cowles family first entered the business when Gardner Cowles, a banker from Algona, Iowa bought the *Register and Leader* in 1903. Five years later, he bought the evening paper in Des Moines, the *Tribune*, and in 1915 the *Register and Leader* became known as the *Des Moines Register*, while the company continued to operate the evening *Tribune.*

The most remarkable feature of the *Des Moines Register* is its coverage of Iowa, a 56,000-square-mile, rural midwestern state with a relatively small population. Because Iowa is a farm state, its citizens are dispersed across a vast area, and in the early part of the century, without adequate means of transportation and communication, this should have made for a very fragmented populace. But as a result of the efforts of the *Register*, Iowa remained relatively close knit.

The Cowles family knew that growth in the newspaper industry could only occur as advertising increased, and this was dependent on the growth of circulation. In order to keep the number of subscribers expanding, the paper instituted a variety of strategies for reaching people and expanding its mandate across the state. In the nineteenth century, the paper was instrumental in advocating the building of the railroads. The railroads were among the most prominent lenders for struggling businesses such as newspapers and would provide loans on condition that their interests not be attacked or compromised in the pages of the newspaper. The newspapers needed more complete railroad systems to facilitate distribution of the paper and to receive information from distant cities before the telegraph was in operation. In rural areas, Gardner Cowles argued, the quality of a newspaper was only one of its selling points; even more important was the ability to get copies of it to customers on the day it was printed. To do this meant devising creative solutions to the problems presented by transportation. Cowles's sons, John and Mike, studied train schedules to find out when editions serving different parts of the state had to be printed, and then re-organized the press schedule around that of the trains. Staggering the printing press to run all night was a more efficient use of the presses, and meant that bundles of papers were ready to be shipped out on each destination's earliest train.

In the twentieth century, the *Des Moines Register* became a proponent of the Good Roads Movement, which aimed to identify the most important routes in the state for paving. Iowa had been known as "the muddy state" for the poor condition of its back roads, and the Iowa legislature sought to make the state more hospitable to the growing automotive industry; the *Register* needed better roads in order to use trucks for delivery. In the 1930s, the Cowleses saved shipping money by piggybacking on an already existing distribution system that was set up to get movies out to theaters across the state. The Iowa Film Delivery System had its own train cars to take film prints out to each town's movie theater, in an era when nearly every small town had one. With so many destinations across the state, theaters became an ideal way station in the distribution of newspapers. The papers were dropped off at the local movie house, where they were picked up by delivery boys who carried them to people's homes by bicycle. With four thousand newspaper boys throughout the state, even the most isolated farmers could receive the newspaper on the day it was printed. To make sure that as many people as possible in a given area became subscribers, the *Register* offered incentives and bonuses to readers who signed up their neighbors.

With circulation booming as a result of these delivery initiatives, the resources were at hand to print a high quality newspaper with comprehensive coverage of state affairs. With three hundred correspondents, the *Des Moines Register* was able to blanket the state and provide the most complete farm coverage, county by county. During the 1930s, this midwestern state became extremely important in setting the agenda for the nation. Not only was the only Iowan in presidential history, Herbert Hoover, elected, but other influential Iowans moved into positions of power as well. Henry A. Wallace, the editor of *Wallace's Farmer* from 1921 to 1933, served as secretary of agriculture from 1933 to 1940, and became vice president under Franklin D. Roosevelt. His father, Henry C. Wallace, had also been an editor of *Wallace's Farmer* and had been appointed secretary of agriculture by President Harding in 1921. That two of the agriculture secretaries in such quick succession hailed from Iowa indicates the principal role of this state in farming matters.

After World War I, prosperity did not reach all Americans equally. As Europe recovered from the devastation of war, it became a stronger competitor in manufacturing and agriculture. For farmers at home, this new competition was hardly welcome. Improved machinery, like Ford tractors, had increased the yields of American farms so much that prices were dropping precipitously, and farmers were unable to pay back loans they had taken out to buy these new machines. With lending institutions overextended, banks were foreclosing and farms were unable to pay back their loans. A generalized economic depression took hold in Iowa long before the stock market crash in 1929 became news to the rest of the country.

The *Register*'s editorial policy remained in favor of Hoover, despite the Great Depression.[2] Farmers did their best to organize and to seek assistance from the federal government by forming a number of associations, including the Farmer's Union and the Iowa Farm Bureau Federation. The paper chronicled these efforts and editorialized on behalf of farmers. Editor Harvey Ingham supported the McNary-Haugen bill in the 1920s, an unsuccessful plan to create a federal body to purchase surplus produce at an artificially inflated price so that farmers were not beholden to lower market prices. The *Register* was a strong supporter of Hoover's efforts to help farmers, but even after proposing the Agricultural Marketing Act, the situation in states like Iowa had not much improved. In 1931, J. S. Russell, the farm editor of the *Register,* noted that "between March 1926 and March 1931, one-seventh of Iowa's farmers had lost their farms through foreclosures. That translated into 33,000 farms and more than 5 million acres ending up in lenders' hands."[3]

On the editorial pages of the *Register*, the nation's issues were highlighted from a distinctly Iowan perspective. Farming and government assistance were foremost to Ingham, and the paper advocated federal aid measures on behalf of its population. Farmers needed government assistance in order to survive, but with Iowa's strong history of frontier individualism, looking to the government was often fraught with controversy. This complicated relationship came to a head in 1931 when the federal government instituted a new program for tuberculosis testing in cattle. Farmers resisted testing on the grounds that the tests were inaccurate and harmful, and that when the disease was found they were not being fairly compensated for the destruction of their herds. In opposing the testing, several incidents of violence broke out in what became known as the "Cow War" of 1931.[4] As a direct result of these protests, the Farmers Holiday Association was formed to help coordinate strikes among farmers. The *Register* reported several cases of milk dumping by farmers protesting the testing practice. After some veterinarians were attacked in Cedar County, the National Guard was called in and martial law was declared. The *Register* urged calm and reason: "The law requiring the testing of cattle for tuberculosis resulted not from despotism but from democratic procedures. It was intended not to oppress farmers but to protect the milk consumers of the state, including the farmers and their families."[5] The *Register*'s paternalistic stance toward the state's inhabitants helped to smooth over these episodes born of exhaustion and frustration.

In 1932 the state and the country shifted tacks and looked to another party to handle the worsening situation. Democrat Franklin Delano Roosevelt and his New Deal defeated Hoover and promised sweeping changes throughout the country, many of which were aimed at bettering the lives of farmers. Welfare programs, farm assistance, public utility projects for rural electrification, foreclosure protection, and bank deposit insurance initiatives were all welcome news to the struggling rural Iowan, and the *Register* kept them abreast of each new day's proposed legislation. The *Register* was such an important source for news in outlying areas that some banks taped its pages to their front windows for passersby to read.[6]

As relevant news for Iowa emanated from Washington, so too did news of Iowa provide the catalyst for change in the capital. Richard Wilson was chosen to head the Washington bureau of the *Register* in 1933, enabling first-person reporting from the source of each day's top news stories. The Washington bureau interpreted events according to the Iowa angle, and often scooped major papers and wire service reports on stories such as the federal farm program.[7] Wilson grew accustomed to seeing his stories printed on the front page back home, and he attracted notice in Washington as well. Roosevelt himself claimed that "Dick Wilson [was] one of the four best reporters in Washington."[8]

The increased pace of important news coming from Washington was good for the newspaper business, as people clamored to find out how new changes would affect them. While many businesses that were connected to agriculture found their fortunes waning, the news business stayed healthy even with less advertising income. Though people were tempted to go without all but the barest essentials, the circulation of the *Register* continued to improve. Most subscribers paid in advance through the mail, but this required having enough money up front to pay for the whole year, which few farmers did. The paper responded to these worsening economic conditions by changing their method of subscription payment for rural readers. Switching to a weekly payment schedule, the *Register*'s circulation department attached small metal cups to rural subscribers' mailboxes, from which carriers could retrieve twelve cents a week.[9]

Having secured a loyal following of readers, the *Des Moines Register* undertook a number of expansions that set in motion what would become a major midwestern media enterprise. Improvements were made in feature reporting, technology, and circulation, and before long an expanded sphere of influence would solidify the reputation of the paper. Managing editor Basil Leon Walters was intrigued with the mechanics of audience research and how to engineer a more reader-friendly newspaper. He contracted Drake University psychologist Dr. Herman Brandt, who designed experiments with a hidden camera to record readers' eye movements. The studies showed that readers rarely read everything on a page and tended to jump around and skip over most of it. His findings were published in his book *The Psychology of Seeing* and helped Walters redesign the paper to capture and sustain the attention of readers.[10]

One of the adjustments that helped the *Register* both connect better with readers and distinguish the Iowan point of view as singular and important came with the hiring of a young University of Iowa doctoral student named George Gallup to survey readers on their preferences, values, and attitudes. Using his own sampling techniques that would reshape the future of public opinion polling, his research sought to "identify which stories had the greatest appeal."[11] Gallup found that local stories written simply were favored by the reading audience. His results led to a new layout, design, and content at the paper, and on Gallup's recommendation the reporters were instructed "to write their stories in the same way they would tell their story to a friend," in the first-person voice whenever possible.[12]

The larger contribution of Gallup to the state of Iowa had much broader effects. By printing the results of opinion polls in the paper, the *Register* was a constant reflection of the mood of the state. The paper published results regularly on a wide range of political, economic, and social issues, and through these polls the state came to have an increasingly coherent point of view on matters that were specific to Iowa. The strategy would be taken up in the 1980s by Gannett's *USA Today*, where it would fulfill a similar function in setting the agenda for national issues. As the Iowa poll gained in importance and the prominence of the state's caucus rose, the twentieth century has seen the ascension of Iowa in determining the political direction of the country.

Other improvements at the paper also helped move the state into the limelight, at least journalistically. The Cowles brothers were aggressive competitors who by 1927 owned all of the newspapers in Des Moines and who firmly believed that a newspaper could only behave responsibly if it had no other competition for readers. By not having to engage in cheap circulation-building tactics, the paper could be free to cover the news in depth. While this was not a widely held belief, the *Register* did seem to prove the exception to the rule of newspaper concentration. The company also became an early media conglomerate by expanding into other forms of media. It created the

Iowa farm, photographed from above. Photo by Wallace Kirkland/Time Life Pictures/Getty Images.

Iowa Broadcasting Company and through it owned three radio stations that were affiliated with the NBC Blue network.[13] Radio could be used to expand the reach of the newspaper and to remind readers of its features, but readers needed to have the paper to have a picture of what was going on, and the *Register* took this charge very seriously.

Learning from the importance of pictures from the tabloids, the *Register* implemented a new rotogravure section in its Sunday paper that was able to illustrate not just people and places, but sequences of events by printing several pictures in a series. In an effort to capture better "play-by-play" action through photography, *Register* photographer George Yates developed a "machine gun camera" with a faster shutter speed that did not require the time-consuming operation of changing plates. Armed with this new technology, the picture quality of fast action events like sports activities was markedly improved. The *Register* was among the first newspapers in the Midwest to subscribe to the Wirephoto service of the Associated Press, and it also claimed a photo archive of a thousand images of its own.[14] By 1937, the centrality of photography at the company was proven in its launch of *Look* magazine, a contemporary of Time Incorporated's *Life* magazine. Published until 1971, *Look* was an extremely popular general-interest photo magazine that often featured celebrities on the cover and blended coverage of politics, fashion, style, and popular culture.

But by far the most impressive development in news coverage at the *Register* came as a result of its purchase of its own plane, the *Good News*, in 1928. The plane enabled reporters and photographers to cover the entire state more quickly and return stories to the press in record time. The plane was outfitted with its own darkroom so that pictures could be developed en route, and it had a trapdoor in its floor to allow for aerial photography. With all of these improvements at the *Register*, the state of Iowa could not help but become more acquainted with itself.

Once a complete picture of the state was established through the *Register*'s efforts in photography, polling, and aerial views, another set of issues emerged which helped to shape the physical space of Iowa. The state became a leader in conservation issues, partly as a result of the predilections of one of its most renowned employees, Jay (Ding) Darling. Darling was the editorial cartoonist at the *Register*, so favored by readers that he was given a prominent spot on the front page, where an editorial cartoon continues to be displayed today. Darling began at the *Register* in 1906 after working as an illustrator and court reporter at the *Sioux City Journal*. He had grown famous enough that the *Register* offered to double his salary. Their investment paid off not only in increased circulation, but also in the paid advertising that they were able to sell with the help of his illustrations. Younkers, the local department store, was particularly keen to have sketches of items for sale accompany their ads.[15] Darling became so popular he was given a job at the *New York World*, but he returned to Iowa after only a short time in the city. The demand for his work remained so great that his cartoons were syndicated by the *Herald Tribune* and carried in 130 newspapers all over the country.[16]

Jay Darling had one of the first pilot's licenses in Iowa, which may have been one of the reasons he became so concerned to protect the natural resources of the state—he had actually seen most of it himself. He developed a relationship with President Theodore Roosevelt, whom he often portrayed in political caricatures, and Roosevelt, for his part, found an ally in Darling for his conservation initiatives. Darling was also a friend of Herbert Hoover, who appointed Darling's publisher Gardner Cowles to a committee to study the management of federal lands. Under Franklin D. Roosevelt, a noted conservationist, Darling was appointed Chief of the U.S. Bureau of Biological Survey (which would become the U.S. Fish and Wildlife Service) under the auspices of Henry Wallace's Department of Agriculture. While Darling held this office, millions of dollars were committed to Works Progress Administration projects, which restored many natural habitats in the state of Iowa. In 1934 Roosevelt signed the Duck Stamp Bill, a proposal of Jay Darling's to raise funds for protection of waterfowl. Darling persuaded the Iowa General Assembly to start a Fish and Game Commission, and also founded the Cooperative Wildlife Research Unit at Iowa State University.[17]

The *Des Moines Register*, along with some of its most talented staff, was instrumental in shaping the state of Iowa. Through extraordinary means the paper made readers more aware of their surroundings and each other, and it constructed and maintained an improved physical place for them to live. It was, for most of its existence, among the top ten newspapers in the United States, and it enjoyed close ties to government throughout, as evidenced by the fact that Cowles wrote Wendell Willkie's presidential acceptance speech in 1940. The centrality of the *Des Moines Register* to the state and to the nation was shown most emphatically in 1949 when Walter Lippmann, perhaps the best-known newspaper columnist of his day, came to the paper for its centennial anniversary. In his remarks he extolled the virtues of localism and what would soon become an anachronistic way of understanding newspapers. He was also praising what the *Register* had accomplished for so large a state: "American newspapers," he said, "large and small, and without exception, belong to a town, a city, at the most to a region."[18]

The Cowles family continued to translate their emphasis on the local into an increasingly successful media empire, purchasing the *Minneapolis Star* in 1935, the *Minneapolis Journal* in 1939, and the *Minneapolis Tribune* in 1941, consolidating them all into the *Star Tribune* in 1982. That same year, the evening *Tribune* stopped publishing in Des Moines. In 1997, the *Minneapolis Star Tribune* was sold to McClatchy Newspapers. Like many other family-owned newspapers with rich journalistic traditions and a strong commitment to localism, the *Des Moines Register* was sold to the Gannett newspaper chain in 1985. In order to make a more profitable newspaper, Gannett cut the breadth of coverage back substantially, so that the once statewide newspaper became primarily a Des Moines paper, with less coverage of Iowa. The Washington bureau was dissolved into the Gannett News Service and two of the Iowa state bureaus were closed. The profit margin of the paper went from 10 percent to 25 percent under Gannett ownership.[19]

The *Emporia Gazette*: Small-Town American Ideal

The function of small-town papers is crucial in supporting local businesses and the overall economic health of the community, while at the same time providing an outlet for a town leader's opinions on the future direction of the town. One of the pioneers of this kind of journalism was William Allen White, whose *Emporia Gazette* was instrumental in providing a public forum for White's vision of how his town, state, and country ought to proceed into the twentieth century. Although White's paper was anomalous for its influence beyond the town's boundaries, the function of the paper in Emporia is an early example of how a newspaper could be used to refashion a community in the editor's image.

White was born in Emporia, Kansas, in 1868, and after apprenticing at the *Kansas City Star* as a young man, returned to his hometown and purchased the *Gazette* at the age of 20. He arrived in town with a dollar in his pocket, but he slowly gained the confidence of local townspeople and bankers and was able to invest in the paper to build it into one of the most important institutions in town. White was adamant in his belief in the small town as a reprieve from the corruption and congestion in the cities of the American northeast. In comparing Emporians to the residents of large cities, White found the latter decidedly lacking: "Man for man, we live better, eat more regularly and have a wider bill of fare, drink less booze, keep out of jail more regularly, and get home earlier.... Also we are more neighborly."[20]

Free from the constraints of the big city, White advocated a plan for living that was based on the strength of a small and cohesive population who shared the same simple values he held, and these values were clearly articulated in the pages of his weekly paper. Residents of the town were made well aware that this was to be a Christian, Republican, middle-class, law-abiding place based on equality and the promise of class mobility for the hard-working and the virtuous. White promoted house building and ownership, cultural institutions, improvements in the town infrastructure in the form of roads and sewers, and the local ownership of utilities. His paper was at the forefront of town building at every level. As he summarized in one editorial, in case people were wondering why the paper continually supported local bonds,

no matter what the bonds are for whether for the municipal band, the public library, the paving, hard surfaced roads, the new High School building, the Memorial hall, the county hospital, the county home, the city market; why we have been for every subscription paper passed in town in a quarter of a century whether for the Y.M.C.A. building, the Y.W., the Welfare Association, with its new building, with its laundry, day nursery and sewing room for working women, for the new College building and the four manual pipe organ—now worth $25,000—for the park improvement, for the fair building, for the livestock sales pavilion; why we have been for enlarging the activities of the city government in every possible way. Well

William Allen White (right), editor of the *Emporia Gazette*, talking to friends in front of a store. Photo by Bernard Hoffman/Time Life Pictures/Getty Images, 1937.

this is the reason—to bring a more abundant life to all the people of this town, to distribute the wealth of this town, by taxation and by gifts and otherwise, and distribute it more equitably, and thereby bring beauty into what otherwise would be a sordid and impossible village life.[21]

The paper reported on town picnics, bridge clubs, baseball teams, county fairs, and all manner of community involvement, with the exception of filmgoing, which was discouraged for being too low-brow.[22] The paper was a chronicle of the activities of the townspeople, who could expect to see their names in print whenever they won a contest, got married, or celebrated an anniversary.[23] Those who transgressed these boundaries were likely to find themselves mentioned in these pages as well, a gentle reminder that spitting, public drunkenness, disrespect for one's parents, or the use of coarse language was frowned upon in Emporia.

Like all other varieties of bad news—especially those indicating economic downturn—crime was mostly avoided in the pages of the *Gazette* for fear that it would lower the morale of residents. The *Emporia Gazette* redefined what was newsworthy on the basis of equality, familiarity, and continuity, in stark contrast to the contemporary news values of disruption, disaster, and discord. As White wrote in an editorial titled "An Editor and His Town,"

> an editor can build up his community only by preaching unselfish citizenship. The booster, the boomer, the riz-razzer who screams in headlines about the glories of the town gets nowhere. But the editor who, by his own practice as well as his own preaching, stands for decent things and encourages unselfish citizenship, glorifies giving and frowns on taking, has a constructive attitude which is sure to help his town. He may not bring more people in; that is as fate wills it. But he certainly can make life better and happier and broader and more comfortable for the people who live in the town. It is better to have 10,000 people living equitably and happy than to have 10,000 people growing fat upon the toil of 90,000 who live lean and sordid lives. The *Gazette* is printed in a community where there are 13,000 people, without a pauper, with every man at work, without a millionaire, with as many telephones as there are homes, as many automobiles as there are families, as many schools as the children need, as many books in the library as the public will read, with a municipal band, a bath tub in nearly every house, no home-made crime. The people in our jails come to town to get there, and we haven't an able-bodied person in the poor house.[24]

Harmony was the foundation of White's booster progressivism; in order for a newspaper to be successful, the community had to thrive.[25] The population had to remain steady or increase, but not at the cost of becoming too big. "Better to have a decent town than a big one," according to White. People had to be encouraged to stay, settle, and have children, and those children had to be persuaded to stay, settle, and have more children. Bad news ran counter to the predetermined need for growth, which was best achieved through the advancement of unity, harmony, and progress.

The scale of small-town papers like the *Emporia Gazette* meant that the editor was in constant contact with his community and therefore could scarcely afford to offend its sensibilities. A negative word about a local businessperson would at the very least run the risk of a confrontation with that person and at worst, lose business for the paper.[26] Readers came to the paper to find what was good and redeeming about their fellow townspeople, not to find what was wrong. The role of the paper in the home was such that any literate member, regardless of age, could be expected to pick it up, and children were encouraged to use the pages of the *Gazette* as a vocabulary primer. In areas not well served by libraries or the book trade, the weekly newspaper functioned as a "circulating library."[27] The paper, therefore, had to be wholesome, uplifting, and dignified.

This approach to news coverage was echoed by the American Society of Newspaper Editors, of which White was the president in 1938, in its 1922 Code of Ethics:

> A newspaper cannot escape conviction of insincerity if while professing high moral purpose it supplies incentives to base conduct, such as are to be found in details of crime and vice, publication of which is not demonstrably for the general good. Lacking authority to enforce its canons the journalism here presented can but express the hope that deliberate pandering to vicious instincts will encounter effective public disapproval or yield to the influence of a preponderant professional condemnation.[28]

The values that the newspaper tried valiantly to uphold were being threatened by a host of new developments in what White variously referred to as the "New Era" and the "Machine Age." Of particular concern was the increasing sophistication and penetration of new communications technologies, and White used the newspaper to warn of their inherent dangers:

> America in these days under the influence of the motorcar, the movies and the radio is getting a lot more economic abundance than spiritual pabulum and moral sense. So we are growing a population more and more permeated with blatant, dull, noisy, cheap half-wits.[29]

More than simply new media technologies, White worried most about the change in individual attitudes he perceived in the postwar boom in both the economy and the population. He found people to be acting more selfishly and immorally, motivated by greater degrees of materialism, while he was trying to advocate neighborliness, stronger community association, and selflessness. Unlike many of his contemporaries, White looked to the government as the standard-bearer for this new model of association, intervening to organize and protect all citizens.

In the 1930s, economic downturn throughout the country forced a host of new recovery initiatives at both the local and national level, and brought many of White's visions of government to life. In the New Deal he had found an ally and a promising return to the earlier days of Progressivism. White was impressed with Franklin Roosevelt's first hundred days in office and supported efforts to help the less fortunate in their time of need. There was a return to the values of small-town America, which were thought to be the necessary salve to the corruption and speculation that had led to the market collapse. White was a leading proponent of these values, and he showed how Emporia could lead by example. As he wrote in *Collier's* magazine in the early 1920s, "In America most of us are Emporians in one way or another. Some of us live in towns ranging from five thousand to a quarter of a million, others were born in or around these towns, and still others of us cherish golden dreams of going back to some Emporia."[30]

White became a national figure through the publication of famously sarcastic editorials such as "What's the Matter with Kansas?" which took aim at backwards politicians whom White found to be working against the best interests of the state. The editorial was reprinted widely in papers across the country and brought the rural editor fame and political influence. He had the ear of presidents, who invited him to Washington to counsel them on policy, and as a literary figure White was welcomed into publishing circles in New York. Although he traveled extensively, White remained closely aligned with Emporia and its *Gazette*, while at the same time writing both fiction and nonfiction for magazines such as *Scribner's* and *Collier's*. He had several books published, some of which were collections of his editorials. With his combination of high-profile cosmopolitanism and small town politics, he succeeded in constructing Emporia as "the Athens of Kansas."

As the spokesperson for Middle America, White and his newspaper were important icons for the 1930s. He was a humble local who had a voice in national politics. As Walter Winchell remarked, "William Allen White assumed that, since Kansas is the geographical heart of America, he was specially equipped to interpret America's soul. In this he was largely correct."[31] As a model for community newspapering, the *Emporia Gazette* and its editor had few rivals.

The *Anniston Star:*
Southern Model Town and Newspaper

The town of Anniston was incorporated in 1879 by the Alabama Legislature, having been founded five years earlier as a company town for the Woodstock Iron Company. After learning of another community in Alabama called Woodstock, the place was renamed Anniston after Annie, the wife of one of the investors, Alfred Tyler. The town was officially opened to the public in 1883, and plans were drawn up to make the settlement a "model city" for the New South. Starting with a population of 3,500 people, it gained notoriety through one of its other investors, Henry Grady, the esteemed editor of the *Atlanta Constitution*, who is credited with coining the phrase "New South." At the opening celebration, Grady gave an address with the city's first mayor, Dr. Richard P. Huger.[32] That Grady, one of the South's most influential newspaper editors, was present at the founding of the city, was an auspicious beginning for both the town and its first newspaper. Both Grady and the newspaper would guide and shape the new town, and the New South, into the twentieth century.

Anniston's first newspaper, owned by the Woodstock Iron Company, was named the *Daily Hot Blast*, after the sound of the ore furnaces. In the inaugural editorial, editor Charles H. Williams wrote, "we will endeavor to publish a paper in keeping with the spirit and progress that has marked the development of Anniston," pledging that the Democratic paper would be "independent enough to speak plainly against all abuses and wrong principles no matter where we find them."[33] Also in the first edition, *Atlanta Constitution* editor Grady wrote a front-page letter extolling the virtues of the city, and quoting the city's founder, Sam Noble, inviting "men of energy and intelligence and moderate capital in what, it cannot be denied, is the model town of the south.[34]

Since the beginning, newspapers in Anniston have been associated with the Ayers family. Dr. Thomas W. Ayers, a local physician, bought the *Hot Blast* in the 1890s but departed for China shortly after to pursue missionary work. Though he took his young son Harry on the trip with him, Harry returned to Anniston after a year and resumed his family's connection to the newspaper industry by writing for local Alabama papers.

Harry Ayers worked as the news editor of the *Anniston Evening Star* under owner J. T. Fain and paid close attention to local politics. Like his father, Ayers was a Southern Baptist with strong ties to the community, and he had many important city elders to counsel him in the absence of his father. One of his closest friends was Thomas E. Kilby, who ran for mayor in 1905 with the help of editorial support from Ayers. Kilby ran on a "business progressive" platform, planning to clean up corrupt town politics, elections, houses of vice, city streets, and parks.[35] Both Ayers and Kilby supported Prohibition—the town remained dry for a century—and though they were not dry themselves, reasoned that the position was the best one to adopt to encourage respectable business interests to come to Anniston.

Local boosterism was not only an editorial stance, it was the livelihood of the newspaper. The most important issue in the development of the town at that time was the railroad, which held local towns like Anniston at their mercy in determining freight costs to transport resources like iron ore and cotton. Without beneficial rates, the city could do little to lure new businesses to town, and neighboring cities and towns all vied to have new tracks go through their territory to induce business traffic. Kilby and Ayers fought for state regulation of the railroads to wrest control of them from northern business interests, despite the conflict of interest inherent in the common practice of newspaper editors receiving free passes on most railroads. Often losing out to Birmingham, Montgomery, or Atlanta, Anniston's boosters not only had to make the city seem attractive to northerners but also to outshine their local competition. The newspaper was crucial to both of these endeavors. As Ayers wrote, "cities like individuals, have to advertise persistently in order to get results. . . . the city today that does not hustle does not make much progress."[36]

In 1910, the *Anniston Evening Star* was purchased by James B. Lloyd, and Ayers continued to run editorial operations. Lloyd was not particularly adept at running the newspaper, however, and the business lost a great deal of money under his direction. The *Star*'s competition continued to come from the *Hot Blast*, which was succeeding on the strength of lucrative alcohol and patent medicine ads that the *Star* refused to print. Seizing an opportunity, Ayers and Kilby, with financial help from a banker in Rome, Georgia, bought the *Hot Blast* from Veazey Rainwater for $7,000. Choosing to stop the publication of vice ads and turning their attention to circulation and advertising improvements, Kilby and Ayers were soon in a position to buy out the *Star* as well, and they consolidated the two papers into the *Anniston Evening Star and Daily Hot Blast*. Before running for lieutenant governor in 1910, Kilby sold his interest in the papers to Ayers so that they could remain editorially "independent" while backing his campaign.

From the offices of the newspaper, Harry Ayers supported the community with membership and influence in as many local organizations as time would allow. He was active in the Rotary Club and was twice voted president of the Chamber of Commerce in 1924 and 1925.[37] He was post commander of the American Legion of Alabama, and using his editorials to insist on more efficient rail connections and improved roads, he was instrumental in helping to bring one of Alabama's most important army bases, Fort McClellan, to Anniston.[38] He was a member of the Southern Research Institute, the Alabama Citizens Educational Advisory Council, the Anniston Community Chest, Chairman of Anniston's Carnegie Library and the YMCA, director of the Southern Newspaper Publisher's Association, and involved in many other organizations.[39] Ayers was a key player in local politics, acting as campaign manager for his friend Kilby as he sought the highest offices in the state, and Ayers himself frequently engaged directly in the process as a delegate and as a nominee in Democratic primaries.

Harry Ayers also fought to keep his newspapers on solid financial ground, despite the exigencies of the local economy. He bought a United Press wire service early, to supply international and war news to his paper, and he was attentive to the business side of the paper as well as its editorials. He invested in a new press that could print thirty thousand papers an hour and created a noon edition of the paper to favor advertisers.[40] By 1928 the population of Anniston had reached thirty thousand, and the *Star* was being delivered to six thousand of them. Though only one-fifth of the population, the reader base of the *Star* represented a larger group of people than those with telephones, electricity, or running water.[41] The central role of the newspaper to a community, as Ayers understood it, was illustrated in a letter from Rex Grover White reprinted by the *Star*:

> It is accepted as an institution by the American public which must do its work, serve all interests, ignore danger, know no sleep, accept abuse, be always polite. It is looked upon as an institution that must give its wares, ie. its columns upon the slightest pretext to the aid of any sort of movement having the slightest tinge of charity, civic advancement, or social welfare. In the same breath it is called upon to protect and destroy, to blow hot and cold, to uphold the courts and to watch them, to support church and liberalism, to befriend the helpless and uphold property rights, to be always right and to be super-human in its swift gathering and presentation of the news.[42]

The *Star and Hot Blast* was frequently used to stir up local pride and sing the praises of the small city, and Ayers was dedicated to the practice of public congratulations for the achievements of local citizens. In 1924 he published a hundred-page "Progress Edition" of the paper, recounting the development of the city and the history of its important citizens and institutions.[43] Harry Ayers's central role in promoting the development of the town was applauded by Leon T. Bradley, director of Alabama Public Utilities Bureau in Birmingham, who wrote in a letter to the editor, "I am certain that the phenomenal growth of Anniston has been materially aided by the *Star*, which has always been a harbinger of good news and the forerunner of progress."[44] This was often accomplished through gentle reprimanding by the paper, which attempted to coax townspeople into supporting their local institutions. Ayers chided shoppers for patronizing stores in Atlanta and Birmingham instead of local businesses and urged parents to send their children to local schools. Ayers argued vociferously for compulsory education as one of the central means by which the New South would modernize, often writing Sunday editorials suggesting to parents which schools they should go to and promoting Alabama Presbyterian College.[45]

Wherever possible, the news in the *Anniston Star* was good news, with Ayers reserving harsh words only for his political opponents. Even the plummeting economy, industrial and agricultural slowdowns, strained race relations, and recurring labor strikes were treated with an optimistic tone. The most important thing to Harry Ayers was business progress, which necessitated investment from the north. In order to portray a functional, orderly, and hospitable home for new business, the default position of the paper was that things were getting better. Displaying characteristic liberalism, Ayers took a progressive position on race in the South, writing that

> an educated and morally trained man, white or black, is an asset to any community. The reverse is likewise true, and the sooner the South raises the standards of living among its black population, the greater will be the economic progress of the South, as well as our generations to come.[46]

In the 1930s the problems in the South were numerous, but the *Anniston Star* attacked them with proposals and suggestions for change rather than announcements of doom. Sharecropping and tenant farming were consistent themes of the paper's editorials, and following Henry Grady in the *Constitution*, Ayers insisted that farmers diversify their cotton crops to avoid losing business. As he wrote in 1935, "we must find substitute crops that will stave off final ruination in a land made poor by the cotton tenant farmer system that so many persons seek to perpetuate."[47] Seeing the farmer as the central figure of the South, who embodied all of the values that would make the region strong, Ayers frequently advocated for their issues. He editorialized that farmers were "the very backbone of our civilization, and the ultimate creators of all prosperity."[48]

The paper maintained a tradition of issue advocacy, choosing strong editorial positions over feigned objectivity—another legacy of Grady. The readers of the South preferred to know where their editors stood politically, and chose papers based on these positions. Ayers fulfilled his role as town advocate emphatically; highlighting the achievements and advancements of the city and often downplaying its shortcomings. Ayers had been a Wilsonian liberal, following the southerner from Virginia in the White House in efforts to improve education and reform government, and in the depths of the 1930s he saw salvation in Franklin Delano Roosevelt. Ayers visited Roosevelt at his summer home in Georgia, and the two developed a relationship that lasted many years. Ayers wanted the *Star* to be the first paper to endorse Roosevelt, and once Roosevelt was in office Ayers often sent his editorials to Roosevelt's home.[49]

The Great Depression hit cities like Anniston particularly hard. War reparations had slowed the export market for locally grown goods like cotton, and the high rate of unemployment from laid-off factory workers left half the population of Anniston relying on public aid. The State was in debt, and some schools were forced to close. Amid this tragic set of circumstances, the New Deal looked like a good deal for the South, long the poor cousin in the union.

The complexity of issues facing the South, and Anniston in particular, left Ayers often equivocal in his positions. While he opposed some of the New Deal policies, he was largely in favor of the President himself. Although aid did not come to the South as much as Ayers had hoped, he found reason to be optimistic with the new administration. Ayers argued for government intervention within the confines of states' rights, wanting and needing help for the region without federal strings attached. He sought help for the textile industry in fighting the railroads, whose rates favored transportation of goods from the East, but when it came to supporting labor his position was often unclear. After witnessing some of the state's most brutal labor strikes in the coal and textile industries, Ayers defended workers' right to strike but rarely supported the strikes themselves.[50]

In 1937 Ayers reversed his position on Prohibition, arguing that being dry led to illegal activity and corruption by bootlegging forces. Instead, he hoped people would engage in voluntary temperance, and that New Deal programs would diminish the reasons for alcoholism. Though a Progressive, Ayers did not support the anti-lynching bill or the Child Labor Amendment, partly out of fear that the need for legislation made the South look backward, but mostly because the business interests in town did not want interference. He was also worried that laws against child labor might hurt his ability to hire young newspaper carriers.[51] In all matters, if there was legislating to be done, Ayers much preferred the lawmakers to be local Southerners, and that the social order of the South be maintained at all cost.

The New Deal was in many ways in conflict with beliefs about states' rights, and government programs often offended the sensibilities of business progressivists. Ayers responded to this clash by increasingly concentrating on education issues, which he saw as the primary impediment to progress in Alabama. Education dominated his editorials, in which he argued that sending people to Alabama universities would create a solid foundation of future local political leaders, "as educated men who are capable of recognizing that Alabama cannot fully develop her wealth of natural resources without a trained leadership and a citizenry that will be responsive to the fundamental needs of the commonwealth."[52]

In 1915, as president of Alabama Press Association, Harry Ayers advocated consolidation in the newspaper industry where towns were supporting more than one paper. Competing newspapers, he thought, led to factionalism, while consolidation would lead to better-quality newspapers. In its present form, the *Anniston Star*, still owned and operated by the Ayers family, has studiously fended off takeovers from large chains. It has maintained its independent status for over one hundred years and has guaranteed that the paper will remain thus in perpetuity through the development of the nonprofit Ayers Institute Foundation.[53] In this, the *Star* has been much more successful than most small-town weeklies, which have increasingly fallen prey to chain buyouts by companies with substantially less investment or interest in community building.

Notes

1. William E. Leuchtenberg, *The Perils of Prosperity, 1914–1932*, 2d ed. (Chicago and London: University of Chicago Press, 1993), 240.

2. William B. Friedricks, *Covering Iowa: The History of the Des Moines Register and Tribune Company, 1849–1985* (Ames: Iowa State University Press, 2000), 99.

3. Friedricks, *Covering Iowa*, 100.

4. "A Gathering of T.B. Objectors," *Des Moines Register*, 18 September 1931.

5. George Mills, *Harvey Ingham and Gardner Cowles, Sr: Things Don't Just Happen* (Ames: Iowa State University Press, 1977), 148.

6. Mills, *Harvey Ingham*, 142.

7. Mills, *Harvey Ingham*, 144.

8. Mills, *Harvey Ingham*, 145.

9. Friedricks, *Covering Iowa*, 90.

10. Charles Whited, *Knight: A Publisher in the Tumultuous Century* (New York: E.P. Dutton, 1988), 120.

11. Friedricks, *Covering Iowa*, 86.

12. Friedricks, *Covering Iowa*, 88.

13. Friedricks, *Covering Iowa*, 84.

14. Friedricks, *Covering Iowa*, 87.

15. David L. Lendt, *Ding: The Life of Jay Norwood Darling* (Ames: Iowa State University Press, 1989), 22.

16. Lendt, *Ding*, 29.

17. Lendt, *Ding*, 37.

18. *Des Moines Register*, 21 June 1949.

19. Philip Meyer, "The Influence Model and Newspaper Business," *Newspaper Research Journal* 25, no. 1 (2004): 70.

20. "Virtue's Own Reward," *Emporia Gazette*, 12 October 1921.

21. "A Great American Novel," *Emporia Gazette*, 23 November 1920.

22. Edward Gale Agran, *Too Good a Town: William Allen White, Community, and the Emerging Rhetoric of Middle America* (Fayetteville, University of Arkansas Press, 1998), 96.

23. William Allen White, *The Autobiography of William Allen White* (New York: MacMillan Co., 1946), 357–359.

24. "An Editor and His Town," *Emporia Gazette*, 4 December 1924.

25. Sally Foreman Griffith, *Home Town News: William Allen White and the Emporia Gazette* (New York: Oxford University Press, 1989).

26. The avoidance of business news that cast aspersions on a newspaper's advertisers was not limited to small-town newspapers. Oswald Garrison Villard demonstrates this behavior at metropolitan dailies in his essay on the relationship between department stores and the Philadelphia Public Ledger. See Villard, *Some Newspapers and Newspaper-men* (New York: A.A. Knopf, 1923).

27. Malcolm McDonald Willey and Stuart A. Rice, *Communication Agencies and Social Life* (New York: McGraw Hill, 1933), 5.

28. Alfred Pratte, *Gods Within the Machine: A History of the American Society of Newspaper Editors, 1923–1993* (Westport, Conn.: Praeger, 1995), 206–207.

29. Agran, *Too Good a Town*, 156.

30. William Allen White, "Blood of the Conquerors," *Collier's*, 10 March 1923, 5–6, 30.

31. Quoted in Walter Johnson, *William Allen White's America* (New York: Henry Holt, 1947), 475.

32. "Anniston and *Star* Have Marched Hand in Hand," *Anniston Star*, 15 July 1945.

33. Kevin Stoker, *Harry Mell Ayers: New South Community Journalism in the Age of Reform* (Ph.D. diss., University of Alabama, 1998), 37.

34. Stoker, *Harry Mell Ayers*, 38.

35. Stoker, *Harry Mell Ayers*, 82.

36. "Southern Commercial Conference," *Anniston Star*, 4 March 1911.

37. Stoker, *Harry Mell Ayers*, 232.

38. Stoker, *Harry Mell Ayers*, 235.

39. Stoker, *Harry Mell Ayers*, 413.

40. Stoker, *Harry Mell Ayers*, 164, 223.

41. Stoker, *Harry Mell Ayers*, 314.

42. Rex Grover White, "The Real Cure for Decrease in Retail Sales is Newspaper Used in Home," *Anniston Star*, 19 February 1922.

43. Stoker, *Harry Mell Ayers*, 271.

44. Leon T. Bradley, letter to the editor, *Anniston Star*, 13 March 1924.

45. Stoker, *Harry Mell Ayers*, 120, 224.

46. *Anniston Star*, 2 December 1917.

47. "King Cotton," *Anniston Star*, 6 March 1935.

48. "Why the *Anniston Star* Opposes Senator Underwood," *Anniston Star*, 22 February 1920.

49. Stoker, *Harry Mell Ayers*, 349.

50. Stoker, *Harry Mell Ayers*, 380.

51. Stoker, *Harry Mell Ayers*, 376.

52. "Heroes of Education," *Anniston Star*, 25 April 1937.

53. "One Newspaper Towns," *Anniston Star*, 23 December 1917. See also James V. Risser, "Endangered Species," *American Journalism Review* 20 (1998).

3

THE BLACK PRESS GOES TO WAR

The *Chicago Defender*, the *Pittsburgh Courier*, and the *Baltimore Afro-American*

On December 13, 1941, the headline of the *Baltimore Afro-American* read, "Mr. President, Count on Us." The story was similar to others in the black press at the time, indicating a strong commitment on the part of the black community to fight in World War II, but as an editorial stance the position was fraught with complications.

On October 9, 1940, President Roosevelt released to the press a new military policy after hearing from several prominent black leaders on the subject. Appealing for more equitable treatment and assignments based on ability rather than race, the Committee for the Participation of Negroes in National Defense put forward a seven-point plan for the integration of the army.[1] Roosevelt's policy maintained a general program of racial segregation with a few minor concessions such as the establishment of more black units. His justification for the weak plan was that the army could scarcely afford a white backlash at such a precarious time in Europe. The black press responded that the black community did not want to harm the war effort; they simply wanted "the opportunity to serve their country to the full measure of their capacity and devotion."[2]

By the start of World War II, the black press was over 100 years old, a powerful voice for African Americans. There were also many African American journals to complement the weekly press; the *Crisis* by W. E. B. DuBois, the *Messenger*, and the *Opportunity* were among the most prominent. Increasingly, news that was by, for, and about the black community was in demand. The mandate of the black press was to cover items that were ignored in the mainstream press, primarily the news, activities, and achievements of African Americans and black communities around the world. By World War II, the circulation of black newspapers in the United States had surpassed one million, a relatively small yet influential force led by the *Baltimore Afro-American*, the *Chicago Defender*, and the *Pittsburgh Courier*. These papers and others were instrumental in moving the black population both geographically and socially.

Freedom's Journal, the first black-owned and -operated newspaper in the United States, was founded by Samuel Cornish and John Russwurm in 1827 in New York City, the same year that slavery was abolished in the state of New York. Although it was in print for only two years, *Freedom's Journal* was a strong advocate for the rights of blacks, including the right to vote. It served mostly freed blacks living in the north and reported on political issues at home and in Africa. It published job listings and heralded the achievements of prominent black community members. The *Journal* was followed by Frederick Douglass's *North Star* in 1847, another abolitionist publication written by an ex-slave. The motto of that paper stated frankly that "Right is of no Sex—Truth is of no Color—God is the Father of us all, and we are all brethren." The paper was edited by Douglass for seventeen years from Rochester, New York, and urged every black man to fight in the Union Army, or as Douglass put it, to "get an eagle on his button, a musket on his shoulder, and the star-spangled banner over his head."[3] Douglass's powerful rhetoric had a lasting and measurable effect on the development of the black press in America, which saw the start of five hundred other black newspapers between the Civil War and 1900.

The *Chicago Defender*

In 1893, as the Colombian Exposition in Chicago was drawing near, black leaders including Douglass and journalist Ida B. Wells noted with dismay that none of the exhibits included participation by blacks. In response, the Exposition organizers set aside a "Colored American Day" in an effort to contain the protests. On August 15, 1893, one thousand blacks came out to celebrate and to hear Frederick Douglass speak. His speech, which was nearly drowned out by white members of the audience, proclaimed that "men talk of the Negro problem. There is no Negro problem. The problem is whether Americans can live up to their own Constitution."

A young printing student from the south, Robert S. Abbott, was among the many audience members. Inspired by the speech and the possibility of a future in journalism, Abbott remained in Chicago to found the *Chicago Defender* in 1905, the weekly masthead of which proclaimed, "American Race Prejudice Must Be Destroyed." With an initial press run of only three hundred, buoyed by World War I and the "Great Migration" of blacks to the North, the paper grew to have a circulation of sixteen thousand weekly copies by 1915.[4]

As much as the paper benefited from the Great Migration, the migration itself was promoted by the paper. The *Chicago Defender* was a major catalyst for the movement of blacks from the South to the North. Black-owned papers in the South operated under threats of violence that kept their editorial positions relatively weak, but in the North, black papers were free to write in a much more confrontational manner. Abbott reasoned that he could expand his readership by sending his papers south, and he could expand his local readership by convincing those in the South to move north. In this prediction he was correct; with encouragement from the *Defender*, the black population of Chicago increased 148 percent between 1910 and 1920.[5] Abbott's migration campaign was undertaken on a number of fronts. Using tabloid-format sensationalism in his paper, including screaming headlines and scandal-ridden front-page crime stories, he emphasized the amount and severity of the oppression in the South by focusing on the harsh violence toward blacks, lynchings, discriminatory hiring practices, and political hypocrisy. By contrast, the North was presented as a free land of job opportunities, plentiful housing, and social harmony.[6] He regularly printed job ads that beckoned southern workers north. The great industrial North, he argued, had an insatiable appetite for skilled labor, with salaries beyond anything possible in the South. Headlines such as "Spring to See Greatest Migration in History," and "Mob Rule Causes Biggest Exodus in History of the South," both reported on and encouraged departure from the South.[7] As further enticement, Abbott printed train schedules—one way—from southern states to Chicago. For large groups, Abbott booked blocks of tickets on the train at a reduced rate.[8] He organized "traveling clubs," promoted "migration fever" in the pages of the *Defender*, and designated particular days on the calendar for "northern drives."

The *Defender*'s style was aggressive, even radical, compared to other printed material available in the South. Abbott, who had trained as a lawyer but was discouraged from practicing because of his color, hurled invective at racial injustice, often using sarcasm to get his point across. He noted in the *Defender* that between 1882 and 1919, three thousand blacks had been murdered by lynch mobs, and he fought against the practice by keeping the story in the spotlight as white papers ignored it. In one editorial on lynching, Abbott noted that there were "five white men lynched, it seems we can have nothing exclusive!"[9] Neither did Abbott use the common terminology of the day to describe his community, often forgoing the words "black" and "Negro" in favor of "the Race." Countering the practice by white papers of parenthetically noting a man's race if he was black,

Abbott began to do the same for white names, resulting in stories that would read "Woodrow Wilson (white) announced today..."

Such tactics were not without risk. Southern black papers had been torched for lesser provocation, and Abbott was incorrigible in his fight for racial justice. Being caught in possession of the *Defender* was dangerous, and selling it was even more so. Using the train porters as delivery mechanisms, the *Defender* was bundled and loaded on trains in Chicago and then thrown from the trains just before reaching stations in the South to avoid detection by local authorities.[10] Landowners in the South tried to stop the circulation of the paper, which was raising race consciousness and depleting their source of cheap labor, but the porters continued to find ways of circumventing officials. The railroads were crucial to the circulation of the *Defender*, which became the first black paper to achieve national circulation. By 1920 the circulation had reached 230,000, two-thirds of which were sold outside of Chicago.[11] The railroads also helped southern newspapers and magazines travel north, allowing Abbott to learn of events there. A regular feature called "News From Your Home Town" kept people up to date on gossip, births, deaths, and weddings from southern locations. Once the papers reached their destinations, it is estimated that each issue passed through the hands of five different people. The papers were read aloud wherever black community members gathered: at church, in barbershops, and in private homes. The *Defender* sold for five cents and was sold through over two thousand vending agents across the country.[12]

The increasing popularity of the *Chicago Defender* and of the black press generally in exposing the harsh realities of race discrimination made them extremely vulnerable to backlash. Southern industry was suffering from the loss of labor to the north, and when myths about blacks not being able to survive in the cold were quickly dispelled, white Southerners sought ways of extinguishing the harmful papers. When sent through the mail, black papers were regularly stopped at the post office for being factious or subversive.[13] When World War I broke out, the government found a new tool to suppress the power of the black press in the Espionage Act. As the black press questioned the degree of loyalty the black community should have to a country still so discriminatory, the government found this harmful to national unity and potentially seditious. The *Defender* repeatedly pointed out the hypocrisy of Wilsonian democracy for the rest of the world when it had yet to be achieved for the black community at home. When Abbott was brought up on charges after printing an editorial cartoon that showed black soldiers fighting the enemy and white soldiers shooting them in the back, it was only by promising to toe the government line on the war that he evaded jail time. He was allowed to resume printing after agreeing to buy war bonds and encouraging his readers to do so. Under such circumstances, editors like Abbott were careful to express their issues in Constitutional terms rather than as disloyalty to the government.[14]

The *Chicago Defender* kept a close watch on the progress of World War I, paying particular attention to incidents of discrimination and segregation of black soldiers, as well as publicizing their military accomplishments, which were ignored in the mainstream press. Peace talks, however, were followed by a summer of upheaval in Chicago, when the city's worst race riots commenced. Abbott's successful resettlement of blacks from the South led to a violent backlash once the war was over, and returning soldiers found unprecedented competition for available jobs.

In what the *Chicago Defender* referred to as the "Red Summer," the city was witness to daily bloodshed. On July 17, 1919, a group of black youths swimming at a beach on Lake Michigan were mobbed by a group of white children, causing one black swimmer to drown. That July, more than thirty people were killed in riots, and over the course of the summer the *Defender* ran a daily box score in the paper tracking how many casualties each side had suffered.

Abbott continued to use his paper to bring people north during the 1920s and to help them assimilate once they arrived. The *Defender* printed useful information for those living in Chicago, including listings of where to look for a job and which businesses not to patronize for fear of overt discrimination. In an effort to help rural farm workers adjust to the new urban environment, Abbott published etiquette tips in the paper and tried to promote social skills, including admonitions to refrain from picking one's nose or fingernails in public. For the newly arrived, ads from the Chicago League on Urban Conditions Among Negroes offered services:

> If You are a Stranger in the City
> If you want a job. If you want a place to live
> If you are having trouble with your employer
> If you want information or advice of any kind
> No charges, no fees

The *Defender* published many such ads for local groups trying to reach the new black urban population, which was both a blessing and a curse. While the *Defender* could not command large advertising revenues from wealthy department stores like the white press, this also meant that it enjoyed an editorial freedom unencumbered by the desires of advertisers. Most of the ads in the early days of the *Defender* were for products of dubious quality or social value, such as skin lightening creams and hair straighteners, but these advertisers made no other demands on the newspaper beyond their own paid space. This left the *Defender* free to print "the truth" about local businesses and to organize boycotts against those that would not hire black workers.

By 1933 Abbott was able to correct for the oversight of the race at the Colombian Exposition of his childhood by promoting Chicago's "Century of Progress." The *Defender* was one of the sponsors of the event and heralded its features in its pages:

> Numerous exhibits at this fair are of especial interest to members of the Race. The Jean Baptiste Pointe De Saible cabin, a replica of the first house built in Chicago, and erected by the city council of Chicago, takes first place because of the fact that De Saible was a "Negro." The National Urban League exhibit in the Hall of Social Science is also attracting unusual attention. Race performers at the Midget Village, the Show Boat, and the Streets of Paris and other scenes in the gigantic exposition offer unusual attractions to the Race visitor who comes to the fair.

The story further encouraged readers to drop by the offices of the *Chicago Defender* for information "on any subject" and to "make our office your headquarters and feel welcome here at all times. It is our contribution to the Century of Progress and we urge you to take advantage of it."[15]

Robert S. Abbott was a prophet for the black press, believing wholeheartedly in its power to transform a people. "The daily press," he wrote, "is a powerful weapon for good or for evil. It speaks to millions throughout the day; it moulds their opinions; it can help hinder or destroy. And it can array nation against nation, race against race with its vicious appeals."[16] He took his role as publisher and community leader seriously, and knew that how he chose to present the news was of consequence for the development of a strong black community. When Abbott died in 1940, the paper was taken over by his nephew John Sengstacke, who was responsible for the newspaper's leadership during World War II and became a celebrated newspaperman in his own right. He gained special renown for installing Harry McAlpin, the first black correspondent, in the White House[17] and starting the Negro Newspaper Publishers' Association (NNPA) in 1940, serving as its first president. The organization was designed to bring together all of the existing associations under one banner, including the Associated Negro Press, which had started at the *Defender* during World War I, and several regional syndicates. The cooperative news sharing arrangement, however, was not welcomed by the *Defender*'s closest competitors at the *Courier* and the *Afro-American*, who

John Sengstacke, right, of the *Chicago Defender*, 1942, a leading African American newspaper during WWII. Courtesy of Library of Congress.

were reluctant to join.[18] The NNPA, however, proved to be an important mobilizing body during the Second World War; it aimed to present a united front to the government on war issues. At the 1942 NNPA meeting it was declared that

> the Negro Newspaper Association is unequivocal in its loyalty to the United States and to President Franklin D. Roosevelt, who is charting our national course in this hour of crisis. Freedom and Democracy must be saved for all the world. The spirit of the Constitution, especially the Bill of Rights, is an inheritance which we must pass on to future generations. To that course, we dedicate our newspapers.[19]

This undiluted support of President Roosevelt was not universally felt among all black papers. The United States' entry into World War II was a watershed event that forced many black publishers to reconsider their position on the president, which had grown quite antagonistic in the years leading up to 1941. Primary among those beginning to question Roosevelt's impending third term was Robert L. Vann at the *Pittsburgh Courier*.

A newsboy selling the *Chicago Defender*, Chicago, Illinois, April 1942.
CORBIS/Jack Delano.

The *Pittsburgh Courier*

During World War II, the main competition for war coverage for
African American readers came from the *Pittsburgh Courier*, which had
achieved a circulation of 277,900 by 1947, to the *Chicago Defender's*
193,900.[20] The *Courier* took advantage of the same shifts in population
that benefited the *Chicago Defender* and the *Baltimore Afro-American*: a
new urban industrial black population recently relocated from the

South that was freer to enjoy new privileges like reading, writing, and community organization. By the second decade of the twentieth century, Pennsylvania had the highest black population of any northern state.[21] The paper was incorporated in May 1910, somewhat later than its two nearest competitors, and its most notable editor, Robert L. Vann, like others in the black press, came to journalism as a secondary career. Like Abbott, Vann had trained as a lawyer and was in fact brought to the *Courier* to act as the paper's counsel.[22] When internal management disagreements left the operation without an editor, Vann stepped into the position, but he never relinquished his primary vocation as a lawyer. It was his dual career that helped to popularize the *Courier*, as Vann could both publicize his legal achievements in its pages as well as use the cases as fodder for newspaper content. He was reluctant to sensationalize serious crime cases in the paper, as Abbott did, for fear that they would run counter to the paper's overall message of racial uplift, but he did not hesitate to buttress his own reputation by heralding his impressive wins. It was with some internal consternation that he realized that his personal victories in the courtroom provided copy that vastly increased newsstand sales.

Vann was unabashedly capitalist in his outlook, and he used his paper to espouse middle-class values and self-sufficiency in the black community. He was wary of the communist leanings of some black editors and supported local black business in its pursuit of the American dream, often to the detriment of other ethnic groups: "There are quite a few stores on the Hill conducted by Jews and others whose patronage is largely made up from colored people. Patronize only those advertisers who patronize us, and you will not only help this paper but the Race. Think over this."[23] Vann berated black citizens for choosing lower-priced goods from white stores over loyalty to black-owned businesses, while at the same time he respected how other ethnic groups were able to survive by knowing and serving their own communities, even if his arguments tended toward the stereotypical. In encouraging blacks to emulate the Jews, he wrote:

> The Jew knows the American people are crazy about clothes. He knows the clothes will sell as long as the people have a dollar in cash or a dollar in credit. Mr. Negro, what is it that your people are crazy to buy? Find out and get into the business of furnishing the thing. Time will build you a wonderful business.[24]

Vann himself tried his hand at a number of unsuccessful business ventures, including a black-owned bank, a black-only hospital, a high-priced black literary magazine, and several investment schemes in West Africa involving mining and export.[25] Most if not all of these endeavors were aimed at giving the black community the means to prosper on its own without having to rely on other groups. It is here that Vann's position on civil rights was distinctly limited to favor the black community. He was emphatically in favor of improved opportunities for blacks, even at the expense of other groups. In fact, Vann was explicitly against new immigrants who came to America to earn money and favored stricter quotas to regulate their entry, like the National Origins Act of 1924. Questioning the immigrant's status as a citizen, he argued that the immigrant

> earns all the American money he wants, and at his own sweet convenience, he leaves for his native fireside, and forgets America until more money is needed.... [Quotas] will reduce the number of half and half citizens whose names and lives are hyphenated to suit their own convenience.[26]

Above all, Vann marshaled a crusade of self-reliance for blacks at every level. "Really, brother, in this day of keen competition, if you expect to succeed, do well that which you find to do and above all cultivate the habits of reliability."[27] This philosophy was reiterated in the masthead of the paper, which preached "Work, Integrity, Tact, Temperance, Prudence, Courage, Faith."[28]

Despite Robert Vann's best efforts at keeping his community afloat, the Depression hit industrial states like Pennsylvania particularly hard. Many blacks had come north in the 1920s as strike breakers in the coal industry, and they were hard hit when coal and steel plants were forced to cut back during the economic downturn. It was partly out of his desire to help that Vann accelerated his efforts in public service, and he was among the first black leaders to advocate a shift from the Republican Party to the Democrats to join in Roosevelt's New Deal programs, even though many of them ran counter to his own philosophy of self-reliance. Vann came out as a Democrat in his famous 1932 "Patriot and Partisan" speech in which he advocated "turning Lincoln's picture to the wall," as a way of signaling that the black community did not have to be forever beholden to the Republican Party for ending slavery. He urged blacks to support the party that served their interests rather than to vote purely out of party loyalty.[29]

For his work in support of the Democratic Party, Vann was made a special assistant to the attorney general in 1933. Thinking this post would grant him the public influence he had always sought, Vann was eager to use the position to give patronage appointments to other blacks. But the position turned out to be less powerful than he had imagined. Roosevelt's New Deal rhetoric contained little that would specifically address the plight of the black community, and Vann had little opportunity to influence national politics in Washington. He was given insignificant tasks to perform in the attorney general's office and had little or no profile in the position.[30]

Though he had a meager impact on national party politics, Vann continued to use his paper to promote the causes that he supported in Pittsburgh and Pennsylvania, and he was vindicated there when the Democrats swept the state elections of 1934. To show their gratitude, state politicians named Vann to five committees, including the Pennsylvania Committee on Public Assistance and the Governor's Commission to Codify the Laws of Pennsylvania.[31] It was from these platforms that Vann pushed equal rights legislation for the state, which resulted in the signing of a bill into law in 1935. Despite this watershed legislation, however, the state found the new equality difficult to enforce, and many white businesses chose to suffer the minor penalties for infraction rather than pay equal wages to minority employees.[32]

The editorial stance of the *Pittsburgh Courier* at this time was anti-union, anti-Communist, and somewhat isolationist, in contrast to many other papers of the black press. When nine black teenagers were accused of raping two white girls on a train from Chattanooga to Memphis in 1931, the Communist Party's International Legal Defense stepped in to defend them, hoping to enlist more black participation in the party. The Scottsboro boys, as they became known in trials that lasted nearly seven years, had at first been taken on by the legal team of the NAACP, which appeared to some to lack the resources needed to mount an effective defense. Vann supported the NAACP's team, editorializing that "Negroes should stand firm for the NAACP and against the blandishments of the reds."[33]

Around the world, military invasions in black countries forced the black press to take a stand on behalf of the black community in America, as a matter of race interest. Despite the fact that the *Courier* was the only black paper to have sent a reporter to Africa to cover events in Ethiopia, Joel Rogers's reports of the Italo-Ethiopian war were not evidence of the *Courier*'s wholehearted belief in intervention. Stories filed from Ethiopia boosted circulation in 1937, when it reached a quarter of a million, but the paper remained circumspect about its level of commitment to other black nations. Vann and his editorialists cautioned that too much attention to race inequity elsewhere might be undertaken at the expense of important battles at home:

> The cost of a good machine gun delivered in Abyssinia will pay a youngster's tuition in a good college for a year.... The purchase and equipment of a Douglas bomber will build one thousand playgrounds with swimming pools.[34]

Notable *Courier* writer George Schuyler wrote that the invasions taking place overseas, with their echoes of colonialism, had important parallels with the circumstance of inequality at home, but he did not advocate black involvement in the fight. "Why," he asked, "should Negroes fight for democracy abroad when they were refused democracy in every American activity except tax paying?"[35] The dilemma was a common one and was found throughout the black press leading up to America's entry into the war. The *Courier* took the position that support for other nations in the race struggle had not been reciprocal, that "while our disabilities have been fairly well publicized throughout the world since Emancipation, no aid has ever come from our brethren across the seas. We have fought our battle alone and they will have to do likewise."[36] As with other issues of international importance, the black press struggled with the tension between helping those abroad and helping to strengthen their own communities at home.

In spite of this general tendency against intervention abroad, the onset of World War II posed a new set of foreign policy dilemmas for the *Pittsburgh Courier*. The paper's advocacy on the issue of military integration was one of the most important circulation-boosting policies for the *Courier*, as it was for many other black newspapers. The *Courier* had long argued for better black representation in the armed forces, and Vann used his connections in Washington to help plead the case. In 1938, when Vann was sixty years old, he conferred with Senator Hamilton Fish of New York and Emmett J. Scott, secretary-treasurer of Howard University, to draft a set of recommendations for improving the status of black soldiers in the military. Senator Fish brought the recommendations to the House in the form of three bills, known as the "*Courier*-Fish" bills, which sought an end to discrimination in the military, entry for two blacks a year to the U.S. Military Academy at West Point, and provision for an all-black division.[37] None of the bills passed the House Military Affairs Committee, however, suffering from entrenched feelings about the inferiority of black soldiers and the fact that the sponsoring Senator was a Republican. Vann also wrote personally to President Roosevelt to ask for an end to the race discrimination in the military and published the correspondence in the *Courier*.[38] For several months following, the *Courier* continuously reprimanded Roosevelt for his weakness on the military question and even supported Wendell Willkie in the 1940 presidential election as a result. Bending to the pressure of prominent black leaders like Vann, an amended Fish bill passed in September 1940, and Roosevelt announced the creation of black air units at the eleventh hour leading up to the election.[39] Shortly before the election had been decided in Roosevelt's favor, however, on October 24, 1940, Robert Vann died.

Along with these more public battles over the role of black service-men in the military, considerably more covert operations were taking place in other branches of the government. What appeared as divided loyalty in the war for democracy in the black press did not go unnoticed by the Federal Bureau of Investigation (FBI). In 1939, the FBI received a report from the Chinese government attesting to the Japanese sympa-thies of the black press. "Japanese Propaganda Among Negroes" named the *Pittsburgh Courier*, among other prominent black newspapers, as Communist sympathizers. In May 1942, Roosevelt held a cabinet meet-ing to discuss the subject of the black press, the result of which was the publication of two reports by the Office of Facts and Figures. The reports analyzed the content of leading black papers and concluded that their overriding theme was discrimination and inequality.[40] This was thought to hurt morale and stir up feelings of disunity, and the reports were followed by several on-site visits to black newspaper offices by the FBI. As the *Pittsburgh Courier* wrote of these visits, "This sort of thing is an obvious effort to cow the Negro press into soft-pedaling its criticism and ending its forthright exposure of the outrageous dis-crimination to which Negroes have been subjected."[41]

One of the more worrisome trends that the FBI noted in its survey was a campaign invented by the *Pittsburgh Courier* that quickly spread throughout the black press. The Double V campaign urged people to think of victory on two fronts: victory abroad and victory at home. The campaign began with a letter received by the *Courier* from a twenty-six-year-old black man named James G. Thompson from Wichita, Kansas, on January 31, 1942:

> The V for victory sign is being displayed prominently in all so-called democratic countries which are fighting for victory over aggression, slavery and tyranny. If this V sign means that to those now engaged in this great conflict, then let we colored Americans adopt the double VV for a double victory. The first V for victory over our enemies without, the second V for victory over our enemies within. For surely those who perpetuate these ugly prejudices here are seeking to destroy our democratic form of government just as surely as the Axis forces.[42]

Beginning the following week, the paper was filled with entreaties to join in the Double V campaign. New York correspondent Edgar T. Rouzeau wrote an impassioned plea under the headline "Black Amer-ican Wars on Double Front For High Stakes," in which he argued that

> reduced to its very essence, this means that Black Americans must fight two wars and win in both. There is the convulsive war abroad. There is the bloodless war at home. The first must be fought with the destructive

"By Executive Order—President Truman Wipes Out Segregation in Armed Forces." *Chicago Defender*, July 31, 1948. Courtesy of Prints and Photographs Division, Library of Congress.

weapons of science. The other must be fought with the pen, in the classrooms and on the speaking platforms. Even in a democracy, freedom is not a bequest but a fruit of conquest.[43]

At the *Pittsburgh Courier*, the war was fought not only with the pen, but also with a wide array of symbols, events, and sponsorships. The paper designed a Double V logo to accompany every story related to the campaign, with one V on top of the other, surrounded by the words "Democracy" and "At Home and Abroad" superimposed over an image of a globe and an eagle. For six months the paper pictured citizens adopting double-V poses with their fingers, arms, and legs and shaving or braiding their hair into the shape of two Vs. Coverage highlighted twins in the double V formation and coworkers on the job making the gesture. The campaign was endorsed by many politicians and community leaders, both black and white. The *Courier* solicited letters from readers that described inventive ways of demonstrating the Double V, and readers eagerly responded with ideas. Pins, buttons, banners, posters, balloons, hats, cars, and window decals all celebrated the campaign as the Double V craze spread across the country in the Pittsburgh *Courier*'s most successful and far-reaching crusade.[44]

This campaign, which embodied the very essence of Robert L. Vann's spirit, was directed by Ira Lewis, who had taken over the paper in Vann's absence. After Lewis's death in 1948, the paper attempted to replicate the paper's success with the Double V campaign with a 1953 campaign called the Double E for educational equality, which was aimed at helping to raise money for the legal fees of *Brown v. Board of Education*.[45] This campaign, too, helped to form the legacy of the *Pittsburgh Courier* as a driving force in the community that supported and developed the city, state, and nation for its black residents.

The *Baltimore Afro-American*

The *Baltimore Afro-American* was started by John Henry Murphy Sr., an ex-slave, in 1892. Murphy was freed in 1863 in the Maryland Emancipation Act, which gave freedom to those who had fought in the Union Army.[46] He merged his *Sunday School Helper* with two other church publications to form a new paper, the *Afro-American Ledger*. The paper raised money by selling stock exclusively to blacks in the community. In 1905 the mission of the paper was declared: "To present to the world that side of the Afro-American that can be had in no other way, and in the second place to as far as possible assist in the great uplift of the people it represents."[47] With its religious roots, the paper that became the *Baltimore Afro-American*, or the *Afro*, as it was more commonly known, was a tool for moral and spiritual guidance. It sought to raise the black population out of its degraded economic state by promoting middle-class values, self-determination, and self-sufficiency for African Americans. Part of this campaign was to be seen in the paper's name itself; chosen as a conscious effort to self-identify as Afro-American rather than Negro.[48] These goals were approached through the educational and political campaigns of the newspaper.

After John Murphy's death in 1922, his children continued the daily operation of the paper, with his son Carl Murphy serving as editor and publisher for forty-five years. Baltimore proved to be an advantageous site for a successful black paper. It was, technically, a northern city, though it maintained a strong cultural connection to the South. After the Civil War, blacks made up 15 percent of the population, and they enjoyed a much higher rate of literacy than in most southern cities.[49] Beyond the city of Baltimore, the *Afro* extended its reach by setting up news bureaus in New York, Washington, and Philadelphia, and at its height there were thirteen regional editions of the paper, including papers in Richmond, Raleigh, Newark, Washington, and Philadelphia.

Outside the United States, the *Baltimore Afro-American* was attentive to world events and the experiences of the race in other countries. The paper was not a member of any press association or wire service in its early years, and thus had to send its own correspondents abroad to cover events. These reporters were sent mainly to countries with large black populations, and the paper's attitude toward blacks in the rest of the world was represented in the graphic on its front page, which depicted the continent of Africa shaking hands with North America.

In its coverage of foreign affairs in the early part of the twentieth century, Liberia, Ethiopia, and Haiti were the main focal points, as the paper paid close attention to colonialism around the world. In general, the paper supported black nationalism wherever possible. Italy's invasion of Ethiopia in 1935 was correctly identified in the black press, if few other places, as the start of another world war, representing the repression of basic human rights. Numerous official delegations of prominent black editors and publishers were sent to African countries in an effort to bind together the black peoples of the world.

The *Baltimore Afro-American*, like most of the black press, saw World War II as an opportunity to prove the patriotism and worth of the black community. Germany's treatment of the Jews was seen as analogous to the treatment of blacks in the United States, and thus a good argument for fighting for democracy on all fronts. This stance was complicated, however, by the *Afro*'s position on Germany during World War I, which was somewhat more equivocal. Carl Murphy, a Germanic scholar who was in Germany when the war broke out, found redeeming qualities in some of their policies, and wrote that the Germans were receiving unfair coverage in America. The May 9, 1931 issue of the *Afro-American* published some of the tenets of the Communist program that the paper found useful for bringing about economic justice for African Americans. The alliance with the Communists had been strengthened after their successful handling of the Scottsboro Boys trial, which divided those in the black press who supported the NAACP at all costs from those who did not. The *Baltimore Afro-American*, with explicit admissions by Carl Murphy and Managing Editor William T. Jones in 1935, was largely pro-Communist, even supporting the Communist Party ticket in the 1932 campaign, although the paper officially endorsed Roosevelt. None of these editorial positions were easily defended when World War II made radical papers suspect and prone to censure by the government, the FBI, and the post office.[50] By 1939, however, the paper had adopted a pro-war stance, offering three justifications for the position:

1. The War would stimulate black migration to the Northern industrial states, a benefit to the race,
2. The War would mean eventual freedom for African Americans, and
3. African Americans were against Hitler because of his race hatred of Jews.[51]

The Baltimore *Afro-American*, like the Pittsburgh *Courier*, supported Wendell Willkie in the 1940 presidential election to oppose Roosevelt's reluctance to help integrate the military: "In this regard, President Roosevelt not only forgot us but he neglected us, deserted and abandoned us to our enemies."[52] These political convictions put the black press in an especially precarious position, as they were both for the war and against the commander-in-chief at the same time.

The *Baltimore Afro-American* was unsurpassed in its war coverage, sending more correspondents than any other black newspaper. Because it did not belong to any press gathering services, the *Afro* stationed its own reporters all over Europe, as well as in Africa and the South Pacific. Among those filing for the *Afro-American* was Vincent Tubbs who, starting in March 1943, was the first black journalist in the Pacific.[53] Elizabeth Murphy Phillips Moss, Carl Murphy's daughter, was the first black female correspondent. Moss traveled around Europe during World War II and completed a series on black troops that she filed from England, under her pen name Bettye M. Moss.[54]

At home, the *Baltimore Afro-American* campaigned for hiring more blacks in city positions, including the fire and police departments. It fought for representation in the state legislature, for a state-supported university, for equal pay for black teachers and for desegregation on railway cars. In one of its most famous crusades, the paper fought for equal access for blacks to recreational areas like city parks, which were racially segregated. Like many other black papers, it supported a "don't buy where you can't work" campaign beginning in 1931, focusing on merchants on Pennsylvania Avenue in an effort to both spare shoppers from potential humiliation and to strengthen the black business community.[55] By 1945, these efforts took shape as the "Orchids and Onions" feature, in which reporters evaluated local businesses on their policies of discrimination and bestowed either an orchid or an onion next to the name of the business in the paper.[56]

The *Baltimore Afro-American* also had one of the most comprehensive approaches to improving the living conditions of black residents of any of the black press. In an exclusive *Afro-American* series entitled "Jim Crow Guide to USA," the newspaper chronicled instances of discrimination across the country. One installment, "How Housing is Kept Lilywhite," began:

> If you are a Caucasian and a Christian, you are more or less free to live anywhere you can afford in the United States.
> If you lack one or both of these qualifications, you will find yourself barred by one or more of such factors as laws, contracts, conspiracies, and terrorism from buying, leasing, renting, inheriting or otherwise acquiring or occupying a residence in many neighborhoods, both desirable and undesirable.[57]

In addition to its regular coverage of issues such as overcrowding, support for low-cost public housing, and tenement health conditions in Baltimore and beyond, the *Afro-American* initiated a neighborhood improvement campaign, an annual event to clean up neighborhoods and reduce crime. The *Afro* Clean Block Campaign was sponsored by the newspaper and conducted by the paper's court reporter Isaac Bannister.[58] The paper outlined a map of the city with each block identified; residents signed up as a block and worked over the summer to improve it by removing garbage, planting flowers, and painting house fronts. A committee of judges would then evaluate each block and award prizes for the best improvements. The campaign was lauded nationally as a successful mechanism for fighting crime locally and promoting community awareness and cohesiveness. As the *Chicago Daily Tribune* wrote in 1938,

> this clean block campaign is an annual community effort sponsored by the energetic *Afro-American*, a newspaper which offers prizes for cleanliness and beautification. This year, with more than 300 blocks

competing, the paper has found it necessary to add a new class of entries which would include suburban blocks. Five thousand children have registered for the campaign. The photographs published in the *Evening Sun*, showing bright and shiny blocks in North Gilmor and Dolphin streets, demonstrate what can be done when the cooperative spirit is aroused in a neighborhood. In some instances, where a vacant house threatened to spoil the appearance of a block, those houses have been given beauty treatments by residents of the block.[59]

The *Baltimore Afro-American* was also influential in the larger cultural life of African Americans, promoting notable black authors, artists, entertainers, and athletes who were being overlooked in the mainstream white papers. The *Afro-American* devoted considerable coverage to Hattie McDaniel after she won an Oscar for her role in *Gone With the Wind* in 1940, and the paper was the best place to read about the victories of black athletes. Sam Lacy, the *Afro-American*'s sports editor, provided extensive reporting of Jackie Robinson in 1947 when he broke the color barrier in major league baseball by joining the Brooklyn Dodgers, following Robinson to spring training in Cuba and chronicling his life in detail throughout the season.[60] Lacy, along with other sports writers in the black press like the *Pittsburgh Courier*'s Wendell Smith, were not only covering the wins and losses of these athletes, but lobbying on behalf of their right to play in the first place. Sports writers at the *Courier*, the *Defender* and the *Afro* were instrumental in pressuring major sports franchises to desegregate.

One of the ongoing concerns of the *Afro* was the use of language itself. It had made a point of emphasizing the importance of naming by calling the paper the *Afro-American* in the first instance, and this crusade was maintained as a priority at the paper. In 1936, the paper began to criticize the lyrics of the Kentucky State song, "My Old Kentucky Home" by Steven Foster, for its use of the word *darky*.[61] Since that time, the paper demonstrated its enthusiasm for the importance of language in naming the African American community as a crucial step in esteem building. These campaigns, which the paper often mounted against books, song lyrics, and films, even took on the Associated Press in 1947 for not capitalizing the word *Negro* in a story.[62]

The *Baltimore Afro-American* is in many ways the quintessential paper of the black press. Its first editor was born into slavery; it made its name crusading against the worst indignities of segregation throughout the twentieth century; it expanded its readership beyond its own city boundaries; above all, it kept the business in the family. When Carl Murphy died in 1967, his daughter became the publisher. There are now fourth-generation members of the Murphy family in charge of what is now the longest continually running family-owned paper in the country.

After World War II, these three papers, the *Chicago Defender*, the *Pittsburgh Courier*, and the *Baltimore Afro-American*, all had national editions, but the war years would prove to be their strongest time. Once the civil rights movement took hold in the 1960s, many of the best black reporters and editors were hired away by larger, white, mainstream papers, and the black press lacked the resources to maintain their dominant position with black audiences. They survived by consolidating and making many of the structural changes that were occurring in the mainstream press. They were constantly competing with each other and for each other's readers. When Robert L. Vann tried to start his own national advertising agency to take over Ziff-Davis, the *Defender* would not join, and Vann was equally reluctant to join Sengstacke's Negro Newspaper Publishers' Association. As Vann wrote when trying to lure the *Defender*'s accounts to his agency, "the success of the *Defender* was achieved in spite of the *Courier*, and the success of the *Courier* was achieved in spite of the *Defender*."[63]

In 1956, the *Chicago Defender* became a daily rather than a weekly paper and was the largest black-owned daily in the world. In an effort to expand through consolidation, Robert Sengstacke acquired other black papers including the *Michigan Chronicle* and the *Memphis Tri-State Defender*. He bought the *Pittsburgh Courier* in 1965, putting an end to one of the most competitive rivalries in the black press.

Throughout its history, the purpose of the black press was explicit advocacy for the black community. It helped to form black communities, raised consciousness of race issues, and elevated the profile of blacks and their accomplishments which were largely ignored by the mainstream press. As Gunnar Myrdal wrote in *An American Dilemma*,

> the press defines the Negro group to the Negroes themselves. The individual Negro is invited to share in the sufferings, grievances, and pretensions of the millions far outside the narrow local community. This creates a feeling of strength and solidarity. The press, more than any other institution, has created the Negro group as a social and a psychological reality to the individual Negro.[64]

Looking back on 115 years of the black press, the *Pittsburgh Courier* wrote equally passionately about the function and significance of the history of the black press, of which it had been a crucial part:

One of the GREATEST contributions of the Negro press has been its part in eliminating SLAVISHNESS and a sense of inferiority from the American Negro psychology.

Week in and week out for 115 years it has told the Negro to straighten up and be a MAN among men.

Week after week it has told the Negro to get an EDUCATION, to demand full citizenship RIGHTS, to measure up to the standards of his environment, to equal and surpass others through sheer MERIT....

The Negro press is the FREEST press in America because it is the ONLY press that consistently advocates freedom and equality for all citizens; that urges strict adherence to the letter and SPIRIT of the US Constitution; that condemns unfairness and prejudice against others because of race, color or creed; that serves its readers FIRST and foremost.[65]

Notes

1. Neil A. Wynn, *The Afro-American and the Second World War* (New York: Holmes & Meier, 1976), 23.

2. "Mr. President, Count on Us," *Chicago Defender*, 13 December 1941.

3. Quoted in Diana Schaub, "The Spirit of a Free Man," *Public Interest* (Summer 2000).

4. Juliet E. K. Walker, "The Promised Land: The *Chicago Defender* and the Black Press in Illinois: 1862–1970," in *The Black Press in the Middle West, 1865–1985*, ed. Henry Louis Suggs (Westport, CT: Greenwood Press, 1996), 9–50.

5. Emmett J. Scott, *Negro Migration During the War* (New York: Oxford University Press, 1920), 102.

6. Allan H. Spear, *Black Chicago: The Making of a Ghetto* (Chicago: University Press of Chicago, 1967), 134.

7. "Spring to See Greatest Migration in History," *Chicago Defender*, 21 February 1925; "Mob Rule Causes Biggest Exodus in History of the South," *Chicago Defender*, 24 July 1926. See also Gareth Canaan, "Part of the Loaf: Economic Conditions of Chicago's African-American Working Class During the 1920s," *Journal of Social History* 35 (2001): 1, 147.

8. Walker, "Promised Land," 27.

9. Robert Abbott (NT), *Chicago Defender*, 9 January 1915.

10. William G. Jordan, *Black Newspapers and America's War for Democracy, 1914–1920* (Chapel Hill and London: University of North Carolina Press, 2001), 33.

11. Roy Ottley, *The Lonely Warrior: The Life and Times of Robert S. Abbott* (Chicago: Henry Regnery, 1959) 139.

12. James R. Grossman, *Land of Hope: Chicago, Black Southerners, and the Great Migration* (Chicago: University of Chicago Press, 1989), 82–88.

13. Walker, "Promised Land," 26.

14. Patrick Washburn, *A Question of Sedition* (New York: Oxford University Press, 1986); Caryl A. Cooper, "The *Chicago Defender*: Filling in the Gaps for

the Office of Civilian Defense, 1941–1945," *The Western Journal of Black Studies* 23 (1999): 111–118.

15. "Chicago's Progress Shown at Fair," *Chicago Defender,* 10 June 1933.

16. Robert S. Abbott, "Breeders of Race Riots," *Chicago Defender,* 11 September 1937.

17. "John H. Sengstacke, Trailblazing Publisher, Dies at 84," *Jet,* 16 June 1997, 4. Blacks were not welcome at Roosevelt's press conferences until 1944.

18. Andrew Buni, *Robert L. Vann of the* Pittsburgh Courier: *Politics and Black Journalism* (Pittsburgh: University of Pittsburgh Press, 1974), 315.

19. *Pittsburgh Courier,* 13 June 1942.

20. Hayward Farrar, *The Baltimore Afro-American, 1892–1950* (Westport, CT: Greenwood Press, 1998), 16.

21. Buni, *Robert L. Vann,* 100.

22. Buni, *Robert L. Vann,* 44.

23. Buni, *Robert L. Vann,* 51.

24. Robert Vann, "The Business Camera," *Pittsburgh Courier,* 5 February 1927.

25. Buni, *Robert L. Vann,* 120.

26. Quoted in Buni, *Robert L. Vann,* 108.

27. Buni, *Robert L. Vann,* 69.

28. Buni, *Robert L. Vann,* 115.

29. Buni, *Robert L. Vann,* 202.

30. Buni, *Robert L. Vann,* 206.

31. Buni, *Robert L. Vann,* 217.

32. Buni, *Robert L. Vann,* 219.

33. Buni, *Robert L. Vann,* 235, 238.

34. Brenda Gayle Plummer, *Rising Wind: Black Americans and U.S. Foreign Affairs, 1935–1960* (Chapel Hill: University of North Carolina Press, 1996), 55.

35. Robert F. Jefferson, "African Americans in the U.S. Army During World War II," in *A Historic Context for the African American Military Experience,* ed. Steven D. Smith and James A. Ziegler, U.S. Army Construction Engineering Research Laboratories, 1998.

36. Plummer, *Rising Wind,* 55.

37. Buni, *Robert L. Vann,* 305–306; *Pittsburgh Courier,* 2, 9, and 16 April, 1938.

38. *Pittsburgh Courier,* 19 February 1941.

39. *Pittsburgh Courier,* 21 September 1940.

40. Washburn, *A Question of Sedition,* 81–82.

41. "America Will Never Be Free Until Its Citizens Are," *Pittsburgh Courier,* 14 March 1942.

42. *Pittsburgh Courier,* 31 January 1942.

43. Edgar T. Rouzeau, "Black American Wars on Double Front for High Stakes," *Pittsburgh Courier,* 7 February 1942.

44. See "Support Grows for Double V," *Pittsburgh Courier,* 14 March 1942, and "Double V Sweeps Nation," *Pittsburgh Courier,* 21 March 1942.

45. Buni, *Robert L. Vann,* 325.

46. Farrar, *Baltimore Afro-American,* 3.

47. *Baltimore Afro-American Ledger,* 28 January 1905.

48. Farrar, *Baltimore Afro-American,* xiv.

49. Farrar, *Baltimore Afro-American,* xiv.

50. Farrar, *Baltimore Afro-American,* 150–151.

51. "We Are for War," *Baltimore Afro-American*, 16 September 1939.

52. *Baltimore Afro-American*, 31 August 1940.

53. Charles G. Spellman, "The Black Press: Setting the Political Agenda During World War II," *Negro History Bulletin* 51, no. 1 (1993).

54. Marion Marzolf, *Up From the Footnote: A History of Women Journalists* (New York: Hastings House, 1977), 91–92.

55. Farrar, *Baltimore Afro-American,* 90.

56. Farrar, *Baltimore Afro-American,* 184.

57. Stetson Kennedy and Elizabeth Gardner, "How Housing is Kept Lily-White," *Baltimore Afro-American,* 31 December 1949.

58. "Isaac C. Bannister, Retired Columnist," *Washington Post*, 8 March 1964.

59. "Bright and Shining," *Chicago Daily Tribune*, 25 August 1938.

60. Farrar, *Baltimore Afro-American,* 188.

61. The *Pittsburgh Courier*'s George Schuyler, on the other hand, was not opposed to Foster's work and supported the naming of a housing complex in Harlem the "Stephen Foster Houses."

62. "Afro Scores Spelling of 'Negro' by Daily," *Baltimore Afro-American,* 25 October 1947.

63. Vann to Franklin, May–June 1939, quoted in Buni, *Robert L. Vann,* 314.

64. Gunnar Myrdal, *An American Dilemma: The Negro Problem and Modern Democracy* (New York: Harper and Brothers, 1944), 911.

65. "National Negro Newspaper Week," *Pittsburgh Courier*, 7 March 1942.

4

POSTWAR NEWSPAPERS, SUBURBANIZATION, AND LAND DEVELOPMENT

The *Los Angeles Times* and the *Long Island Newsday*

Postwar American newspapers brought the news of peace, jobs, and prosperity. Advertisements for new consumer goods heralded the shift toward domestic production and a new way of life for American families, while surrounding news stories told of the threat of the Cold War, the Communist menace, and bomb shelters in the backyard. Among the new circumstances facing returning soldiers were a reorganization of the economy and a radical shortage of housing. New housing starts had slowed dramatically during the Depression and had not kept pace with the birth rate or the new arrivals of immigrants. Returning soldiers added to the crisis, when, armed with veterans' benefits and an eagerness to start new families, they sought out single-family dwellings in developing areas outside of cities. As people moved further away from city centers and into newly developed suburbs, the newspaper found itself under threat from the new medium of television, but it continued to be the prime mover in constructing new communities of people. In this era, newspapers were central to the development of a new suburban way of life that came to define the American dream.

The *Los Angeles Times*

In the history of place making, there is no more powerful newspaper force than that of the *Los Angeles Times* in the construction of Los Angeles. Though rarely thought of as a suburb, the settlement pattern of the city is characterized most notably by sprawl, and this pattern of development was largely determined by the interests of the family that owned the famously partial leading daily newspaper.

General Harrison Gray Otis, the first owner of the *Times*, used the paper to promote settlement in the area through his dedicated efforts to bring northerners and midwesterners to California. When competition in the railroad industry made transportation from the Midwest out to the coast affordable to even the least fortunate, dramatic land speculation began. Abandoned land left from the drought of 1864 left unlimited acreage available to developers, and those eager to cash in on gullible country folk paid handsomely to advertise their plots in the local papers, for which the *Times* quickly distinguished itself as the most effective venue.[1] General Otis started the Los Angeles Chamber of Commerce in 1888 and through it coordinated the railroad companies to improve their efforts at bringing new migrants to the area, initiating a campaign of boosterism unparalleled in any other major paper.

As founder of the "All-Year Club," Otis's son-in-law Harry Chandler advertised the area in every major newspaper and magazine across the nation. The *Times* was among the primary sponsors of the club, which aimed to promote Southern California to the rest of the country as more than a temporary winter tourist destination. *Times* writers were used to write editorial copy for posters and pamphlets boasting of Southern California's assets for permanent residence, and this promotional material blanketed the country. This copy was supplemented by the midwinter edition of the *Times*, published each January and sent to the north and east free of charge, and it reminded readers in northern towns—at the height of winter—about the balmy temperatures and lush foliage they were missing in California. Years later, Chandler would initiate the "Make a Friend for California" campaign, which challenged residents to ask their friends from out of state to join them in sunny California.[2]

There were few discernible boundaries between the interests of the newspaper owners, the newspaper, and the fate of Los Angeles. The legacy of General Otis, carried on through Harry Chandler, was to engineer the rebirth of Southern California from a lawless frontier town into a thriving metropolis, and the paper advanced the cause of the city on every front. The family became large landowners through canny purchases of land tracts in California and Mexico that would later be subdivided and sold, but they came into some of their land by happy accident, when would-be speculators could not afford to pay their bills for placing classified ads in the papers, and were forced to pay in the form of land deeds instead.[3]

To make their land holdings even more profitable, the family at the helm of the *Times* promoted a number of related causes. An automobile page was started in 1905, and the new activity of motoring soon garnered an entire section. A population enamored of driving supported all of the industries that the Chandler family had interests in, including automotive manufacturing, oil, rubber, and aerospace technology. The paper redrew the map of transportation in the state, lobbying for the development of roads, rail, ports, and harbors that were located to take advantage of the land that the family owned.[4] An editorial in the paper boasted that

> because we have had the good judgment to build roads and more roads. Because we have constructed highways leading from the center of this metropolis to every point of the compass. Almost unconsciously we have developed a system of communication which is making for prosperity, convenience, happiness, and assuring future development.[5]

"In Southern California," the paper wrote, "it was the *Times* that was first and foremost in a campaign for good intercity, intercounty and interstate highways."[6] With the help of the Chandlers' support of the automobile, Southern California had more cars than any other part of the country in the interwar period.[7] The underdeveloped public transportation system of present-day Los Angeles is a legacy of the Chandlers' desire to promote cars and freeways rather than buses and subways.

The *Times* worked ceaselessly to present the area in its best possible light. In the early years, crime, natural disasters, and other discouraging news was either underreported or avoided altogether. It was not uncommon for the paper to move earthquakes away from Los Angeles and into Santa Barbara and San Francisco in news reports.[8] As part of the *Times*'s boosterism of Los Angeles, the city of San Francisco was described as the place where evil menaced:

> Otis constantly boomed Southern California's climate, its real estate values, its fertility, its growth. His general Order No. 1 read simply "Push things." By contrast, he described San Francisco as "the buckle on the Northern Murder Belt."[9]

Harry Chandler in Charge

After General Otis's son-in-law, Harry Chandler, took over the daily operation of the *Times*, the paper grew less caustic but no less partial to the Chandler family businesses.[10] For those looking to the *Times* for information about Los Angeles, there was an abundance of good news to be found. A casual reader of the *Los Angeles Times* in the early part of the twentieth century would find much to recommend the Los

Angeles area for business and living. The *Times* was relentless in its harassment of labor organizers in order to keep the area free of unions. Harrison Gray Otis revealed his growing hostility toward labor following the Typographers Strike in 1890 which hit all four Los Angeles newspapers. He employed non union workers to work in his printing plant while other papers settled. After the Railroad Strike in 1896, he tried to break the unions by organizing the Merchants and Manufacturers Association and encouraging other business leaders not to give in to unions. On October 1, 1910, several explosions destroyed the *Times* building and injured many workers, catalyzing both sides of the labor issue and strengthening Otis' convictions against them:

> The scoundrels successfully attempted to destroy those whose courage to oppose them they could not daunt. They did not hesitate to plot to ruin a building which is being constructed for the public benefit.[11]

As the "father of the Los Angeles aqueduct," in 1913 Chandler organized the diversion of water from the Owens River toward Los Angeles so that the arid land could support the growing population. This newly irrigated and fertile land, combined with perfect year-round weather, created the ideal conditions to lure people and investment to Southern California. As the *Times* wrote in 1930,

> The metropolis of an area rich in raw materials and agricultural produce, strategically located for the development of industry and foreign trade and gifted with ideal living conditions, Los Angeles has enjoyed a continued growth that has aroused the wonder of the world.[12]

The pro-growth agenda of the newspaper was also seen in the development of one of the country's first newspaper real estate sections in 1901, although the whole paper was used to promote land and speculative home building. Other sections of the paper also came to reflect the creation of new locations and preoccupations: the Southland Farm and Garden section was renamed Southland Homes and Gardens in 1934. "Southland" was the *Times*'s way of renaming the area and extending its purview beyond the limits of Los Angeles. In 1921 the Los Angeles Realty Board voted Chandler the city's "most useful citizen"; Chandler owned more land than any other single Angeleno, and, without being a real estate agent himself, likely sold more of it than any other resident as well.

Harry Chandler was the director of more than forty corporate boards and organizations, including the State Chamber of Commerce, the Community Development Association, the Merchants and Manufacturers Association, the Matson Navigation Company and Security-First National

Bank, Stanford University, and the California Institute of Technology, founded to ensure a continuous supply of qualified workers for local industries. Through partnerships with other businessmen and investors, Chandler envisaged and built the Los Angeles Civic Center, the Union Railroad Station, the Hollywood Bowl, the iconic Hollywoodland sign, and numerous hotels for prospective land buyers to stay in, including the Beverly Wilshire. Harry Chandler's wife Dorothy was responsible for the fundraising that created the Los Angeles Music Center, and the paper's lobbying efforts helped to bring the 1932 Olympics to Los Angeles.[13]

When a new *Los Angeles Times* building was opened on July 1, 1935, Chandler made his interests in the development of the city clear in that day's editorial:

> The best interests of Los Angeles are paramount to the *Times*. They have always been. The city and this newspaper have grown up together. With humility, those in charge of its conduct realized that it grew because it was, in a certain sense, the voice of a lusty, energetic, progressive community. That it prospered because it echoed the call of a triumphant pioneer spirit.[14]

As the most significant of "those in charge," Chandler's efforts proved extraordinarily successful: the population of Los Angeles went from 319,000 in 1910 to over 1,238,000 in 1930. The population of Beverly Hills alone grew 2,500 percent in the 1920s.[15] One of the most potent indicators of the Otis-Chandler family's successful efforts was the issuing of over 62,000 new building permits in 1923.[16]

Financially invested in Hollywood though the ownership of land and support of Warner Brothers studios, the *Times* also became a patron of the growing motion picture industry. The paper began its coverage of the film industry in 1909, publicizing screenings and covering the studios in "behind the scenes" features. The *Times* started reviewing films in 1913, beginning with "Reincarnation of Karma," and the newspaper offices were used as a location in Charlie Chaplin's first film, "Making a Living," released in 1914. The *Times* was soon the preeminent movie newspaper, issuing glossy magazines about film celebrities, like "Pre-View," inaugurated in 1923.

Norman Chandler and the War Years

Harry's son Norman Chandler began working at the paper as a young man and became vice president and general manager in 1936. Under his direction, the paper maintained its staunch Republicanism, rallying against Roosevelt, labor, Communists, and all manner of social forces seen to be working against free enterprise. The format of the paper was expanded and became more accessible in response to increased competition from Hearst's *Examiner*. The columns were widened and more pictures were added, and the paper was honored with the Ayer Cup for typographical excellence in 1937.[17]

The *Times* described the period preceding Norman's takeover as one of adversity, while acknowledging that the greatest challenges still laid ahead. Looking back on sixty years of publication, the *Times* praised its own perspicacity:

> The decade of 1920–30 was one of postwar adjustment, speculation and greed. The *Times* fought to checkrein the wild horses and warned of the follies which inevitably follow such saturnalia, but its advice went unheeded and the 1930–40 period found the country in the throes of crackpot ideas which always follow disaster. The *Times* battled these fallacious schemes with all its vigor and will continue to do so.[18]

The *Times* story, published just days before the attack on Pearl Harbor, continued,

> a scourge has swept the continents of Europe and Asia and threatens the Americas. Its goal is the destruction of the way of life we have known for 150 years. It would take from free men the hard-earned liberties gained through the centuries and substitute an onerous form of slavery—both economic and social.... It is a grim challenge and the *Times* would be faithless to its glorious past if it equivocated or pussyfooted.[19]

The war brought 632,000 new workers to the Los Angeles area to work in munitions factories and related industries.[20] The population swell was a boon to the growing *Los Angeles Times*, but serious investments in infrastructure had to be made in order to accommodate all of these new Angelenos after the war was over. The paper contributed to this effort both materially and editorially.

As chairman of the Newspaper Publishers Committee, Norman Chandler also wrote a series of syndicated advertorials that appeared simultaneously in over 350 American newspapers during this period. In them, Chandler argued on behalf of the importance of a maintaining a free press as a necessary safeguard against the Communist threat. In his personal entreaties to keep newspapers strong as a way of strengthening America, Chandler wrote with strident rhetorical flourish:

> The newspapers in any totalitarian state give their readers glowing tales of the goodness and rightness of the *Leaders* and paint horror pictures of

> "those stupid people in America who try to govern themselves!" This
> pleases their masses—and satisfies them.[21]

His strength of conviction on the issues of freedom, democracy, and
the press in America and the views he proclaimed weekly across the
nation provided the solid foundation on which to lay the claim that
California was the place for patriotic Americans to settle after the war.

By the end of the 1940s, the population of Los Angeles had reached
four million, and the paper continued to boost the population and
residents' esteem in doting essays and editorials. Labor diatribes were
conflated with Communism, and red-baiting was used with little or
no news pretext. The paper unequivocally supported its own favored
political candidates, and in one much-heralded case, helped to get
Richard Nixon elected to Congress by labeling his opponent a Red.
With the *Times*'s support, Nixon's participation on the House Un-
American Activities Committee helped him to secure a place in the
Senate in 1950.

The Times Company hedged its bets against potential competition in
all media, and in the postwar period it expanded to serve the growing
population that was spreading throughout the area. In October 1948 it
started an afternoon tabloid called the *Los Angeles Mirror,* which operated independently of the *Times* and had a separate company headquarters and staff. The *Mirror* was modeled on the *New York Daily News*
and was designed to appeal to a working-class audience with short,
breezy stories and color photography. Its orientation, according to the
Times, was speed, "the objective being to clip minutes, even seconds off
the operation. We will give readers impartial, objective and factually
accurate news as fast as it is humanly possible to do it."[22]

The same year, the company also joined forces with CBS to start a
television station, KTTV. It was the first newspaper company to do so.
As the president of CBS, Frank Stanton, noted at the time,

> the *Los Angeles Times* occupies a distinguished position in Southern
> California. It has been identified throughout with the whole area's
> remarkable development and holds an outstanding reputation among
> the nation's leading newspapers.[23]

The paper supported its television business with the introduction of
Walter Ames, a television reporter, who helped to make the *Times* a
necessary companion to the enjoyment of television.[24]

The format of the *Times* changed to reflect the shift in demographics that the community was undergoing. New sections of the
paper were created to make the paper more relevant to each demographic. There was more emphasis placed on sports and women's

news, and a daily comics feature was added to appeal to children.[25] Content was tailored to specific suburban neighborhoods, which effectively prevented local papers from emerging as viable competitors. To meet the needs of the growing population of readers and advertisers, the *Times* purchased a paper mill in Oregon that was capable of producing eighty thousand tons of newsprint a year, which helped to cover the circulation that reached 765,000 on Sundays.[26]

Building New Neighborhoods

Much of the paper's bulk was a result of its advertising, and among the ads, the most notable were those for new houses and neighborhoods. The Chandler name was found frequently among the many stories describing new subdivisions, as land that Norman Chandler owned was parceled out for development. Thousand Gardens, one of many similar areas just being invented in the 1940s, was heralded in the paper as being "pronounced by international experts to be the nation's outstanding residential enterprise." The area, on the former Rancho Cienega, comprised 105 "well favored" acres "at the foot of the gentle northerly slope of Baldwin Hills." Listed among the owners of Thousand Gardens, Inc., were Norman and Ralph Chandler.[27]

One of the most successful developments crafted and promoted by the *Los Angeles Times* was the San Fernando Valley. The land was irrigated by the aqueduct project, and contained sixty thousand acres, previously known as the Van Nuys ranch, owned by a Harry Chandler–led syndicate. The group built a paved road through the land to make it accessible from Los Angeles and encouraged the ownership of automobiles by prospective landowners. The location of the land tract was also perfectly suited to the postwar ideology that favored isolationism, containment, and the dispersion of settlements away from densely populated cities, which were considered to be at risk by targeted bombing. As a suburb for the middle class, which grew to accommodate returning soldiers, the San Fernando Valley's agriculture was also commended for its wartime efforts:

> It's an important contribution to the victory, this production of food in one of the nation's largest and most important cities, and so, too is the year-around yield of the thousands of Victory gardens in the municipal limits...Now's the time for the patriotic and frugal home gardener to be bestirring himself![28]

Hundreds of housing ads in the mid-forties cluttered the pages of the paper, beckoning returning GIs to settle in newly developed subdivisions with government-backed loans and "no down payment" offers. Advertising for new houses could even be found in the news columns, with sketches of plans adorning stories about the increasing rate of new housing starts. In 1948, the *Times* reported that building in San Fernando Valley had increased almost tenfold in the previous five years, with 6,822 building permits issued in the summer of 1948 alone.[29] By 1950 there were 500,000 people living in the Valley, and the *Times* projected a population of one million by 1960. War veterans were the happy beneficiaries of the housing explosion, and their arduous struggles were featured regularly even in the real estate section:

> The home Lloyd Griffiths dreamed about in a Japanese prisoner of war camp is his today in Van Owen Park, a new residential development on Vanowen St. between Vanalden and Corbin Aves., San Fernando Valley.[30]

The real estate section blended the news of new homes and neighborhoods with the social and political realities of homeowners, and both provided opportunities for the *Times* to sing its own praises in the development process:

> Since the war, there have been vigorous doses of facelifting and beautifying ingredients. Thousands of new, comfortable homes. Exquisitely designed office buildings. Beautiful, serviceable industrial plants. And miles of time-saving highways and freeways. This rash of building spilled over into Los Angeles County and fanned out to include the entire Southland.[31]

By January 1961, the New Year's predictions focused on Los Angeles's overwhelming growth, with an eye toward the future. In a story liberally illustrated with sketches of split-level homes and new high-rises for a "Southland megalopolis," the headline foresaw a population of 28 million by 1980.[32] The area delineated as "Southland" was the 250-mile area from "north of Santa Barbara to the Mexican border, and east from the city of Santa Monica 75 miles to the triangle of cities comprising Riverside, San Bernardino and Redlands." The parameters of this land were carefully outlined to cover the area in which the Chandler family had substantial holdings, and the area's virtues were relentlessly extolled to flatter existing and future residents:

> Southern California is fortunate in that its economy is diversified. There is not dependency on one basic industry.... Another major economic advantage has been the attraction of imaginative people with vigor from other regions.... Those who buy now and buy right will enjoy a future harvest. Happy New Year to all![33]

Through the promotion of this settlement pattern, the *Los Angeles Times* became the leader in advertising, most of which was for land and new homes. The paper led American newspapers in advertising linage in 1957 with 20,823,586 lines, "the fifth consecutive year that the Times has had national leadership in classifieds."[34] By 1965 the *Los Angeles Times* would break records by running over one hundred million lines of advertising, still more than any other paper in the country today.

The *Los Angeles Times* was a family-owned and -operated business that had the development of Los Angeles at the top of its agenda throughout most of the twentieth century, but never so powerfully as in the postwar era. Harry Chandler retired from official management of the newspaper in 1941, but continued to go to the office until his death in 1944. His son Norman, who had been vice president since 1936, became president and general manager of the Times-Mirror Company following his father's retirement. Phillip Chandler was elected vice president and assistant general manager, Harrison Chandler was vice president and manager of the Times-Mirror Printing and Binding Division, and Harry's wife, Marion Chandler, was secretary of the company.[35] Norman Chandler was succeeded by his son, Otis Chandler. The Times Mirror Company went public in 1964 and was listed on the New York Stock Exchange, the first newspaper company to do so. The company would lose much of its conservatism in the years to come, but it continued to be the primary booster for the Los Angeles area and the multitude of other industries in which the Chandler family had interest.

Newsday Comes to Long Island

With its spectacular oceanfront shoreline, Long Island had been an enclave for wealthy industrialists long before the turn of the twentieth century. Inland, however, Long Island was a series of disconnected small towns and burgs. Nassau County was created following the annexation of western Queens County to the City of New York in 1898. The remaining towns of Hempstead, North Hempstead, and Oyster Bay joined the rest of Long Island rather than the newly five-boroughed city. By 1900, the Pennsylvania Railroad had taken possession of the Long Island Railroad line and was providing service from Manhattan, bringing the previously rural area into closer contact with the city and laying the foundation for future suburban development.

Among the grand estates on the north shore of Long Island were those of Harry Guggenheim and Alicia Patterson, both given to them as wedding gifts from their respective fathers. A common interest in aviation,

Alicia Patterson, co-founder and publisher of the Long Island newspaper *Newsday*, at her desk in Hempstead, New York, Monday, September 27, 1942. Courtesy of AP/Wide World Photos.

one of the growing industries of Long Island, brought the neighbors together. They divorced their spouses and married each other in 1939.

When S. I. Newhouse closed his *Nassau Daily Journal* following insurmountable labor disputes, a printing plant in Hempstead was left vacant. In short order, Patterson had the area surveyed to see if Long Island could support a new paper to compete with the *Nassau Daily Review-Star*, an organ of the Republican Party, which held a majority in the area. In her estimation, there was no news outlet serving northern Nassau County, and Patterson convinced Guggenheim to buy the plant for her. She went forward on the theory that if she could start a paper with an expanded breadth—beyond the commercial zone of Hempstead—her paper would find a readership. In actuality, she would engineer the population growth in order to create potential readers, using the newspaper as her tool.

Patterson's decision to become a newspaper publisher in 1940 placed her squarely in the tradition of her famous publishing family: her great-grandfather Joseph Medill had founded the *Chicago Tribune*, her father's cousin Colonel Robert R. McCormick had been its most illustrious publisher, and her father, Joseph Medill Patterson, started the *New York Daily News*. Her aunt, Eleanor (Cissy) Patterson, ran the *Washington Times-Herald*.

Launched after Labor Day 1940, *Newsday* was a small, amateur, and somewhat scrappy 32-page newspaper. The initial print run of thirty thousand sold for three cents and was published only on weekdays.[36] Patterson chose the tabloid format against advice from her father at the *Daily News* and hired Harry Davis from the *News* to be the managing editor. Patterson and Davis held a contest to name the paper, but in the end they preferred the name that they had already chosen— *Newsday*. The population was small, and the staff was inexperienced. Some employees were borrowed from other papers, but many had never worked at a paper before.

The war was a mixed blessing to Long Island and its new daily. New aircraft manufacturing plants brought industrial development and workers to the area, but wartime rationing made putting out the paper increasingly challenging. Gas rations made it difficult for people to get around to cover stories, and the paper rations meant that even getting enough newsprint to put the paper out was a primary concern. The amount of newsprint each operation was allowed to have was based on the previous year's circulation, favoring long-established papers over upstarts whose circulation was climbing at a faster rate. *Newsday* cut back advertising to save paper space, and when the shortage was especially dire, Patterson borrowed rolls of newsprint from her father at the *News*.

It also became increasingly difficult to staff the paper, since the draft hurt the *Newsday* newsroom more than most. Unlike the newspapermen at more established papers, Patterson's reporters, circulation crew, and advertising salesmen were young and draftable. This left the day-to-day business of newspapering to Patterson and a staff made up mostly of women. Relying on favors from Patterson's family, borrowing occurred in staffing as well, as when Alan Hathway from the *Daily News* became the general manager of *Newsday*, replacing Davis, who had also come from the *News*.

When help was not forthcoming from Patterson's father, *Newsday* relied on its co-owner Harry Guggenheim for financial backing. Guggenheim maintained 51 percent control over the company, an arrangement that was an impediment to Patterson throughout her career. She managed daily editorial operations, but he made all final financial decisions. She believed that high-quality newsgathering was a necessary expenditure, while he preferred a more conservative fiscal approach. She often had to fight her husband on editorial issues, and once threatened to sell her 49 percent stake to a rival paper.[37] Despite Patterson and Guggenheim's professional and marital difficulties, however, *Newsday* continued to thrive, and a second Suffolk County edition was added in 1944, printed from a Bay Shore office. With the added edition, *Newsday* was poised to become the dominant newspaper on Long Island.[38]

The Housing Problem

What the paper needed most for its survival was a bigger population base, and Patterson found a way to capitalize on returning soldiers by luring them to Long Island with the thing they needed most: affordable housing. There were over 765,000 war veterans returning to the New York area alone, and the shortage of housing was so dire that the army had constructed temporary shelters out of surplus tents in settlements in Brooklyn and the Bronx.[39] The federal government under President Truman consolidated all of its housing programs under the Housing and Home Finance Agency in 1947 in response to an increasingly powerful housing reform movement.[40] At the same time, wartime rent control legislation was extended to keep the rent inflation at bay, and in 1949 the Housing Act provided funding for new public housing units, slum clearance, and mortgage insurance. Housing was suddenly a national priority and a national crisis. Conditions were so poor and so apparently underconsidered that it seemed necessary to state in the 1949 Housing Act that every American deserved a "decent home and a suitable living environment." This was the first time the federal government intervened in the development and shaping of cities and towns in such a direct manner; newspapers had been doing it all along.

Newsday editorialized the housing crusade from the war's end, but no initiative was as powerful as the one advertised in the May 7, 1947, issue of the paper. Two thousand new homes were made available at sixty dollars a month in the area known as Island Trees, Long Island. The development would create the country's largest suburb and the most potent symbol yet for postwar American life: Levittown.

Levittown was the first of many important crusades for *Newsday*. Even before the houses went up, Patterson was central in the fight to get the plans approved in the town council. A previously existing zoning law requiring all new dwellings to have basements had to be

Aerial view of Levittown, New York. April 13, 1949. Bettman/CORBIS/
Arthur Green.

overcome, since Levitt's designs were built on concrete slabs for
building efficiency. By mobilizing prospective renters around the
issue, *Newsday* brought hundreds of people to the council meeting to
argue that this bylaw be reversed.[41] In return for their favorable
coverage of the project, *Newsday* employees were rewarded with their
choice of Levittown homes.

Brooklyn-born William Levitt had secured the Island Trees land
before the war, and was determined to build on it on a large scale. He
designed the enormous subdivision of nearly identical houses on 60-
foot by 100-foot lots, using assembly-line construction techniques,
cheap materials, and nonunion labor. Following the announcement,
the overwhelming demand led Levitt and Sons to expand the plan to
include over six thousand homes. Within four years, over seventeen
thousand houses had been built. In order to provide this new population with the necessary amenities, the plan was also broadened to
include a shopping center, restaurants, a bowling alley, gas stations, a
swimming pool, and a playground.[42] *Newsday* once again helped to
rally public support for these projects, including the renaming of the
town. As Levitt remarked to the *New York Times*, "We had long
cherished the idea of having a community such as this bear our name,
but we hesitated to do so until about a month ago when the local

newspapers published certain reports in which the residents them-selves appeared to be in favor of it."[43]

The development was laid out in a series of quadrants that made the huge space seem smaller in scale. Adding to the village atmo-sphere, the streets of Levittown were named thematically in groups. Some were named after planets, others flowers, and others birds. This was no doubt useful in navigating the endless identicality of the homes. These attempts to bring natural life to the subdivision were evidence of the difficulty of inventing a town virtually overnight that people would choose to live in; there was no history, no neighbor-hood, nothing known at all about what life in Levittown would look like. But the developers did not have to worry. The housing shortage, the desire by newly married couples to get out of their parents' homes to be on their own, and the low cost of the homes were motivation enough to cause a frenzy when the houses came on the market. War veterans and their wives lined up at Levitt's office to fill out applica-tions by the tens of thousands. If the homes themselves were generic, their occupants were comparably homogeneous. Ethnic restrictive covenants prevented non-Caucasian applicants from gaining entry to the new community, despite the fact that such covenants were ruled unconstitutional in 1948. *Newsday* editorialized that the decision of where to live should be left to the individual, rather than the state, implicitly supporting the racist policy of Levittown.[44] Houses were assigned in bulk and in an orderly fashion at the leasing office, such that new renters were often placed in homes in alphabetical order. With neighbors often all sharing a last name, the common bond of community was enhanced even further.[45]

The support of this new suburb was key to the success of *Newsday*. Not only did it manufacture an instant community of readers, it was a community that was young and growing. With this new population, *Newsday* finally had a readership base that was not only large enough to support a newspaper but was also loyal and indebted to the paper for the very homes they lived in. *Newsday* became the residents' beacon, their voice, and their advocate.

The postwar baby boom saw the births of seventy-six million babies in the U.S. in the years between 1946 and 1964, and this growth in family size was integral for growing suburban papers like *Newsday*. By 1954, the circulation of *Newsday* had reached 213,813, up from only 64,000 in 1946.[46] Young children with bicycles were given paper routes to distribute the papers, and housewives became a significant new consumer force. The growth of the economy would come through the efforts of these young families who were prevailed upon to buy the products of the new civilian production schedule. For newspapers this meant that large advertisers could be secured to purchase space in the paper, which in Patterson's case came at the expense of older papers in the city like her father's *Daily News*. As department stores and car dealerships followed their customers to the suburbs, inner-city papers saw a decline in their advertising pages. With the arrangement of populations such as Levittown's, newspapers were also better able to segment their readers demographically in order to package and target them more directly for advertisers.

The new postwar lifestyle was apparent in another key feature of Levittown homes: each one came with a new television in the living room, preinstalled and set into the paneling under the stairs to the second floor. For many families who would not have been otherwise able to afford such a luxury, this detail was a persuasive selling point, and the television would help to socialize them into a new consumer lifestyle. Appliances and household design became the new necessities, as seen in the ethos of home improvement that was developing in Levittown. One year, *Life* magazine even held a contest for the best Levittown house, pitting neighbor against neighbor for national exposure. Local community centers held home improvement seminars that instructed new residents on the finer points of interior decorating and design.

Television also brought the politics of the postwar period into the homes of Levittown, and particularly the politics of fear that came with the new world order. Many Levittowners built bomb shelters in their backyards, and as in Los Angeles, the suburban lifestyle choice was supported over city living largely on the basis of the impending bomb threats of the Atomic Age. In 1954, the McCarthy hearings were on television for five weeks straight, which helped to reinforce the ideologies of fear and containment both nationally and locally.

Although her paper benefited from the growth of suburbanization, Patterson understood that newspapers had to be tirelessly local in their coverage if they were to counteract the competition from magazines and television.[47] She worked throughout the 1950s to strengthen *Newsday* by bringing more rigor to the copy desk and hiring a team of young, energetic, and well-educated journalists who worked overnight rewriting the work of the daytime reporters. With a 7 a.m. press time, *Newsday* had the luxury of time to go deeper on stories than did morning papers. They could use the night to follow up on leads, get deeper background, and take more time to craft the structure of each story. By the time the paper came out in the afternoon, it typically had more analysis and depth than either the morning papers or television coverage. This was significant in securing the place of the paper in the home, as it was most often read there rather than on buses, trains, or subways like other tabloids. Not wishing to completely ignore television, however, Patterson hired Jo Coppola to be the paper's first television critic.[48]

1954 was a benchmark year for the paper. It was on much more solid financial ground following the closure of the *Review-Star* in 1953. In September Alicia Patterson was on the cover of *Time* Magazine, and the story detailed her lone-woman successes at the start-up paper and her astute anticipation of suburban growth, which the paper continued to shape. Following an undercover investigative report of local nursing homes by reporter Madeline Ryttenberg, the paper was honored with a George Polk Memorial Award, and the paper received its first Pulitzer Prize the same year for meritorious public service. The award was given for the investigation of William DeKoning Sr., a corrupt labor leader, that led to his conviction for extortion and larceny in connection with racetrack gambling and construction contracts. The exposé in *Newsday* resulted in his year-long prison sentence at Sing Sing Prison and a higher profile for the newspaper. In recognition of its new status, Managing Editor Alan Hathway was appointed to the Pulitzer jury in 1956.[49]

Newsday gained a reputation for exposing corruption in local government and social services and undertook campaigns on behalf of its readers to build hospitals, schools, and better roads for the community. *Newsday* reporter Bob Greene was appointed to the New York Anti-Crime Committee, which went after the Teamsters, and Arthur Bergman wrote a series called "Suffolk's Unsolved Murders: The Case for a County Police Force."[50] The paper also mobilized around the adoption of a new county charter that would unify the local government. In these efforts, *Newsday* was redrawing the map of Long Island and working to build the necessary amenities for the ever-growing population.

Through Alicia Patterson's relationship with Robert Moses, the most influential figure in twentieth century urban renewal, *Newsday* was always at the forefront of the reshaping of the greater New York area. Though Moses was plagued by controversy for most of his career, *Newsday* typically supported his grand schemes, especially when they had to do with improving access between the city and Long Island. Moses was the president of the State Parks Commission; and as the architect of all major roadway, bridge, power, state park, and beach plans on Long Island, he was a crucial ally in forwarding Patterson's vision. Patterson supported Moses's plan to build a road from Staten Island to Montauk that would cut through Fire Island, despite the plan calling for an elevated roadway atop large sand dunes. Facing charges from other newspapers that *Newsday* employees stood to gain if a highway went through because their own vacation property would increase in value, the Fire Island highway became a heated political contest. Not least among the concerns was the ecological damage likely to affect the shoreline. Eventually, but too late for many residents, *Newsday* supported the preservation of Fire Island by backing its application for National Seashore Status.[51] In revisionist histories, Alicia Patterson is credited with stopping Robert Moses from putting a highway through Fire Island.

In 1955, when a B-26 bomber crashed into a residential community in East Meadow, it landed on the home of *Newsday* compositor Paul Koroluck.[52] This and similar accidents were fueling a debate about the continued utility of the Mitchel Field Air Force Base in East Meadow. In the midst of the Cold War, many residents supported the location of the base out of fear that it was needed to protect New York City from foreign threat. Many residents also feared the effect its closing would have on the local economy. As development in Long Island encroached on its perimeter, however, civilians were increasingly at risk from the proximity to active aircraft, and accidents were becoming common. Robert Moses and *Newsday* were again central to the debate, and Patterson met personally with President John F. Kennedy to seek support for these land use issues. On November 29, 1960, the Kennedy administration announced that Mitchel Field would close, and the huge tract of land it had occupied was made available for public use. The land grant allowed for the expansion of Hofstra University's campus and provided 135 acres for Nassau Community College.[53] Alicia Patterson served as a trustee of both of the schools and promoted their causes frequently in *Newsday*.

Patterson's meeting with President Kennedy was only the last in a long history of political entanglements. She was a committed Democrat, in part because returning vets were likely to be Democrats, and they comprised her core readership. Patterson supported Roosevelt and the New Deal as well as backing Eisenhower in the 1952 presidential election, but she had to hedge her bets when Adlai Stevenson was the Democratic candidate because of her close relationship with him. She supported John F. Kennedy in 1960 and was vindicated in her choice when he helped her achieve many of her goals for Long Island. The paper, however, was equivocal on matters of party politics, since Harry Guggenheim was a Republican and insisted on making his endorsements known in the paper. In election years, *Newsday* ran opposing "He Said/She Said" editorials on facing pages that were authored by the husband and wife.

Alicia Patterson died following stomach surgery in 1963 at the age of 56. She had created a successful paper with a circulation of 375,000, and left her 49 percent ownership to four of her nieces and nephews.[54] Harry Guggenheim became the publisher of the paper, and Patterson's nephew, Joseph Medill Patterson Albright, was made his assistant.[55] In 1967, Bill Moyers, President Johnson's press secretary and advisor, was made the publisher of *Newsday*, and Guggenheim resumed his title of president and editor-in-chief.[56] In 1970 Harry Guggenheim's health was declining, and he began to entertain offers to sell *Newsday*. The Times Mirror Company, owner of the *Los Angeles Times* and by then the third largest publishing company in the United States, offered $75 million in stock to buy the paper. Although the minority shareholders were unwilling to sell, Times Mirror acquired Guggenheim's 51 percent in May 1970. Following the announcement, Bill Moyers resigned as publisher, and William Attwood was named as his replacement by Otis Chandler, vice chairman of the board of the Times Mirror Company.

The dramatic shifts in population that were engineered by these two papers were emblematic of the power newspapers had in changing the social landscape. With their merging in the Times Mirror Company, they were also paralleling the next most significant phenomenon in American newspapers in the twentieth century, the growth and concentration of chains. In the next chapter, two of these chains will be investigated.

Notes

1. David Halberstam, *The Powers That Be* (New York: Knopf, 1979), 104.

2. Dennis McDougal, *Privileged Son: Otis Chandler and the Rise and Fall of the L.A. Times Dynasty* (Perseus, 2001), 107.

3. McDougal, *Privileged Son,* 66.

4. Halberstam, *Powers That Be*, 94. See also: Marshall Berges, *The Life and 'Times' of Los Angeles: A Newspaper, a Family, and a City* (New York: Atheneum, 1984) and Robert Gottlieb and Irene Wolt, *Thinking Big: The Story of the* Los Angeles Times, *Its Publisher, and Their Influence on Southern California* (New York: G.P. Putnam, 1979).

5. F. F. Runyon, "Our Southland," *Los Angeles Times,* 15 March 1932, 12.

6. *Los Angeles Times*, 1934.

7. McDougal, *Privileged Son,* 163.

8. Piers Brendon, *The Life and Death of the Press Barons* (London: Atheneum, 1983), 224.

9. Brendon, *Press Barons,* 224.

10. Harry Chandler was officially made the publisher of the *Times* when General Harrison Gray Otis died in 1917, but he had been running it for many years prior to this.

11. "Pin Crimes to Unionites," *Los Angeles Times*, 3 October 1910, 14. See Mike Davis, *City of Quartz: Excavating the Future in Los Angeles* (New York: Vintage, 1990).

12. Edgar Lloyd Hampton, "The Great Migration," *Los Angeles Times*, 2 January 1930, C7.

13. *Los Angeles Times*, 24 September 1944.

14. McDougal, *Privileged Son*, 130.

15. William E. Leuchtenburg, *The Perils of Prosperity, 1914–1932*, 2d ed. (Chicago and London: University of Chicago Press, 1993), 183, 225.

16. Rob Leicester Wagner, "Mergers, Acquisitions and Front Men," chap. 4 in *Red Ink, White Lies: The Rise and Fall of Los Angeles Newspapers 1920–1962* (Upland, CA: Dragon Flyer Press, 2000).

17. McDougal, *Privileged Son*, 124.

18. L. D. Hotchkiss, "*Times* Steers Its Future Course by Beacon Lights of Experience," *Los Angeles Times,* 4 December 1941.

19. ibid., *Los Angeles Times*, 4 December 1941.

20. Zeanette Moore, "City's Needs Told as World Crossroads," *Los Angeles Times*, 8 March 1945.

21. Display Ad, *Los Angeles Times*, 11 February 1941.

22. "The Mirror, New Afternoon Paper, to Appear on Oct. 11," *Los Angeles Times*, 3 October 1948.

23. "Times and CBS Unite in Television Project," *Los Angeles Times*, 28 April 1948.

24. McDougal, *Privileged Son*, 180.

25. McDougal, *Privileged Son*, 179.

26. "*Times* Buys Large Oregon Paper Mill; Newspaper's Expansion to Match Los Angeles' Growth Now Assured," *Los Angeles Times*, 17 April 1948.

27. Charlie Cohan, "Bird's Eye View of Huge Housing Development," *Los Angeles Times*, 30 March 1941.

28. "This 'Farm City'," *Los Angeles Times*, 18 February 1945.

29. "Valley Building Grows Tenfold," *Los Angeles Times*, 28 August 1948.

30. "War Prisoner's Dream of Home Now Realized," *Los Angeles Times*, 17 December 1950.

31. Ray Hebert, "Southland Area Facelift Spurred," *Los Angeles Times*, 2 February 1958.

32. Al Johns, "California Leading Nation in Population Growth; 28 Million Set for 1980," *Los Angeles Times*, 1 January 1961.

33. Al Johns, "Down to Earth; Soaring Sixties Now on Horizon," *Los Angeles Times*, 1 January 1961.

34. "*Times* Leads U.S. in Main Ad Lineage," *Los Angeles Times*, 2 February 1958.

35. "Times-Mirror Co. Elects Norman Chandler President," *Los Angeles Times*, 26 February 1941.

36. Roy Silver, "No 1 at *Newsday* Still Guggenheim," *New York Times*, 15 December 1966.

37. Robert F. Keeler, *Newsday: A Candid History of the Respectable Tabloid* (New York: William Morrow, 1990), 242.

38. *Editor & Publisher*, 1 July 1944.

39. *New York Daily News*, 5 July 1998.

40. "Foley Named Head of Housing Agency," *New York Times*, 8 August 1947.

41. Keeler, *Newsday*, 134.

42. "Community Takes Name of Levitts," *New York Times*, 4 January 1948.

43. ibid., *New York Times*, 4 January 1948.

44. Keeler, *Newsday*, 136.

45. See *Wonderland*, the 1997 film directed by John O'Hagan.

46. "Thumping for Readers," *Wall Street Journal*, 9 November 1954.

47. "Publishers Warned of TV Competition," *New York Times*, 21 September 1954.

48. Keeler, *Newsday*, 281.

49. "Pulitzer Jurors Named by Board," *New York Times*, 5 January 1956.

50. Keeler, *Newsday*, 255.

51. Keeler, *Newsday*, 307; *Long Island Business News*, 24 January 2003.

52. "Bomber Falls in L.I. Street, Crew of 2 Die, House Burns," *New York Times*, 3 November 1955.

53. "U.S. Revises Plan for Mitchel Land," *New York Times*, 12 May 1962.

54. "Alicia Patterson is Dead at 56," *New York Times*, 3 July 1963.

55. "Guggenheim Takes Post as Publisher of *Newsday*," *New York Times*, 9 July 1963.

56. "Man With Many Hats; Billy Don Moyers," *New York Times*, 15 December 1966.

5

FLORIDA IN CHAINS

The *Miami Herald* and the *Tampa Tribune*

When the Times Mirror Company purchased *Newsday* on Long Island in 1971, it was following a pattern of ownership that was becoming increasingly common across the country at that time. Newspaper chains had been developing since the turn of the century, but in the postwar era, as the threat from television and suburbanization plundered dailies across the country, new growth strategies were developed. Many newspaper chains that had been growing slowly, acquiring papers one at a time, began buying entire chains at once. Where newspaper chains in the first half of the twentieth century tended to be extensions of their owners' personalities and agendas, chains in the second half of the century were more likely to be composed of random and generic holdings.

Adding new pressure on bottom-line returns in the newspaper industry was the fact that many newspaper groups went public in the 1960s. With profit margins in the newspaper industry rivaling some of the best stock performers, Wall Street encouraged more and more companies to list on stock exchanges, shifting the burden of performance from reader satisfaction to shareholder value. Selling stock in order to get cash to pay for expansions and acquisitions created a double bind for companies that in many cases had been held in private family control for generations. In order to get the needed revenue, they had to be willing to give up more and more control of their enterprises, and as the boards of directors grew larger, the oversight of individual papers grew more distant.

This chapter looks at two Florida newspapers that became parts of larger newspaper chains and the shift in responsiveness to their local context as their parent companies grew into larger, more sophisticated organizations. Newspapers were central movers in the development of

Floridian towns and cities from the earliest days of the state. Considered as an American frontier of sorts, the swampy Florida landscape has resulted in a tumultuous history of boom and bust. Perhaps more than any other state, Florida exists at the mercy of its geographical location, its weather patterns, its vast coastline, and its inconsistent land quality. Generations of newcomers have been lured by the promise of sunshine, only to be scorned by hurricanes, floods, insect-ridden crops, and droughts. It has been a destination for those seeking a better life and for those escaping the rigid conventions of the north. Refugees and retirees have fueled population growth for over one hundred years, as have the military, shipbuilding, and citrus and tobacco crops. Enduring these same unique Florida conditions were the daily newspapers, constructing, promoting, and cultivating the state alongside and just as often in advance of all other industries.

The *Miami Herald*

Fort Dallas was incorporated as the City of Miami in 1896, and the nascent outpost brought entrepreneurs in railroads and manufacturing looking to capitalize on what they dreamed might become a major southern port. Indiana lawyer Colonel Frank B. Shutts had come to the city to work for the U.S. Treasury Department, and while he was there he took possession of the failing *Miami Morning News-Record* when it went into receivership. Shutts purchased the paper with Henry Flagler,[1] a partner of John D. Rockefeller's in the Standard Oil Company and one of the newly minted railroad tycoons who were appearing on the Miami scene, and they changed the name to the *Miami Herald*.

Flagler, who appreciated the importance of the press to a developing place, financially supported many Florida papers, including the *Gainesville Sun,* the *Pensacola News,* and the *Jacksonville Times-Union*, which he would later own with other partners in the railway industry. Most of his newspaper investments, however, were kept private; Flagler didn't want to appear to have the influence over them that he did. He made pronouncements against his interest in newspapers, declaring in 1890 that "there is not a particle of truth in the rumor that I am about to start a newspaper. If I had to take my choice between a den of rattlesnakes and a newspaper, I think I would prefer the snakes."[2]

The papers were a central part of his public relations campaign to develop Florida, and he used them to promote the importance of railway development. Flagler also provided free railway tours of Florida to newspaper editors from the north in the hopes that they would write positively about the area.[3] With public, state, and federal approval and support, Flagler would be the first to lay down rail lines connecting the previously isolated southern city to the rest of the continent. The railroads helped the land development, bringing building supplies south at a pace that soon could not keep up with demand. Flagler's Florida East Coast Railway had already linked Jacksonville to Miami when he set his sights on the next leg of rail southward to Key West, and the *Herald* wrote glowingly of the project.[4] Most travel up and down the coast to this point had been reliant on watercraft, as areas of swampland made much of the inland territory impassable. With the coming of rail lines, more of the interior of the state was made accessible, and rail magnates soon imagined new towns springing up around terminals, with skyrocketing land values at each point.

Coming to Miami after similar work in St. Augustine and West Palm Beach, Flagler became the "father of Miami." He lowered the ocean floor in the harbor to allow larger boats to arrive, created new islands, built beaches, and developed hotels, like the Royal Palm Hotel on fifteen acres on Biscayne Bay.[5] He donated money and land for a public school building and a hospital to fight the yellow fever epidemic, established a waterworks system, and started Miami Light and Power Company from a generator at the Royal Palm.[6] In an effort to promote the good weather news to the rest of the country, he gave land to the United States Weather Bureau for a station in Miami.[7]

For Shutts, however, the best reason to be in the newspaper business was the advertising. By the 1925–26 winter season, there was so much land speculation that Miami papers were unmatched in advertising linage, setting records that remain unbroken. In the first six months of 1925, the *Miami Herald* averaged over 200,000 column inches in a month, more than either the *Chicago Tribune* or the *New York Times*. In the summer of 1925, the *Miami Daily News* came out with a 504-page issue, mostly comprised of real estate ads, setting a record for the largest newspaper ever printed.[8] The buying and selling of property, traded via land deed binders like sports cards, reached a frenetic pace. People drove from all over America to get a piece of the action, and traffic jams snarled on Flagler Avenue. There were an estimated 25,000 agents working to sell lots, and a city ordinance was passed to prevent the selling of property in the street.[9]

The growth spurt was short-lived, however, and when a hurricane hit in 1926, the growing town and its newspapers suffered major losses. The hurricane was a major disaster by any measure: 115 people were killed and thousands were left homeless. News reports in the *New York Times* and elsewhere would estimate damage to be in the hundreds of millions, but to the reader of the *Miami Herald*, damage was minimal. The paper was eager to get past the storm and

Close-up of real estate sign. Photo by Ed Clark. Courtesy of Time-Life Pictures/Getty Images.

quickly downplayed its toll so as not to frighten potential settlers or business investors:

> The normalcy that has come is in the minds of the people. They are still just a little bit dazed, but they are sane—there is an absence of any of the hectic outbreaks that nearly always accompany disaster.... Miami has not yielded to the emotional temptations that come in such a time as has been experienced here. Mental normalcy means the most rapid rehabilitation of the city that is humanly possible.[10]

As part of the continued booster campaign, the paper looked the other way on the cheaply built housing stock, the devastating loss of life of African American laborers, and strategies for emergency preparedness. The only advice the paper would offer was for residents to stop talking about the disaster, warning that rumors were themselves more dangerous than hurricanes. One editorial cartoon, "The Wind That Does the Most Damage," claimed: "exaggeration—that is the latest foe to be conquered."[11] The fight against storm-related smear campaigns, which the editors of the *Herald* believed opponents engaged in out of jealousy, was among the few occasions when hurricanes were mentioned at all:

> Miami and Florida object to having such storms designated as belonging to them.... The business bodies of this community note that the tempest hurrying northward is often branded as the Florida hurricane, and think this is unfair, that something ought to be done about it, but what they know not. Neither do we.[12]

In a short-lived attempt to solicit help for rebuilding the city after storm damage, the Mayor E. C. Romfh and *Miami Herald* owner Frank Shutts began a fundraising campaign. They quickly ended their efforts when they realized that the funds received would not outweigh the negative publicity garnered through the asking.[13]

As dependent on the weather as the Florida economy was, there were other things that kept the place going even in the midst of such natural disasters. As a town of sin and vice, Miami was popular with tourists and gangsters alike, who came to experience something of the exotic without having to leave the United States, though in many ways they must have felt as if they were in another country. The local laws were relaxed and unenforced, and the frontier mentality made gambling, racketeering, prostitution, and rum-running from Cuba the preferred vices of the day. The anonymous beach community beckoned those escaping stricter laws elsewhere, and those who simply wanted to disappear. Miami became a magnet for northern crime syndicates, and for public enemies like Al Capone, who was one of Miami's more famous part-time residents living in a mansion on Biscayne Bay.

Little of this criminal underworld was found in the *Miami Herald* under Shutts, who preferred to keep news cheery in order to lure more tourists. In the 1930s, bank foreclosures, grisly murders, and courtroom corruption did not warrant headlines.[14] Tourists, he reasoned, were coming to enjoy the liquor, cigars, and women that were plentiful in Miami, and it was not considered good business for a newspaper to threaten a town's most attractive qualities. The *Herald* even played down one of the most sensationalistic stories of the decade, when federal agents killed bank robber "Ma" Barker and her son in a standoff near Ocklawaha, Florida.[15]

Miami came to be known as "Chicago South," a lawless town run by gangsters and corrupt politicians. Newspaper expertise was also imported from the crime capital of the Midwest, notably in the form of Moses Annenberg, who came from Chicago to purchase the *Miami Tribune*, the main competitor to the *Herald* in 1933. The Chicago-style newspaper circulation wars were reenacted in Miami, with rival papers simultaneously trying to outdo, and then outbid, each other. Annenberg's *Tribune* did not follow the same principle as Shutts's *Herald*, and in tabloid style his paper was the record of all that was seedy in Miami, from sex scandals to corrupt cops.

There were circulation contests, centerfolds of bathing beauties, huge photos of train wrecks, banner headlines, and gory details of crimes. There was also responsible and penetrating reporting of life in the black communities, including stories on joblessness and problems with health and the lack of basic utilities, the kind of reporting that most papers did not do, certainly not the *Herald* or the *Daily News*.[16]

Tourists enjoyed a taste of the lurid, and street sales of the tabloid were strong. After the cover price was cut to a penny, the *Tribune*'s circulation reached fifty thousand.[17] One of the *Tribune*'s biggest scoops came when the U.S. Weather Service warned of an impending hurricane in 1935, and Flagler's Florida East Coast Railway sent a train to the Keys to evacuate people in advance. When the train did not return, the *Tribune* went to investigate and discovered washed-out roads and rail and more than four hundred dead. It blanketed the story in a photo-laden extra, while the other papers remained quiet.[18] The *Tribune* was a scrappy, crusading paper that went after stories the other "establishment" papers would not, but with few political allies, Annenberg did not have the protection that the other papers had. When FCC hearings began on telephone monopolies, it was revealed that AT&T had been leasing lines to Nationwide, Annenberg's *Daily Racing Form* bookie service empire that was worth $6 million a year. The *Herald* and the *Daily News* finally found an exposé they could champion.

In 1937 Jack S. Knight and his brother James purchased the *Miami Herald* from Shutts, in what would become the Knight brothers' most important newspaper acquisition. The Knight newspaper chain had grown slowly out of the *Akron Beacon Journal,* started in 1903 by their father, Charles Landon Knight. Jack Knight inherited the Akron paper in 1933 and began to expand the holdings of the company with the purchase of *Massillon Independent* in Ohio. From these modest beginnings, the second-largest newspaper chain in the country would grow, but despite the eventual size of the operation, Jack Knight would continue to live in Akron and was a central figure in the community until his death.

When the Knights came to Miami to buy the *Herald*, they imme-diately made an offer on Annenberg's *Tribune*. Annenberg took $600,000 and the *Massillon Independent* in exchange for his failing paper, and Knight closed the *Tribune* that same day.[19] The remaining local paper, the *Miami Daily News*, was owned by James M. Cox, the three-term governor of Ohio and Democratic presidential candidate in 1920, a race that he lost to Warren G. Harding, publisher of the *Marion Star*. This convergence of business, politics, and newspapers was common in the early days of Florida expansion, and Miami would prove fertile ground for the development of large newspaper chains. Cox had come to Miami from the *Dayton Daily News*, a paper he purchased in 1898, where he rivaled C. L. Knight's *Akron Beacon Journal*. He bought the *Miami Metropolis* in 1923 and renamed it the *Daily News*.[20]

A proponent of the "no news is good news" school, Cox was skittish about reporting news that might hurt the economy. When the stock market crash hit, Cox issued the order to minimize the story across his chain, arguing that the plummet was

> nearly if not quite over and yet all of our newspapers are filling the public mind with the idea of disaster. This can easily develop a psychological condition hurtful to the general interest. The great masses of the people who are not involved can pursue, uninterrupted, their part in commerce. Otherwise, the impression will grow that we are on the verge of a serious industrial depression. My thought as publisher was to help our public forget the panic. . . .[21]

The Knights' $2.5 million purchase price of the *Herald*, though high for the time in a country in the depths of the Depression, was a calculated risk that was more than certain to pay off. With the *Tribune* out of the way and wartime expansion on the horizon, the *Herald* was perfectly situated to take advantage of the growing market. The Knights set about building their adopted city from the ground up, focusing on the local infrastructure in their coverage. The foundation of the place had to be laid, starting with the local utilities. The ownership of the power supply company, water, and the railroads were constant fodder for the newspaper, which tried to balance busi-ness entrepreneurship with reliability of service. The streets needed paving for all the celebrity automobiles, hotels needed to be built, and beaches had to be cleaned.

The issue of gambling and corruption was a constant one. On one hand, new businesses could be encouraged to relocate in Miami if they were assured that practices were fair; on the other, the system had been corrupt for so long and existed at so many levels that rooting it out would necessitate a complete overhaul of the police, the elected representatives, and the judiciary. The money supporting all of these men in power came from those who were themselves building the place up, the railroad tycoons, the hotel and restaurant developers, and most of all the home builders. It was impossible to replace one side of the operation without impinging on the rights of the other. News coverage had to be somewhat delicate in covering politics in order to promote the benefits of free-flowing capital, and this meant balancing investigative reports with exaggerated civic boosterism.

At Cox's *Daily News*, a crusade began against the influx of gangsters and took Al Capone as its target. It supported a local ordinance against vagrancy that periodically resulted in Capone being picked up. Unsatisfied by this temporary solution, Cox urged the federal government to intervene at a higher level, by means of income tax evasion:

> That was the beginning of Capone's end. In due course he, with other members of his crowd, was on his way to prison. The *Daily News* was left to make this fight alone. This should not imply that the other newspaper was at all in sympathy with Capone. In too many places, if one newspaper begins a bold and necessary crusade, its competitors deny the movement either sympathy or support. The fact is not creditable to the profession, but it is a fault which will be admitted, I think, by most publishers and editors.[22]

Knight, an avid gambler who regularly frequented casinos and racetracks, was nevertheless against the placing of bets in his editorials, a contradiction that was not lost on his newspaper competitor. He attempted to use his own paper as a standard bearer against conflict of interest and corruption, as he editorialized in the *Herald*:

> Free meals, free drinks, trips to Cuba, "publicity" jobs and other manifestations of life on the cuff have been accepted for so long among Miami journalists that mere mention of the fact produces bored expressions of mock surprise. But the public has a right to look to newspapers as protectors of its interest. That interest cannot be guarded when reporters receive this sort of outside compensation.[23]

Despite the best efforts of the *Herald*, the vice city got more than its share of attention from federal bureaucrats looking to set their own example, and the owner of the *Herald* would have to reconcile his own propensity to spend time in casinos with his editorials which advocated their banishment.

Jack Knight was a Republican, he was anti-Roosevelt and anti–New Deal, and he was a pre–World War II isolationist, but the paper was as politically independent as a large newspaper operation could afford to be. The overriding mandate of the *Herald* was the support of the local economy, with an emphasis on news coverage that would bring in the most advertising. As James Knight put it:

> When we buy a newspaper, we spend money to improve the editorial product. That brings us more readers who read the paper more thoroughly, producing better results for advertisers. More revenue from added circulation and advertising produces better profit. And this we plow back into improving the editorial product still more.[24]

Under his leadership, the *Herald* added columnists Walter Winchell, who documented the celebrity Miami scene of gangsters and starlets, Heywood Broun, and Eleanor Roosevelt,[25] all of whom had previously published in the *Tribune*. For many readers the most important column was the one written by Jack Knight himself, "Editor's Notebook." The column would appear in all of his newspapers, setting the general tone and political orientation for the entire chain.

When war broke out, Miami was in the center of the action. By then a crucial port, a major manufacturer, and an army base, Miami prospered from the influx of workers that came to work in munitions factories and in shipbuilding. But the war was closer to south Floridians than many other Americans, and vigilance over the waterways was an ongoing effort. German submarines were never far offshore, and the proximity to Cuba was a constant source of distress. As Cox remembered,

> the early scenes of war preparation in the Miami area were unforgettable. Golf courses, vacant areas and boulevards were full of marching men at the very crack of dawn. Five hundred thousand young Americans came to the Beach to be trained and then classified for service elsewhere. Fifteen thousand young officers were trained for the Army Air Corps. These stalwart youths exemplified the human resources which make the nation's strength. General Arnold of the Air Forces characterized it as the West Point of the air. All up and down the coast great airfields were built with runways in some instances miles in length. The airplanes and blimps were to be seen and heard day and night.[26]

Domestic wartime activities provided ample fodder for newspapers, but papers like the *Herald* were caught in the double bind of having more news than usual as well as greater demand on the part of readers but less and less paper on which to print. The *Herald* made a strategic decision in wartime that would help to seal its fate as a high-quality newspaper with a loyal following well into the postwar era: they cut circulation and asked people to share their copies, and they covered news at the expense of ads. By limiting advertisers' space to one page of basic information and classifieds to wartime necessities only, the *Herald* became the most trustworthy source for news in Miami, despite the severe profit losses it suffered from the lack of advertising.

After the war, returning vets chose Miami as a good place to settle. Some had been stationed there for training, and others had simply heard about the good weather and abundant resources. Demand for housing soon outstripped supply, and the city would experience yet another boom, reminiscent of the heyday of the 1920s.

Reporters and editors returning from the war found an increasingly prosperous *Herald*, but the labor movement would take hold at newspapers as it would across many other industries. Pressmen went on strike at the *Herald* on January 5, 1947. Rather than stop the paper, Knight moved the production to the presses at the *Miami Daily News*, and when the *News* went on strike, the *Herald* returned the favor. The inability of striking workers to shut down operations was a serious obstacle to the effectiveness of strikes in Florida, and replacement workers were always easy to find, garnering Miami the nickname "Scab City." Nevertheless, tension between union and nonunion labor was intense and sometimes violent. A fire at the presses on October 1, 1949, caused major damage to the *Herald* plant and to its stock of newsprint, which could not be saved.[27]

Just as J. Edgar Hoover had turned his attention to Miami in the interwar period, so Senator Estes Kefauver would make his career there in the postwar era. His Senate Crime Committee held hearings on the state of graft, gambling, and greed in Miami, once again revealing the dark underworld of the city to the rest of the nation. The investigation was helped by the *Herald*'s own ongoing investigation of criminal behavior, and the files it had been keeping for a regular feature called "Know Your Neighbor," which pictured known criminals and listed their addresses.[28] James Knight was involved in a local Crime Commission, and both he and his brother became objects of scorn within the mob. The tide on organized crime had turned, and official public sentiment seemed no longer willing to tolerate it. The *Herald* maintained steady coverage of mob malfeasances and won the Pulitzer Prize for public service for its crime reporting efforts in 1951, just as the *Miami Daily News* had done in 1939.[29]

The chain was growing at a rapid pace, with Knight making acquisitions across the country and shutting down the local competition as he had in Miami. In 1940 he bought the *Detroit Free Press*, and four years later the *Chicago Daily News,* which he sold in 1959. In between, the *Charlotte Observer* and the *Charlotte News* were added to the chain. In Charlotte, the two existing papers both continued to operate for some time. First sales and production facilities were merged, and in 1985 the *News* was closed down, leaving only one newspaper in Charlotte and no competition for advertisers or readers. In the mid-1960s, the Knights purchased the *Times* in Coral Gables and the *Tallahassee Democrat*, shifting their emphasis toward the growing suburbs and the state capital.

Knight's regional acquisitions were closely mirrored by his local rival at the *Daily News*. James L. Cox continued to expand his empire in Ohio with the purchase of the *Canton Daily News* and the *Springfield Morning Sun*. As Knight would do in Charlotte, Cox acquired the *Atlanta Journal* in 1939 and the *Atlanta Constitution* in 1950, which soon merged into the *Atlanta Journal-Constitution*, now Cox Newspapers' flagship paper in a corporation that includes broadcasting, cable, direct mail, and automotive auctions.

Knight Newspapers maintained its focus on newspapers. Though the chain was not centrally managed, its profits soared in each of its markets. In Miami, local coverage continued to focus on downtown redevelopment, and the *Herald* contributed with its own new, six-story, block-long building with impressive new presses and offices along Biscayne Bay. One of the tenants of the new building was the Cox-owned *Miami Daily News*, which used the *Herald*'s business facilities in exchange for abandoning their Sunday edition, giving the *Herald* a monopoly on Sundays.[30]

It was from this new headquarters that the *Herald* took on its greatest news challenge of the 1960s, the ongoing Cuban crises 228 miles away. The Bay of Pigs invasion put the paper at odds with the new President, as the *Herald* sought to match foreign policy coverage with the growing population of Cuban exiles in Florida. All of south Florida waited apprehensively as the Soviets backed Cuba in the missile crisis of October 1962. In the end, Knight, a committed Republican, wrote in support of Kennedy's leadership. He welcomed the President at the Inter-American Press Association meeting in Miami, both favoring stronger alliances with Latin America, four days before Kennedy was assassinated in Dallas, Texas.

Knight fought for freedom of the press in South America as the best way to end conflict and bring about hemispheric peace. The realm of influence of the *Herald* was also growing, with more foreign correspondents and an English-language *Herald* edition that was started in 1946 and circulated by air to South America. By controlling the image of Miami to South Americans, the *Herald* would help entice more immigrants to the state and set the agenda for South American relations.

The Miami shoreline. Photo by Herbert Gehr. Courtesy of Time-Life Pictures/ Getty Images, 1941.

After the purchase of the *Macon Telegraph* and *Macon News*, the Knight chain had the fifth largest circulation in the country.[31] Knight disliked the word *chain* to describe his holdings, preferring instead to call it a group, one that was increasingly profitable with papers in Akron, Charlotte, Detroit, Miami, and Tallahassee, as well as three weeklies in Florida. The size and structure of the company was also expanding, and a new hierarchy of leadership was created to reflect its size. Jack made his brother James chairman and chief executive officer, and the publisher of the *Detroit Free Press*, Lee Hills, was made company president and executive editor. Jack oversaw the operation from the position of editorial chairman, and in this role he was awarded the Pulitzer in 1968. This new series of titles was in preparation for the most important strategic decision made by the company, which was to go public in 1969 with a listing on the New York Stock Exchange.

Knight was reluctant to take the company public, but the decision was finally made. Among his board of directors, his vote was typically the lone voice against expansion, as it was when the acquisition of the Philadelphia papers was being deliberated. The demands of being a public company meant more structure, process, and memos than he was used to, and there was always the fear that shareholder value would be at the forefront of the decision-making process, above journalistic integrity. In the end, however, the tax burden of the private company led the directors to choose public stock ownership as the only viable path. The public offering was accompanied by several other newspaper acquisitions, a signal to prospective stock buyers that the company was continuing to expand. Following the purchase of the *Macon Telegraph* and *News*, the *Boca Raton News*, the *Milledgeville Union-Recorder*, and two papers in Philadelphia, the *Inquirer* and the *Daily News*, were added. A regional pattern was beginning to emerge in these acquisitions, as the company focused on eastern papers, many of which were in the South.

A few years later, the company would join another newspaper chain that had also gone public in 1969, Ridder Publications. Founded in 1892 with Herman Ridder's New York–based German newspaper, *Staats-Zeitung*, what appeared to be a single-paper business targeted to the immigrant population began growing into a chain with the purchase of Samuel Morse's *Journal of Commerce*, also published in New York, in 1926. Following this acquisition, Ridder followed much the same pattern as did Knight, buying, for example, the *St. Paul Pioneer Press* and the *St. Paul Dispatch* in 1927. The *Pioneer Press* had been Minnesota's first daily newspaper, started in 1849, and as with the rest of the acquisitions of two newspapers in the same city, they were merged in 1985.

Knight Ridder grew through the purchases of the *Lexington Herald*, the *Lexington Leader*, the *Columbus Ledger*, and the *Columbus Enquirer*. The company's Florida holdings were extended with the *Bradenton News*. In most cases, as in Lexington, where the papers were merged in 1983, and in Columbus, where the two papers were merged in 1988, the acquisition by the chain meant the demise of independently owned newspapers that had been in operation since the early nineteenth century. The *San Jose Mercury News* was already a mostly merged paper before it was purchased by Ridder in 1952.

This geographic concentration helped the papers expand their sphere of influence by delivering larger audiences to advertisers from wider geographic areas. As people continued to flee inner cities in favor of suburbs, newspapers raced to follow them by swallowing suburban weeklies that ringed larger cities and centralizing their printing into one common press facility. In 1995, Knight Ridder bought the Contra Costa papers in California, and combined five papers into a single Sunday edition. In the northeast, the company bought Pro-Media Management, a company of suburban weeklies around Philadelphia, and Consumer and Community News in New Jersey, serving the surrounding areas with weeklies and shoppers. The deals were getting larger, as entire groups of papers were being traded at a time, often with other large chains. More and more newspapers were considered portfolio assets rather than organs of news. When Knight Ridder took over the *Monterey County Herald* in 1997, it was purchased in exchange for Colorado papers that it then sold to the rival Scripps Howard chain. The experience in Monterey illustrated the darker side of chain ownership. In addition to staff cuts that resulted in twenty-eight lost jobs, the new company did not recognize the union, and the new management's presence in the newsroom and in the community was seen as hostile. Just as the Knights were accused of being "foreign owners" in Miami, their new acquisitions across the country would be met with allegations that a company of its size whose first priority was its shareholders would be unable to tend to the needs of the local constituencies of their smaller papers. Increasingly, this charge proved correct.

The *Tampa Tribune*

The *Tampa Tribune* was started by Wallace Stovall as the *Tampa Morning Tribune* in 1893 with the commitment that

> its language shall be plain, its intelligence reliable, its scope broad and its great aim to give all the news. It will aim to be reliable, fair and useful. All parties and men will be treated as their merits, positions or actions deserve. It will be independent in everything but neutral in nothing where right, justice or the public good requires outspoken opinion, severe censure or full investigation.[32]

At the turn of the century, Florida was the growth capital of the country, outpacing many other states in population growth. The paper was a sponsor and booster of a February 1908 three-day migration festival, to be held at the state fair. Invitations were sent far and wide to politicians, civic leaders, and newspaper editors across the country. The *Tribune* wrote that the conference "would doubtless result in a plan of magnificent proportions to induce settlers to enter the south."[33] When census figures confirmed a growth rate in Tampa of 143.2 percent in 1910, counting forty thousand residents, there was a Census Celebration in honor of the achievement.[34]

Stovall was an unparalleled civic booster, using his paper to support the building of Union Station, a Carnegie library, and the Florida State Fair. His *Tribune* was also the motor behind the Gasparilla Festival, commemorating the apocryphal pirate past of the region by staging a mock pirate invasion every year. Town leaders donned earrings, headscarves, and eye patches in a made-up reenactment of the founding of the town, a newspaper-invented tradition that is still celebrated today.

Cigar manufacturing was the main industry propelling the growth of Tampa, and it was also the source of labor struggle that would pit the *Tribune* against the Cuban and Spanish populations with their radical and revolutionary politics. The Cuban independence movement, originating in Ybor City in Tampa, quickly grew into the Cuban Revolutionary Party, and with it arrived calls by the city's newspapers for containment of the agitators. The *Tribune*'s position on the striking laborers was not only based in a belief in free enterprise unfettered by organized labor; the publisher had investments in cigar companies and the *Tribune* itself had cigar manufacturers on its board, members who had a vested interest in the news agenda of the day. As in Miami, the rival paper, the *Tampa Times*, was owned by a politician, in this case, three-term mayor D. B. McKay. Both papers, therefore, were united in their attempts to run labor leaders out of town, often advocating illegal measures in getting rid of them. Local citizens were urged to fight the "agitators" and form Citizen's Committees, who by means including deportation, intimidation, and violence sought to purge Tampa of its labor threat.[35]

News stories were told from the point of view of business leaders, who knew that the cigar industry was central to the economic health of the city. Events were covered, therefore, from the perspective of law and order and from the interests of management rather than labor:

> What might have turned out a serious situation was nipped in the bud yesterday morning by Constable W. M. Allen and Deputy Sheriff J. J. Miller, who were called to the cigar factory of J. D. Greenlee ... by the

proprietor. The officers found a score or more employees, lying about heavily armed and apparently determined to make trouble.[36]

During a seven-month strike by cigar workers in 1910, the newspaper editors rallied citizens against labor leaders with nativist rhetoric. After months of violence and lynchings, police squads were called in to quell the uprisings, but the revolutionary fervor was unabated.[37] The *Tribune* editorialized steadfastly against the strikers:

> The crowd of reds operating in this city under the guise of anarchists, bolshevists, socialists, or anything else they may call themselves are put on notice that the first aggregation of them caught attempting to hold a protest meeting on May 1—or any other day—is going to be awfully sorry.[38]

Such threats did not go unnoticed by the workers, and the *Tribune* office itself was soon under threat by arsonists. Spanish and Cuban residents were well organized and politically astute, and they demonstrated not only against the local labor conditions at the factory, but also against repressive regimes in Spain and Cuba.

Though it dealt a blow to the economy of Tampa, the decline in the vogue for cigars made for a more peaceful city. During the Depression few could afford to buy hand-rolled cigars, and the popular preference for machine-made cigarettes moved the industry northward to Virginia. Many Cuban and Spanish residents of Florida followed the manufacturing and service economy north, and shipbuilding took over as the main industry of the region.

The new motoring craze brought out-of-town tourists, called "Tin Can Tourists" because of their stores of canned supplies, to the warm state. After World War I northerners came for the ride, and many of them stayed beyond the season to settle. The *Tribune* detailed the comings and goings of tourists in regular features of the paper, listing the arrivals like a ship's manifest in a regular column called "The Passing Throngs."[39] The car mania also added a new supply of advertisers to the paper, a new page of auto news, and editorials promoting the Good Roads Movement. Henry Ford's five dollar a day minimum wage made for more cars on the road and drivers with more money, both of which Florida welcomed, especially when motoring visitors decided to purchase one of the many properties for sale. The turnover in land deals was so high that from week to week and season to season tourists and residents alike were buying and selling lots without ever taking possession of them. Everyone, teenagers included, was getting rich on the land boom, which showed no signs of abating in the 1920s, despite regular hurricanes, storms, and swindle stories. All provided excellent content for the newspaper business.

The speculation frenzy itself was a self-sustaining goldmine for the newspapers:

> The first step involved publicity in the local daily newspapers. All were civic boosters and eagerly reported the claims of developers in the news columns. Then you advertised heavily in those same newspapers, both to keep the free publicity coming and to lure the prospects to the sales office. At the sales office, maps and drawings and even a scale model presented a gorgeous picture of the development when completed. Then you clinched the sale with visions of profit, reminding the prospect of the fabulous resale prices investors had been getting during the land boom.[40]

In 1924 Stovall started a "Development Page" in the paper and for the first time began to count real estate advertising revenue separately; he found it was worth double that of department stores and automobiles. For 1925 the *Tampa Tribune* showed a profit of $400,000.[41] The relationship between land development and the *Tampa Tribune* was solidified further through people like Truman Green, who left his job as the ad director for Davis Island's development for the ad manager's job at the *Tribune*.[42] Just as Henry Flagler had done in Miami, David P. Davis dredged the bottom of Hillsborough Bay to create new islands for resort development. By the end of 1924, tourists had spent over $1,683,000 on Davis Island property.[43]

The newspapers were instrumental in the development of this almost frontier town, with newspaper owners themselves often becoming large landowners. Stovall is credited with building much of Tampa's skyline himself; his own house, a sprawling mansion on Bayshore Boulevard, was built in 1926, and several office buildings downtown that were speculative ventures changed the city dramatically in the late 1920s: the Wallace building, twelve stories tall; the Stovall Professional Building, eight stories; and the Stovall office building, seven stories.[44] Beyond the city limits, Stovall's land holdings extended down to the Everglades. "At the crest of the boom, he was rated the city's largest individual property owner as well as one of its most wealthy citizens," according to his biographer.[45]

In his biography of Wallace Stovall, Dudley Haddock writes that Stovall and his *Tribune* "were among the most forceful factors in the modern development of the state and South Florida in general and the City of Tampa in particular."[46] Haddock credits the newspaper war between the *Tribune* and the *Times* with laying an important civic foundation in the city:

> Because virtually all of their squabbles were predicated upon topics having to do with Tampa's progress its people thus became thoroughly

informed concerning every phase of civic development. This familiarity with community needs inculcated in Tampa's early citizenship the spirit that resulted in the building of the dynamic city around which revolved the economic life of nearly one third of Florida's population.[47]

Wallace Stovall died on March 10, 1950. His obituary in the *Tribune*, written by Ed Lambright, was headlined, "A Builder Rests":

He built a village weekly into a widely circulated and prosperous city newspaper, which he sold for more than a million dollars; he built a dream of Tampa's future into massive structures. His enduring monument is in Tampa's towering skyline.[48]

At what looked to be the height of the *Tribune's* profitability in 1925, the paper was sold to Lulette Gunby, a New York woman fronting for a land speculator, a banker, and several local advertisers for $1.2 million. Immediately regretting the sale, Stovall tried to start his own rival paper with the proceeds, with limited success.

In 1927 the paper was taken over by Samuel Emory Thomason from Chicago and John Stewart Bryan of Richmond. Thomason was a *Chicago Tribune* veteran, who started and continued to run the tabloid *Chicago Times*. The newspaper war between the *Tribune* and the *Times* in Chicago was replicated by the newspaper war between the *Tribune* and the *Times* in Tampa, with Thomason in charge of one of each. The *Chicago Times* was sold in 1947 to the *Chicago Sun* and merged with it in 1948, but Thomason's experience of running a picture tabloid in Chicago would prove useful in the new gangster playground in Florida. Bryan was the publisher of the *News Leader* of Richmond, Virginia, and was from one of Richmond's most prestigious families. He would later serve as the president of William and Mary College from 1934 to 1942. The *News Leader* and the *Richmond Times-Dispatch* formed Richmond Newspapers, Inc., with the Bryan family holding 54 percent of the company's stock. This company would later take over the *Tampa Tribune* and would eventually form the basis of Media General.

The prosperity of the Tampa Bay area soon stagnated, and the 1930 census reported that Miami had taken pride of place in Florida's population race. The building boom was compromised by bad weather, single-track railroads that were unable to handle the volume of needed building supplies, and an already saturated market of suckers. Many workers left for New York after the once-booming cigar industry collapsed, and local crops fell prey to insect infestations and drought. Many Florida towns no longer had the money to pay for basic infrastructure to support the overdevelopment, and road, drainage, and sewage projects languished. Nearby St. Petersburg had the highest debt in the nation in 1927, forecasting the crash that would come to the rest of the country two years later. The New Deal Works Progress Administration projects would help to restore the area by building up Bayshore and the University of Tampa, restoring Plant Park, paving Drew Airfield runways, and clearing brush for Hillsborough State Park. Peter O. Knight Airport was named for the executive of the Tampa Electric Company, the gangster cousin of Mayor McKay. New causeways helped to connect the water-locked area, and airports provided new gateways to South America.[49] At home at the *Tribune*, a beautiful art deco building went up in 1935 to house the paper's operations on Lafayette Street.

Cars, land, and weather provided an ongoing source of news that Florida newspapers did not have to expend much effort in gathering. Weather, which ran to extremes in Florida and had the potential to wipe out crops, towns, and neighborhoods overnight, was one of the most important beats. Like Miami and the rest of the state, Tampa strained to keep such disruptive news to a minimum. Many local boosters thought it unfair that bad news seemed to hover around Florida, and used the newspapers to set the record straight, as Peter Knight did following a 1935 hurricane:

> When San Francisco was visited by an earthquake, the press of the country did not talk about the California disaster. When Chicago had its great fire, the press of the country did not talk about the Illinois disaster. When Galveston was destroyed, no one spoke of the Texas disaster. . . . And now when but a small portion of Florida has been affected by the hurricane, the country refers to this as the great Florida disaster.[50]

Added into the mix was the state's unofficially equivocal stance on Prohibition. Tampa was well placed along liquor smuggling routes from Bahamas to Cuba, helping the illegal import of alcohol to become a lucrative side business for Tampa's fishermen. Inland, distilleries churned out homemade beverages. Cuban and Spanish residents resisted the ban on alcohol, and the underpaid and easily bribed police force allowed hospitable conditions for speakeasies and nightclubs to flourish. As in Miami, antivice crusades were not popular for fear they would affect needed tourism, but the *Tampa Tribune* did go after slot machines in 1930,[51] and covered its share of the gambling, shoot-outs, racketeering, and mob wars that marred Ybor City. It was Thomason's policy, however, to show neither bodies nor snakes in the *Tribune*.[52]

Tampa turned 50 in 1937, but the local circumstances were dire on most fronts. The rival *Florida Times-Union* out of Jacksonville came under the ownership of Henry Flagler and three railroad companies, who reaped the reward of one of the few remaining sources of advertising. The *Tribune* would have to wait for World War II to bolster the failing economy by bringing the shipbuilding industry back to life. The paper successfully campaigned for a new airfield, and a $10 million base was granted in July 1939.[53] Named for Colonel Leslie MacDill, it served as a giant air training base for the war. By the middle of the war, circulation had reached ninety thousand daily and a hundred thousand on Sundays. On the paper's fiftieth anniversary, the *Tribune* noted that

> both Tampa and Florida have grown and developed marvelously in those 50 years. This newspaper has grown and developed with them and has had some part, some influence, in that growth and development.[54]

In 1944, the Tribune's only war correspondent, Gordon Grant, left for Europe. At home, the paper organized its carriers to sell defense savings stamps and war bonds to subscribers, and civil defense ads were a new, much-needed source of income.[55] Soldiers took over the apartments, houses, and hotel rooms once occupied by tourists, and another housing boom began.[56] After the war, assembly-line construction, prefabricated houses, and the new technology of air conditioning encouraged more newcomers, and suburbs began developing to the north of the city. In fact, so many houses were going up for returning veterans and new residents that an illegal trade developed in construction materials.[57] Greater distances to new subdivisions brought more cars and with them more car advertising in the *Tribune*. Florida State University was constructed to handle all the returning veterans going to school with the help of the GI Bill.

The war also brought more vice when the soldiers attracted flagrant open-street prostitution and brothels. The crime and corruption brought renewed vigor to the *Tribune,* which began crusades to clean up local government. Its reform efforts were aimed at the alderman and ward system of government, which it viewed as an antidemocratic and inefficient machine marred by favoritism and closed patronage. The paper began by surveying government structures that it found to be cleaner and more open elsewhere and completed a series on twenty-five American cities run by city managers.[58] Locally, it pushed the idea on civic groups and real estate developers and gave special mention to neighboring St. Petersburg, already operating under a city manager. It would be one of managing editor Virgil M. "Red" Newton's biggest crusades, which ran

> eight years and more than 1,500 stories and pictures before victory was declared in 1953 with a newly elected legislative delegation that

increased the area of Tampa from 21 to 68 square miles and added 91,000 people to the city's population.[59]

Other campaigns included those against oil companies, who were avoiding taxes and threatening the landscape with their refineries and promotion of individual car ownership at the expense of public transportation. The Tampa Electric Company sold the efficient and charming trolley system that connected downtown Tampa to a consortium called National City Lines. National City Lines would replace the electric streetcars with gasoline-fueled buses to serve their own interests in gasoline, auto manufacturing, and rubber. It would later be revealed as a syndicate of General Motors, Firestone, and Standard Oil, who were convicted of criminal conspiracy in 1949.[60] The inefficient bus system was made even less so by ensuing bus strikes which made travel around the region even more dependent on private cars.

In other conspiracy news, investigative reporter Jock Murray's underworld investigations for the *Tribune* led another antigambling crusade.[61] Newsmen at the *Tribune* were harassed and threatened by the mob, but the paper continued in its efforts to demonstrate that political graft and payoffs were linked to organized crime. A list of local politicians and their connections would bring Senator Estes Kefauver to Tampa as he had been brought to Miami. Longtime gangster and Ybor City resident Charlie Wall testified in 1950 at the Senate Committee to Investigate Organized Crime in Interstate Commerce, five years before he would be found murdered in his home by a homemade blackjack filled with birdseed.[62] Despite the rampant gangland activity in Tampa, it was considered to be a less important site than Miami had proven to be a year earlier, and the Senate Commission did not stay long. A *Time* magazine article, however, gave the *Tribune* and Red Newton credit for their longstanding crusade in an article called "Red's Reward."[63] Newton later gained prominence in the fight for the Freedom of Information Act, signed into legislation at long last by President Johnson.

The paper gained a reputation for its crusades and its in-depth investigative reporting, having successfully worked against corrupt elections and inhumane prison conditions. In the 1950s, it took aim at public education, helping to improve a system that was considered by many to be failing and in need of repair. But when *Brown v. Board of Education* was handed down, Florida, like many southern states, took a purposely slow and gradual approach to integrating schools. The *Tribune* editorialized that *Brown* was

deplorable to the extent that it is disruptive and destructive of the law, custom and the social order in those states which have maintained segregation since the slaves were freed by Lincoln's proclamation.[64]

The paper supported the 1957 "interposition resolution" in the Florida legislature, which prevented the Supreme Court from ending segregation in the public schools.[65]

After the war, the *Tampa Tribune* became a statewide paper with bureaus in Tallahassee, Sarasota, Bradenton, Lakeland, Clearwater, and Sebring–Avon Park,[66] and became the third largest employer in Tampa after the telephone and electric companies. With a high proportion of retirees moving into the state, newspaper readership was also unusually high, even after television entered the field.[67] The *Tribune*, like many other newspapers across the country, faced the threat of television head-on, lobbying the FCC for a broadcasting license in order to add television to their radio operation. A license to broadcast on Channel 8 was granted in 1955, and like the *Tribune's* radio station WFLA, the channel carried NBC feed.

After nearly sixty-five years of rivalry, the *Tampa Times* finally fell to the *Tribune* in 1958, when it could no longer compete with the dominant daily. The Tribune Company, consisting of the *Tribune*, the *Times*, WFLA-TV, and WFLA-radio, was acquired by Richmond Newspapers, Inc., in 1965, then headed by John Stuart Bryan's son D. Tennant Bryan. The company became known as Media General in 1969, with Richmond Newspapers as a wholly owned subsidiary, and a year later, like Knight Ridder, Media General went public with a listing on the American Stock Exchange. The *Times* and *Tribune* operated alongside each other in a merged capacity as the *Times-Tribune* until 1982 when the *Times* was closed altogether.

Mergers such as these became commonplace in the early 1970s for several reasons, all of which made newspapers more lucrative assets inside larger and larger companies. Mergers between two newspapers in one location produced economies of scale through cutbacks in payroll and content sharing across the chain, and with many companies turning to public stock ownership, these closures helped secure the immediate profits shareholders were seeking. The newspaper industry was also aided by the 1970 Newspaper Preservation Act, which exempted newspapers from antitrust laws and made Joint Operating Agreements common among two-newspaper towns. Though intended to keep struggling second-place newspapers from closing in order to preserve two editorial voices, the consequence of these agreements was that papers shared production expenses and profits, while also fixing prices for advertising. In many cases, the afternoon paper closed after only a few years of joint operation.

Afternoon papers were the hardest hit in these mergers because of changing reader demographics. Suburbanization and longer commutes encouraged more people to seek their newspaper news in the morning, while turning to television news in the evening. More women were in the paid workforce, and younger readers were less inclined toward newspaper readership. In cities, taller apartment buildings presented challenges for delivery, because of the difficulty in gaining access to the inside corridors. As a result of diminished afternoon readership, advertisers who had grown used to buying space in both papers at combination rates started to insist on buying ads in the morning papers only.[68]

The *Tampa Tribune* was also typical of its era in its approach to new press technology. Video display terminals were added to the newsroom, and subscriber lists were computerized. Offset printing allowed several newspapers in one area to be printed on a common press, encouraging the purchase of locally concentrated groups of papers. As new production facilities were seen to reap greater and greater rewards in cost and time savings, however, there was also a need for new capital investment to pay for the machines. Among many of the cost-cutting measures were cutbacks in local news coverage and content-sharing agreements, both resulting in newspapers that were less responsive to their local environments. For many failing newspapers, editorial luxuries such as comprehensive local news had to be forfeited until short-term cost cutting could get them back together, and in the meantime, readers were lost. In order to increase revenues, chain owners were much more likely to raise advertising rates, often without making any real gains in circulation. With corporate owners usually located at a headquarters in another state, they were more immune from the immediate effects of backlash from local business owners when rates were raised.

The *Tampa Tribune*'s Richmond-based corporate parent, Media General, led by chief executive officer J. Stuart Bryan III, initiated many of these new strategies. The company was a fully integrated media operation with holdings in newspapers, television stations, and new media. With twenty-five daily newspapers in Virginia, North Carolina, Florida, Alabama, and South Carolina and as many television stations in the same regions, Media General is both vertically and horizontally integrated in the Southeast. In addition to its 40 percent interest in the *Denver Post*, its holdings include another one hundred periodicals including weeklies, shoppers, and trade magazines.

In March 1999, the Tribune Company moved into its new fully converged News Center, which now incorporates Tampa Bay Online, NewsChannel 8, and the newspaper in a twenty-four-hour news production facility. Newspaper journalists write content that is used for both television and Internet broadcasts, and the $40 million complex is completely digital so that broadcast feed can be immediately streamlined on the Web site. Broadcast anchors can write copy for the newspaper and the Web site, and newspaper journalists may appear on camera. The high-tech News Center serves as a model for future media convergence across the industry, and the *Tampa Tribune* is one of the fastest growing newspapers in the United States.[69]

Despite their chain ownership, the *Miami Herald* and the *Tampa Tribune* continue to flourish as flagship newspapers in large corporations. They have strategically purchased surrounding suburban papers to discourage rivals from entering the field, and they publish separate editions in Spanish—such as the twenty-five-year-old *El Nuevo Herald* in Miami—to serve the growing Hispanic population. Yet they continue to operate under corporate performance pressure to produce extreme profit margins, which takes money away from costly investigative reporting enterprises. By contrast, the *Tampa Tribune*'s rival across the bay, the independent *St. Petersburg Times* is widely regarded as one of the best in the state, and does not have public shareholders. The newspaper is supported by a trust started by Nelson Poynter, called the Poynter Institute for Media Studies. The Institute functions as a nonprofit journalism school to train newspaper workers. Although the *Times* receives frequent buyout offers, the trust stipulates that the paper must continue to operate independently and in the public interest and that profits be reinvested in the company.[70] The *St. Petersburg Times* is the exception that proves the rule that large chains and corporate management techniques are not necessary for growth, profit, or quality in the newspaper business.

Notes

1. Edward N. Akin, *Flagler: Rockefeller Partner and Florida Baron* (Gainesville: University Press of Florida, 1992), 167. Akin claims that Flagler bought the *Metropolis* and changed the name to the *Miami Herald* in 1910.

2. Akin, *Flagler*, 204.

3. Akin, *Flagler*, 184.

4. See *Miami Herald*, 22 January 1913, for a glowing report of the extension upon its completion.

5. Akin, *Flagler*, 163.

6. Akin, *Flagler*, 165.

7. Akin, *Flagler*, 184.

8. William E. Leuchtenburg, *The Perils of Prosperity, 1914–1932*, 2d ed, (Chicago and London: University of Chicago Press: 1993), 183.

9. Frederick Lewis Allen, *Only Yesterday: An Informal History of the 1920s* (New York: Harper and Row, 1931), 235.

10. *Miami Herald*, 30 September 1926; "Do Not Believe Rumors," *Miami Herald*, 21 September 1926, quoted in Theodore Steinberg, *Acts of God: The Unnatural History of Natural Disaster in America* (New York: Oxford, 2000), 54.

11. "In Today's News," *Miami Herald*, 16 September 1926.

12. "Naming the Hurricane," *Miami Herald*, 14 September 1935.

13. "To the American People," *Miami Herald*, 23 September 1926.

14. Charles Whited, *Knight: A Publisher in the Tumultuous Century* (New York: Dutton, 1988), 52–53.

15. Christopher Ogden, *Legacy: A Biography of Moses and Walter Annenberg* (Boston: Little, Brown, and Company, 1999), 152.

16. Ogden, *Legacy*, 151.

17. Ogden, *Legacy*, 153.

18. Ogden, *Legacy*, 153.

19. It would be from the Annenbergs that the Knights would also purchase their other major urban dailies, the *Philadelphia Inquirer* and the *Daily News*.

20. James M. Cox, *Journey Through My Years* (New York: Simon and Schuster, 1946), 309–314.

21. Teresa Zumwald, *Dayton Ink: The First Century of the Dayton* Daily News (Dayton: Dayton News, 1998).

22. Cox, *Journey Through*, 316.

23. "Editor's Notebook," *Miami Herald*, 31 March 1940.

24. "James L. Knight, Interview" *Miami Herald,* 12 March 1972.

25. Whited, *Knight*, 80.

26. Cox, *Journey Through*, 320.

27. Whited, *Knight*, 153.

28. Whited, *Knight*, 166.

29. Whited, *Knight*, 166–167; Cox, *Journey Through*, 318; John Hohenberg, *The Pulitzer Prize Story: News Stories, Editorials, Cartoons, and Pictures from the Pulitzer Prize Collection at Columbia University* (New York: Columbia University Press, 1959).

30. Whited, *Knight*, 237.

31. Whited, *Knight*, 271.

32. Reprinted in the 30 August 1908, edition.

33. Quoted in George E. Pozzetta, *Immigrants on the Land: Agriculture, Rural Life, and Small Towns* (London: Taylor and Francis, 1991), 176.

34. Bentley Orrick and Harry Crumpacker, *The* Tampa Tribune*: A Century of Florida Journalism* (Tampa: University of Tampa Press, 1998), 80.

35. Darien Cavanaugh, *Huelga! Labor Activism and Unrest in Ybor City: 1886 to 1950* (Tampa, FL: Ybor City Museum Exhibit Catalogue, 2003).

36. *Tampa Tribune*, 10 May 1907.

37. Cavanaugh, *Huelga*, 10.

38. "No Protest Meeting for Tampa," *Tampa Tribune*, April 27, 1919.

39. Cavanaugh, *Huelga*, 15.

40. Orrick and Crumpacker, *Tampa Tribune,* 103–104.

41. Orrick and Crumpacker, *Tampa Tribune,* 106, 108.

42. Orrick and Crumpacker, *Tampa Tribune,* 129.

43. William Frazer and John J. Guthrie Jr., *The Florida Land Boom: Speculation, Money, and the Banks* (Westport, CT: Quorum Books, 1995), 135.

44. Michael Canning, "The Colonel's Tampa Legacy," *St. Petersburg Times*, October 4, 2002.

45. Dudley Haddock, *Wallace F. Stovall: A Publisher's Publisher* (Tampa, FL: publisher unknown, 1949), 6.

46. Haddock, *Stovall*, 3.

47. Haddock, *Stovall*, 6.

48. Ed Lambright, "A Builder Rests," *Tampa Tribune*, 10 March 1950.

49. Orrick and Crumpacker, *Tampa Tribune*, 165.

50. "Florida Damage of Local Import," *Wall Street Journal*, 8 October 1926.

51. Orrick and Crumpacker, *Tampa Tribune*, 141.

52. Orrick and Crumpacker, *Tampa Tribune*, 192.

53. Orrick and Crumpacker, *Tampa Tribune*, 196.

54. *Tampa Tribune*, 31 December 1944.

55. Orrick and Crumpacker, *Tampa Tribune*, 206–207.

56. "Soldier Families and Shipyard Workers Fill Up City, Not Tourists," *Tampa Tribune*, 4 February 1944.

57. Orrick and Crumpacker, *Tampa Tribune*, 246.

58. Orrick and Crumpacker, *Tampa Tribune*, 236.

59. Orrick and Crumpacker, *Tampa Tribune*, 236.

60. Orrick and Crumpacker, *Tampa Tribune*, 246.

61. Orrick and Crumpacker, *Tampa Tribune*, 255.

62. Orrick and Crumpacker, *Tampa Tribune*, 313.

63. Orrick and Crumpacker *Tampa Tribune*, 284.

64. Orrick and Crumpacker, *Tampa Tribune*, 300.

65. Julian Pleasants, *Orange Journalism: Voices from Florida Newspapers* (Gainesville: University Press of Florida, 2003), 6.

66. Orrick and Crumpacker, *Tampa Tribune*, 269.

67. Reese Cleghorn, "Florida's Newspapers Set a Fast Pace," *American Journalism Review* 18, no. 9 (1996), 4.

68. Peter Benjaminson, *Death in the Afternoon: America's Newspaper Giants Struggle for Survival* (Kansas City, MO: Andrews McMeel & Parker, 1984).

69. Karissa S. Wang, "Tampa's Media Barn: New Complex Unites WFLA-TV, *Tampa Tribune* and TBO.com," *Electronic Media*, 27 March 2000.

70. Leonard Downie Jr. and Robert G. Kaiser, *The News about the News* (New York: Vintage, 2003).

6

THE COMMUNITY NEWSPAPER

From the *Village Voice*, the *East Village Other*, and the *Chicago Seed* to CNHI and the *Hazard Herald*

Beginning in the 1950s, the trend toward larger, chain-owned newspapers was countered by the localism of independently owned community newspapers. These small papers were typically antiestablishment, haphazardly and irregularly printed, and experimental, but many grew to be large and profitable operations. Most were initially located in the nation's largest cities, but they quickly spread to smaller areas, creating a network of alternative and underground news. The growth in such underground papers was helped by the growing ferment in youth culture that was increasingly dissatisfied with the status quo of mainstream society and by the production advancement from moveable type to offset printing that allowed new players to enter the newspaper field with relatively little initial investment. The "underground" and "alternative" press, although not synonymous, nevertheless shared an opposition to mainstream news and the dominant political system, and were primarily identified with youth culture.[1]

The local alternative press took the mainstream press as its target, seeing in its "objective" news style an obfuscation of the truth. In response, newsrooms in the underground papers were nonhierarchical and often staffed by nonprofessionals. News was written through first-person accounts, not by bystanders but by participants in events. The writing was by definition subjective and partial; the goal of these papers was to bring about change. Most writers on local alternative papers were activists, artists, and organizers first and writers second. This style of writing came to be known as New Journalism, defined by its "atmosphere, personal feeling, interpretation, advocacy and opinion, novelist characterization and description, touches of obscenity, concern with fashion and cultural change, and political savvy."[2]

The community that was constructed through this writing was inherently youth oriented and frontierist. Since the first alternative papers were located in neighborhoods that were outside mainstream residential areas, the press was intently focused on issues emerging from the built environment in which they operated, including safe and affordable housing, rent control, air quality, preservation, zoning, redevelopment, and social amenities like schools and hospitals. In reporting and debating these issues, the alternative press literally shaped the neighborhoods where they operated on behalf of their readers.

The *Village Voice*

One of the first local alternative papers was the *Village Voice,* founded in Greenwich Village in 1955. Although there was already one community newspaper, the *Villager,* in the area at the time, Ed Fancher, Dan Wolf, and Norman Mailer, with little newspaper experience among them, came together to put out one of their own. It began as a regular local newspaper, with a heavy emphasis on criticism and the arts. It would grow to become an indispensable guide to the Village, and in the process it came to define for both residents and foreigners, members and nonmembers alike, what the Village was and what it meant to be bohemian in the 1950s.

Fancher and Wolf met as students at the New School for Social Research in the Village in the 1950s, and from the start their paper staunchly identified with the community of which they were a part. It detailed everything about Village inhabitants, what they looked like, what they wore, what they ate, what they liked and disliked. The paper was a daily compendium of Villagers' political leanings, their sexual proclivities, their habitats, and their moods, even as it disputed whether there was such a thing as a Villager and engaged in a routine debate about the life and death of Greenwich Village. As Dan Wolf put it,

> our idea for a paper was a ruggedly individualistic journal unhampered
> by surveys and statistics, a paper where people could speak to people in
> a community that is one of the most vital and knowledgeable in the
> world.[3]

Fancher and Wolf brought Norman Mailer into their operation to write a column about the literary establishment, of which he was a reluctant, sometime member. He had by that point published the very successful *The Naked and the Dead* and the not-so-successful *Deer*

Park. His columns grew increasingly into rants, provoking letters from readers who saw him as both part of the problem and part of the solution. He had a troubled relationship editorially and financially with his partners that would lead him to quit the paper, rejoin it, and quit again. Typical of his aggressive, audience-unfriendly approach, was his first column:

> Greenwich Village is one of the bitter provinces—it abounds in snobs and critics. That many of you are frustrated in your ambitions, and under-nourished in your pleasures, only makes you more venomous. Quite rightly. If I found myself in your position, I would not be charitable either. Nevertheless, given your general animus to those more talented than yourselves, the only way I see myself becoming one of the cherished traditions of the Village is to be actively disliked each week.[4]

Fancher performed the role of publisher and secretary-treasurer, and Wolf was president and editor. The rest of the masthead at the "weekly newspaper designed to be read" included Jerry Tallmer as associate editor and Dan Balaban as assistant editor. Published at 22 Greenwich Avenue, the paper cost subscribers three dollars a year. Though Fancher and Wolf were not newspaper veterans by any means, they shared an enthusiasm for the Village that rivaled any small-town editor's boosterism.

The early years of the paper had to contend with the growing conservatism of 1950s America, and closer to home, the powerful Mafia operations in the Village. But regardless of the external forces affecting the rest of America, inside the Village the readers cohered around a growing sense of shared community. The Village *was* a village, and members knew who they were. As one reader wrote: "At last I have found—and unhappily will not find again—excitement, frivolity, and seriousness in a small town newspaper."[5] The readers may have thought of their paper as a small-town service, but it grew rapidly in scope, with contributions by some of the leading artists and writers of the day. Ezra Pound, e. e. cummings, and Allen Ginsberg wrote poetry. Underground filmmakers did film reviews; fiction writers and playwrights wrote and critiqued their craft. The writers who were drawn to the *Voice*, at first unpaid in exchange for total freedom of content, developed their own new style of journalism, personalizing and politicizing the events of the day, and always writing with humor. Jules Feiffer's cartoon, "Sick, Sick, *Sick*..." mocked the self-righteous sincerity of conformists and nonconformists equally. Internally, the *Voice* had many voices, with critics often contradicting each other in their reviews, and editorials often clashing with reported pieces. It was a lively reflection of the cacophony outside, as Dan Wolf acknowledged in an early editorial:

> Our policy—designedly elastic, indeed often contradictory (at least to the superficial eye)—is to give voice to all the many divergent factors, pressure groups, attitudes, and conflicting personalities of the Village.[6]

It was not only in the letters section that Villagers came together as a community, but also in the classified ads section, which quickly became famous for its nontraditional appeals for services, items for sale, and mates. Here and in the rest of the *Voice*'s pages, a new dialect was being formed, a dictionary of hipster language used in the bohemian environment as another way of letting insiders know who was in and who was out. A civil war between Hipsters and Squares was being waged, downtown versus uptown, artists versus ad men, hippies versus suits. Friends found friends around the country and around the world by speaking the same language and creating an underground network of like-minded allies. The "Village Bulletin Board" charged $1.50 a line and advertised arts societies, body toning, home sketch classes, drama workshops, all manner of auditions, underground films, and companion seekers.

The *Voice* campaigned on behalf of the people against illegal evictions of tenants and against the brutal conditions at the Women's House of Detention. When teenagers descended upon the area to drop out and live outside the confines of conformist society, they turned to the *Voice* as their guide. Its pages chronicled the local music scene, explained how to find an apartment, and detailed where to find girls. When heroin began to take the lives of these teenagers, Ed Fancher, along with the minister of the Judson Memorial Church, Howard Moody, started the Village Aid and Service Center on West Fourth Street to provide help for youths with drug problems. Fancher, in addition to being the publisher of the *Village Voice*, also ran his own private psychotherapy practice and was chair of the New York Neighborhoods Council on Narcotic Addiction.[7]

This was only one of the causes that the *Voice* would champion, helping to build the institutions that would define Village life and campaigning against the demolition of landmarks integral to the area, such as the Jefferson Market Courthouse (saved) and Pennsylvania Station (lost). In a retrospective of 1956, the *Voice* recounted all that had been lost in the previous year, including the Wannamaker building, Rhinelander Gardens, and the old Studio Building. At the same time, the paper looked cautiously on as the three academic institutions in the area, New York University, the New School, and Cooper Union, all announced plans for expansion.[8]

As interest in the area grew, old inhabitants grew nervous about what might be lost to the influx of monied newcomers. Things were becoming more expensive and, according to the *Voice*, decidedly less bohemian:

> On every side the Bohemian found himself in 1956 beleaguered in his traditional haunts. The indispensable $20 a month cold-water flats are being fitted out with radiators and inside toilets, by order of the city. Rents are rising accordingly. The beards in the White Horse and Julius's hide the chins of account executives as often as those of artists.[9]

These changes were taking place at the *Voice* as well as it gained readership and began to attract the notice of advertisers. But the paper's more financially stable position was not universally regarded as positive by its readers. As one wrote in 1957,

> to everyone's surprise it succeeded beautifully, and the lack of dollars was ameliorated. Even the public-utility companies gave it ads. But to practically nobody's surprise, other things happened too. VV became (always excepting Feiffer) dull, timid, lifeless, meaningless. One after another her columnists who really had something to say and said it strongly disappeared: Mailer, Tucci, Flower. One after another her ideas dried up and blew away. Bit by bit her progressive, openminded, realistic tone sank to a whisper.[10]

The paper's successes also helped it to mount larger, more indelible campaigns. In 1954, the City Planning Commission had declared a thirty-block area of the Village a slum, making it eligible for clearance by the city. The *Voice* helped to publicize the actions of the Greenwich Village Association's Housing Committee to prove that the area did not qualify as "blighted" because it was not overcrowded, delinquent in real estate taxes, or suffering from building violations.[11] The slum clearance was part of a federal program to raze small, often poor and African American communities and replace them with large-scale apartment buildings built by private investment construction, as well as arenas, concert halls, and performance spaces that catered to middle-class, white audiences.[12] By the early 1960s, the *Voice* was reporting a "furor over the city's proposal to rehabilitate 14 blocks of the West Village," and in March of 1961, the news was that

> six busloads of tenants and well-wishers arrived at City Hall in the rain. Wearing 'Save the West Village' emblems, the crowd filled into the Board of Estimate chamber and took up almost every seat.[13]

It was reported later that year that "Mayor Wagner and the Housing and Redevelopment Board, headed by J. Clarence Davies, responded to pressure from the West Villagers and dumped the City Planning Commission's project for the West Village"—sparing many of the Village's quintessential streets but not before many blocks were torn down to make room for high-rises.[14]

Perhaps most importantly, the *Voice* helped to prevent the city's master planner, Robert Moses, from putting a highway through the middle of Washington Square Park, long considered to be the "heart" of the Village. In a years-long battle with the city, in which everything from

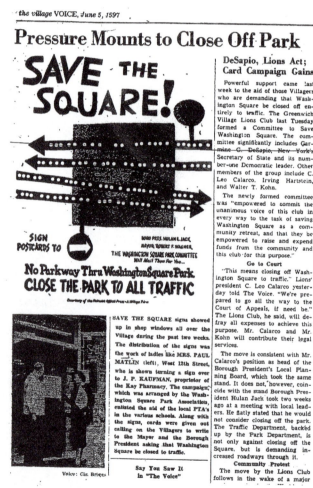

"Save the Square" ad campaign. Courtesy of the *Village Voice*.

a sunken roadway to an elevated expressway to a four-lane highway through the park was proposed, Villagers grew increasingly vociferous and well organized around the roadway plan, arguing that it would ruin the village-like tranquility of the area and cleave the park in two. Warning of a post-highway future of the Village, Dan Wolf editorialized,

> of course, Greenwich Village will remain; maps and guide books will note it and nostalgia will breathe into it a spurious vitality. But all the same it will cease to be a reality...Washington Square Park is a symbol of unity in diversity. Within a block of the arch are luxury apartments, cold-water flats, nineteenth century mansions, a university, and a nest of small businesses. It brings together Villagers of enormously varied interests and backgrounds.[15]

The *Voice* reported on community and council meetings in each week's issue, often with front-page stories and dozens of editorials. Led by Shirley Hayes, chair of the Washington Square Park Committee, the growing momentum against changes to the park was perhaps the paper's longest-running and most emphatic crusade. Unwilling to take the park plans as inevitable, residents organized into many different groups to oppose them.[16] Reprints of "Save the Square" protest postcards appeared in the pages of the *Voice*, and photos of people hanging posters in shop windows showed the popularity of the campaign.[17] Ed Fancher spoke regularly at council meetings against politicians and planners.[18] In an editorial titled "The Rape of the Square," the *Voice* urged readers,

> if Villagers don't want to see that ditch go through, they'd better express their feelings NOW, in no uncertain terms, to Hulan Jack, to Carmine De Sapio, and to other political leaders in and out of this community.[19]

The paper advertised local panel discussions at the Cooper Union school with themes such as "Greenwich Village Takes Stock of Itself," "Greenwich Village and the Traffic Problem," "Making Greenwich Village a Better Place to Live," and "Greenwich Village as a Cultural Community."[20] In a powerful guest editorial, the comments of speaker Jane Jacobs, urbanist, Village resident and organizer, were reprinted:

> Here is the Village—an area of the city with power to attract and hold a real cross-section of the population, including a lot of middle-income families. An area with a demonstrated potential for extending and upgrading its fringes. An area that pays more in taxes than it gets back in services. An area that grows theaters all by itself, without arguments between Mr. Moses and Mr. Albert Cole. All this without the benefit of bulldozers, write downs on land cost, or tax exemptions.[21]

In October 1958, the paper reported a "major victory" after the city announced a trial closing of the park to traffic.[22] After sixty days, "Traffic Commissioner T. T. Wiley, an advocate of a four-lane roadway through the Square, has admitted that the closing has caused no congestion."[23] The temporary closing became permanent, and the *Village Voice* proved that it could rally its readers and prevail, even when fighting City Hall.

Village Voice map of local services. Courtesy of the *Village Voice*.

As Jane Jacobs argued in her public talks, it wasn't only the ability to protest that defined the Village; live theater was also becoming central to its identity. The *Voice* was a strong supporter of the local theater scene and backed what became known as off-Broadway theater, distinguishing the downtown scene from the one uptown. Maps of the area were printed in the *Voice*'s pages, showing where all the new theaters were springing up, and listings for showings, readings, and casting calls surrounded serious-minded reviews. Jerry Tallmer even started an awards ceremony to honor off-Broadway performances, initially called the *Village Voice* Theater Awards, and soon given their permanent name, the Obies. In the ceremony's first year, 1956, awards went to Jason Robards for his role in *The Iceman Cometh*, and *Uncle Vanya* was voted best play.[24] The paper continued to herald the work of the not-yet famous, including Robards, Steve McQueen, Al Pacino, and the *Voice*'s young office janitor, James Earl Jones.

Besides theater, live music was the *Voice*'s next most important subject, and its listings and reviews made it an indispensable aid to life in the Village. As with theater, performance spaces were as important to the paper's politics as the performances themselves. The *Voice* rallied against the parks commissioner, who tried to ban folk music concerts in Washington Square Park, writing,

> it is not that Mr. Morris is a stickler for purity, it is just that his nature demands that our parks be raped only under the highest auspices, like those of the Fifth Avenue Coach Company and Huntington Hartford. What he objects to is not folk-singers: he and friends really cannot stand the fact that those itinerant musicians are not eminently and richly sponsored. . . . There is nothing so painful to the Institutionalized Man as unsubsidized spontaneity.[25]

Such campaigns were crucial to the community-building efforts of the *Village Voice*, and readership increased along with the feverish pitch of each new issue. Readers were also coming from further and further outside the Village, with approximately one out of every five readers living beyond its boundaries. Subscribers were found in the outer boroughs and even in other states. Such reach helped the paper to sell advertising space to businesses located outside the Village, and its sales efforts moved further uptown to find owners of record, book, and clothing stores who could be persuaded to take out space. The advertising strategy of the *Voice*, such as it was, was to spread the base of advertisers widely so that no one business could have influence over the content of the paper. Consequently, ads were small but numerous, and they came from businesses that were not inclined to advertise in more mainstream papers, whose rates were prohibitive.

The *Voice* sold well on newsstands, saving the paper money on mailing charges. Its distribution method was often improvised, but demand for the paper eventually led newsstands to take the paper less begrudgingly than before. The cover price of the paper was raised from five to ten cents in 1957, though many copies were left free at cafés and theaters, presaging its future cover price. By 1960 the circulation was over sixteen thousand. The biggest boost to the *Village Voice*'s circulation came not from any sales technique, but from the *Voice*'s competitors uptown. In New York's longest newspaper strike, from December 1962 to March 1963, the New York Typographical Union closed down all area presses except the *Voice*'s, which was located in New Jersey. With nothing else to read, New Yorkers clamored for the downtown tabloid. Its pages increased from twenty to thirty-two, and its weekly circulation rose to forty thousand. When the *World Journal Tribune*, a merged paper made from New York's *World*, *Sun*, *Journal*, *Herald*, and *Tribune*, finally closed in 1967, the *Voice* was left standing among the victors of a decade-long and merciless newspaper war. With only the *New York Times*, the *Daily News*, and the afternoon *New York Post* left, the *Voice* was able to carve out a growing niche of readers, who often took the *Voice* alongside more mainstream papers like the *Times*. Mocking this fact, it taunted its local competition in ads that read "Keep Ahead of the Times."[26]

On newsstands in New York, the *Voice* was outselling the *Atlantic*, *Esquire*, *Harper's*, *Newsweek*, *New York*, the *New Yorker*, and *Saturday Review*.[27] By 1967, the paper began to claim that it was the best-selling weekly in the United States, with a circulation of ninety thousand copies a week.[28] The cover price rose to fifteen cents, and the yearly subscription to four dollars. With a quarter of its readers coming from outside New York and twelve hundred subscribers outside of the United States, some feared that the *Voice* was becoming too popular for its own good.[29]

The popularity of the paper was matched by its growing size. The *Voice* was becoming the best advertising medium in the city for entertainment listings and apartments for rent. The most widely read feature in the paper was Jules Feiffer's cartoon strip, which was syndicated in one hundred papers across the country.[30] The big news stories of the 1960s provided the raison d'être for the *Village Voice*, and it struggled to cover them with writers on every front: From Freedom Summer 1964 to Black Power Summer of 1966 to the Summer of Love in 1967, from the assassinations of John F. Kennedy, Martin Luther King Jr., and Robert F. Kennedy to race riots, antiwar protests, and the Democratic National Convention in Chicago, from sit-ins, be-ins, and love-ins to Woodstock, Altamont, and Stonewall, and from Che Guevara's funeral to Jack Kerouac's. As political reporter Jack Newfield summed up the news agenda, "We don't support the Establishment on any issue."[31]

In 1969, with circulation at 138,000, Wolf and Fancher sold 80 percent of the *Village Voice* to Carter Burden, a city councillor, splitting $3 million from the sale but maintaining editorial control.[32] By the spring of 1970 they had moved the operation to larger quarters at University Place and Eleventh Street and raised the price to twenty cents, and four years later the paper would balloon to 132 pages.[33] Circulation peaked in the 1970s at 150,000.[34] Under the new owners, Burden and Bartle Bull, the ad ratio would also go as high as 75 percent in some issues, causing the news hole to shrink and stories to jump as many as a dozen times throughout the paper.[35]

The success of the *Village Voice* as an advertising medium was obvious, and so was the success of the Village itself as a direct result of the paper. Despite increasing numbers of high-rises and a rising crime rate, the *Voice* had romanticized the Village to such an extent that many of its writers had priced themselves out of the neighborhood. As much as they wrote about urban renewal projects and fought against the lifting of rent controls, the neighborhood was getting more expensive, and many of the *Voice* staff had to move further away. The owners and editors, on the other hand, were becoming wealthier and choosing to live in more upscale doorman buildings uptown. In both cases, the charge that the writers at the *Voice* were becoming removed from their cause was not without some merit.

The Other Village Newspaper:
The *East Village Other*

That the *Village Voice* had become too straight and mainstream and that it had sold out were among the claims made a few blocks east, where a new publication was seeking to push the envelope of underground newspapers. Begun in October 1965 by Walter H. Bowart, the *East Village Other* soon brought writer John Wilcock, concurrently and then formerly of the *Voice*, to join. Serving as managing editor was a poet named Allan Katzman. All three were under thirty when they started this enterprise.

The *Other*, named for Carl Jung's definition of the other as that which is outside normal, also referred to the "other Village," the one to the east of Greenwich Village that, as an upstart community, could claim the *Village Voice* as the Establishment. To Wilcock, who did not leave the *Voice* amicably, his old paper had "become a community newspaper for Greenwich Village, while the *Other* serves an international community of the underground."[36] The rivalry was certainly felt more strongly at the *Other* than at the *Voice*, but in one revealing editorial the *Other* accused the *Voice* of glamorizing the East Village as a strategy to rid themselves of some of its own tourist burden:

> The cross town paper doesn't really know what's happening in the East Village and in their ignorance could be sending ladies from Long Island, in search of a cheap thrill from bohemian contact, to their death.
>
> Summer in the ghetto is always violent and the summer in the east side is no exception. Within the past few weeks in a four block area, there has come to our attention four muggings.... These happen every day and our "East Village" is not ready to receive visitors unless it somehow handles these problems....
>
> Certain East Village merchants are happy to see the influx of tourists. And one cannot complain about a natural urge for increased business. But the cross town paper, it appears, would save their precious Macdougal Street by sending tourists to Viet Nam.[37]

The *East Village Other* was one of the decisive architects of the East Village, drawing its boundaries, constructing and explaining its contents, and even popularizing the name "East Village." The *EVO* was the proud guardian of the area bounded by Houston, Third Avenue, Fourteenth Street, and the East River in Manhattan, an area overlooked, ignored, and largely unknown to mainstream New York society in the postwar period:

> There is no doubt in the minds of the editorial staff that it is a slum occupied by divergent groups: Puerto Rican, Negro, Ukrainian, Russian, Polish, Hassidim, Beatnik, Artist, Creep, Bar Fly, Bum and Policeman. Each of these groups is here with different reasons: Some can't help it; some won't help it; some don't help it; some are passing through; some take it seriously; and some find it sacred burial ground where they shed the last vestige of their worth.[38]

Like the *Voice*, the *Other* worked on behalf of neighborhood groups and associations to slow the gentrification process and quell the rezoning ambitions of city planners, though with somewhat more provocative rhetoric than the *Voice*. When a Cooper Square redevelopment project was announced, a story called "No, I Will Not Go" outlined the problem:

> These proposed new dwellings are not being designed for the people who will be displaced by the demolition of the existing buildings. Rather, the Planning Commission cites in its release 'increased demand from people who can afford City rents and wish to live near their work.' That is, they figure the middleclass suburbanites are getting sick of

EVO map showing the territory of the East Village. Courtesy of the *East Village Other*.

commuting and want to move back into the City, and are now making enough money to live here if the appropriate dwellings can be constructed for them. The rezoning will spur such construction. Which would turn Cooper Square into a lilywhite ghetto of nine-to-fivers. No more artists. No more hippies. No more young single people looking for mates. No more beautiful fat old Ukrainian ladies mumbling down the sidewalk like R. Crumb cartoons. No more Puerto Ricans playing backgammon on the sidewalks listening to portable radios playing Spanish music. No more Hassids.[39]

In a typical entreaty to action, the writer pushes further: "The idea is to demonstrate to the City, once and for all, that there is a community on the Lower East Side—a community that some of us feel humbly is the most beautiful in the City, if not the country—a community that will not be told, 'Move out. Now.' In the weeks to come this paper will consider the Cooper Square Redevelopment Committee in detail, starting with the outline of the Committee's Alternative Plan for Cooper Square Redevelopment, devised with the assistance of Licensed City Planner Walter Thabit." Readers were invited to "get in touch with the committee at their storefront headquarters at Fourth Street and Second Avenue."[40]

While the *Other*'s readers sought revolution and the demolition of most traditions and conventions, they were also historic preservationists seeking to keep the neighborhood fabric intact. The only aspect of the status quo that they wished to maintain was the existing built environment of small-scale walk-up apartment buildings and other local amenities. As the paper noted, "one of the few aspects of the past which most New Bohemians hold sacred is the old and sentimental architecture that so statically surrounds them."[41]

In addition to being a provocative and activist community newspaper, the *Other* was also a graphic exercise in psychedelia. Its bold and swirly graphics were its signature, its haphazard layout evidence of its nonconformist approach. It was to be the first "electric" newspaper, mimicking the contrast and motion of television. The format was fluid and always experimental, changing weekly and undermining traditional layout rules. Headlines and stories were run sideways, in circles, and off the page. Its letters section was titled "lettersafreakfilledforum." It delighted in the use of four-letter words, forcing the *Voice* to become more blue in its language as well, some say. The *Washington Post* called it a rag "that has to be seen to be believed."[42] Part of the visual impact of the paper came from two of its cartoonists, Art Spiegelman and R. Crumb, who would both go on to gain fame for their work and help to start the underground interest in comics.

The psychedelic layout was the graphic manifestation of the central political issue of the *Other*, which was the legalization of drugs. "Since *EVO*'s editorial policy has it that every head should know how he got that way, we mean to detail the latest information available to us on the New Psychedelics."[43] News frequently reported who had been arrested and on what charges. In a feature called the "East Side Survival Bulletin," there appeared short daily items such as "SUNDAY: three arrests—one cat for standing on the corner, paroled in night court, and two others for possession after they were stopped and illegally searched."[44] A typical classified ad read, "Grass, hash and acid dealers take notice: Al Woodard is a finger man. Blond, 5 feet, 7 inches, boasts of contacts, drinks, street cat. I'm serious. A Service Announcement."[45]

Timothy Leary's column, "Turn On, Tune In and Drop Out," was originally published in the *Other*, and helped to propagate his philosophy of "better living through chemistry." Members of the *Other* staff testified in the Senate hearings on juvenile delinquency, advocating that senators try LSD before legislating on it.[46] Ads with bubble letters advertised the wares of local head shops and strobe light providers, and gardening features described the best light, shade, and soil conditions for growing marijuana.[47] The paper also featured a regular cartoon called "Captain High," in which a pot-smoking, omniscient superhero, seen only from the legs down, flew around to warn people of impending police raids.

The drug agenda of the paper was partly based on a study of its subscribers that revealed that 71 percent had attended college, 13 percent had gone to graduate school, 98 percent had tried marijuana, and 77 percent had tried LSD. According to the editors, the paper represented "an artistic group which is interested in the youth of the world and the youth revolution. We are suprapolitical and basically moral because we are reacting to an America whose ethics no longer rest on responsibility but on the loophole."[48]

The *East Village Other* was printed at a shop at Tenth Street and Avenue A, and by 1966 the biweekly paper had a circulation of ten thousand. By 1967 circulation had reached fifty thousand copies,[49] and two years later it had gone to a weekly press run. A one-year subscription in 1969 cost six dollars. At that point it was a solid enough operation to employ a ten-person staff, with each person earning between fifty and eighty dollars each a week. It looked as though the paper might at some point rival the *Village Voice* for influence in its community.[50] Disputes over management, politics, and artistic vision led the *East Village Other* to fold in 1971, but its rate of growth by that point had made it a significant player on the alternative field. In four years its circulation had grown from five thousand to sixty-five thousand. It had taken the established *Village Voice* fourteen years to achieve that measure of growth.[51]

The *Chicago Seed*

From New York, the fervor for underground news and alternative newspapers spread west to Chicago and to California, making notable stops in East Lansing, Michigan, at the *Paper* and in Milwaukee at the *Kaleidoscope*. One of the significant second-generation underground papers in Chicago was the *Seed*, which started in April 1967 and lasted for about seven years. The *Chicago Seed* was founded by Don Lewis, a local artist, and Earl Segal, who owned a poster and button store.[52] The

Seed community developed around the "hip strip" of Wells Street in the Old Town district, formerly a neighborhood of German immigrants called North Town. In the 1960s the area became the midwestern center of the "Bohemian Renaissance." With its coffee houses, folk and jazz music clubs, head shops, and clothing stores, Wells became known as "the poor man's Carnaby Street."[53] Teenagers came to see performances at the Plugged Nickel, the Midas Touch, the Earl of Old Town, and Moody's Pub, where Joan Baez once came in to play an unannounced performance.[54] Unofficial performance spaces sprang up everywhere, like the Steppenwolf Theater, which started in a church basement. Like the *Voice* in New York, the *Seed* was the source for finding out about these happenings, and the paper also worked to secure permits from the city for performances, demonstrations, and concerts so that the movement it supported could exist in a more official capacity.[55]

The offices of the *Seed* on North LaSalle Street also served as the Chicago headquarters of the Youth International Party ("Yippie") movement, and Editor Abe Peck took to signing his editorial columns Abraham Yippie. The paper was concerned with the formation and maintenance of this movement and its existence as a subculture of Chicago and across the country. Its coverage was comprised mostly of movement plans, debates, and demonstrations. Like its associate papers in New York, the *Seed* had psychedelic graphics, provocative and agitational writing, and comics by R. Crumb. The *Seed* was known for its participant journalism; its writers and editors were reporting on the community and demonstrations that they themselves were a part of. Writing for the *Seed* was understood as part of the larger organizing effort, and *Seed* readers, known as Seedlings, were likely to participate in all manner of militant actions. The offices of the *Seed* were open to groups who needed the use of darkroom facilities or the photostat machine for printing flyers for their causes,[56] and the editorial collective was a loosely structured and nonhierarchical formation of friends and fellow travelers.

The focus of the paper was youth rebellion and revolution, and in this way it was used, like other local alternative papers, as a guidebook for how to get along outside the mainstream. It was instructional, as in the 1969 article called "How to Commit Revolution," and it was practical in its regular column called "Making It," which explained how to survive in Chicago. As Abbie Hoffman, leader of the Yippie movement, noted in *Steal This Book*, the *Seed* provided "the best advice on crashing and the local heat scene."[57]

The *Seed* distinguished itself through its coverage of the Democratic National Convention in 1968, which it anticipated for several issues leading up to the event in August. Organizers planned to get people out to protest the convention and the war in Vietnam under the guise of putting on a music festival, but Abe Peck, by then editor of the *Seed*, warned against the ruse:

> The word is out. Many people are into confrontation. The Man is into confrontation. . . . Chicago may host the Festival of Blood. . . . But people are still into the Festival flash. . . . The only way to end the sham is to withdraw our permit request. . . . New York Yippies have told us to expect a lot of static for this decision. That's cool. We refuse to pose as front-men for an alternative that no longer exists. . . . Don't come to Chicago if you expect a five-day Festival of Life, music and love.[58]

Though there was a Festival of Life music concert with local bands playing in Lincoln Park, the Yippies' intention was to counter what it was calling the Convention of Death. In preparation for the convention, the paper printed several predemonstration articles and an information piece titled, "What to Do in Case of Arrest." Where the mainstream papers printed the official political agenda, the *Seed* printed the demonstrators' agenda.[59]

The atmosphere in Chicago was heated even before the conventioneers and out-of-state protesters arrived. In April, the assassination of Martin Luther King Jr. had incited riots on Chicago's west side that killed nine people and burned out twenty blocks of a neighborhood. June saw Senator Robert F. Kennedy's assassination by Sirhan Sirhan at the Ambassador Hotel in Los Angeles, and a week before the convention was to start, the Soviets invaded Prague, crushing the reform experiment known as "Prague Spring." Locally, a seventeen-year-old Sioux named Dean Johnson was shot by police on Wells Street the day before the convention opened. By the time the politicians arrived, the city's youth and young people from across the country were on hand to disrupt the order of things.

At the same time, those in charge of official law and order were becoming more frequent targets of attack in the *Seed*. The front cover of a 1968 issue had an illustration of a Chicago policeman as a pig, with the words, "The policeman is not there to create disorder, the policeman is there to preserve disorder" coming out of Mayor Daley's mouth.[60] On the front cover of the *Seed*'s issue covering the convention, an illustrated parody of a *Chicago Tribune* extra was headlined "PIG WINS," with a story that began "Mr. S.P. Pig has been elected President."[61] The convention opened on August 26, and leading up to it crowds of Yippies had gathered to camp out in Lincoln Park, which they were legally permitted to do until the opening day of the convention. From the park, crowds marched toward the convention hotel, and once there found bodies crushed together and police shoving demonstrators and reporters through the plate glass windows of the Conrad Hilton Hotel. A bullet had also found its way through the front window of the *Seed* office.[62] Following what later came to be known as a "police riot," several arrests were made for "incitement of violence," a newly punishable crime according to the 1968 Civil Rights Act. The trial for inciting violence included Yippies Abbie Hoffman and Jerry Rubin and Black Panther leader Bobby Seale. The rallies outside the courthouse turned into riots themselves, and more days of rage ensued. Clubs and restaurants along Wells Street were closed following the riots as police pursued the hippies.[63] The *Seed*'s participant news coverage was told through the riots and police brutality that were glossed over in the mainstream, aboveground press, which came to be referred to as "Pig Media" in the *Seed*.[64] Following the tumult of 1968, the *Seed* kept close watch on police relations, paying particular attention to instances of race prejudice on the force. A 1969 issue featured a strip of "Racist Pig Comics" by Skip Williams.[65]

By 1969 the paper had reached a circulation of twenty-three thousand, and when it merged with *Chicago Kaleidoscope*, circulation topped forty thousand. The last cover of 1969 mourned Malcolm X, Che Guevara, Lenny Bruce, Ho Chi Minh, Martin Luther King Jr., and John Coltrane in a collage.[66] Editor Abe Peck left in 1970 after not being able to overcome censorship and what he saw as the growing dominance of the right. In the spring of 1971, six of the remaining staff members left, exhausted from the endless obstacles to the success of the movement, including harassment by the federal government. The last issue that carried a cover price was published in December 1973. The *Seed* lasted as a free newspaper for at least two more issues, but died after a defeated staff could no longer fight.

It was during this time that a number of alternative papers became less radical in their approach and began to prioritize entertainment over ideology. Some of this shift in focus was brought about by external pressures such as the Federal Bureau of Investigation's close watch on the daily activities of these small papers. In some cases, the FBI was able to discourage large advertisers such as Columbia Records from supporting the papers, which were unable to survive without this revenue.[67] The *Seed* was eventually overtaken by the *Chicago Reader*, which was modeled on Boston's *After Dark*, targeting students and young professionals and downplaying radical politics. After 1973, the underground press, "like the movements it covered, had both succeeded and withered."[68]

The Underground Press Syndicate

In an attempt to deal with the issues facing the alternative press, including government harassment, censorship, and copyright difficulties, in 1966 five alternative papers banded together to create the Underground Press Syndicate (UPS). The problems of the underground press were legion, according to Peck: "We had no press cards. Our sellers got arrested. Our office was shot up on two occasions."[69] The syndicate operated as an exchange for news and features, and all members were free to use one another's material, which was sent through the UPS newsletter, the *Free Ranger Intertribal News Service*.[70] The original members were the *East Village Other*, the *San Francisco Oracle*, the *Los Angeles Free Press*, the *Berkeley Barb*, and the *Paper* of East Lansing, Michigan, but the organization grew to include over one hundred publications shortly after it was established. Others included the *Chicago Seed*, the *New York Rat*, the *Detroit Fifth Estate*, Philadelphia's *Distant Drummer*, Boston's *Avatar*, Cambridge's *Old Mole,* the *Great Speckled Bird* in Atlanta, the *Bay Area Ramparts*, *Resist* in Palo Alto, and the *Pittsburgh Peace and Freedom News*.

When different political allegiances began to create a rift at the UPS, the new Liberation News Service (LNS) was created in 1967. LNS provided prepackaged news and graphics to its subscribers without fear of copyright infringement, so popular graphics would be reprinted across hundreds of issues.[71] Together, UPS and LNS provided broader coverage to local and small-town newspapers without their own news-gathering resources. LNS had approximately six hundred subscribers, and its goal, like that of most alternative newspapers, was to provide a different view of events than did the mainstream media:

> Liberation News Service provides a totally different alternate medium for those of us who are fed up with hearing there were 'some 25,000 to 40,000 demonstrators' when we ourselves saw at least twice that many; hearing them say the 'police acted with appropriate restraint' when we saw the guy next to us getting his skull busted just because he had long hair; hearing that we . . . are 'sincerely working for peace' and that we are 'supporting and defending democratic government in Vietnam,' when we see our government destroying a countryside, waging an undeclared war of attrition on helpless women, children, and farmers in the name of one totalitarian puppet regime after another, with no sane end in sight.[72]

By 1969 five hundred underground papers had a combined circulation of 4.5 million copies; by 1971 they claimed a circulation of between ten and twenty million.[73] As the member papers themselves began to become less radical in order to stay in business, attracting new "hip consumers," the Underground Press Syndicate also decided that a change was necessary. Seeking greater legitimacy and credibility, it decided to change its name to the "Alternative Press Syndicate" in 1973.

These sharing agreements helped small papers stay afloat against powerful resistance from mainstream papers, since more and more the

alternative press was forced to behave economically and organiza-
tionally like the mainstream. As in the mainstream press, the struggle
for advertisers was constant as the alternative papers tried to strike a
balance between providing a forum for businesses that could not or
would not advertise elsewhere, like tattoo and massage parlors and
adult classifieds, and trying not to alienate more lucrative legitimate
businesses. And as with the mainstream press, many small papers were
closed in the 1970s and 1980s, while others were sold into chains.

To improve circulation, several of these papers, including the *Village Voice*, eliminated their cover price and began to claim much
higher readership numbers as readers-per-copy increased. The free papers became some of the best vehicles for classified ads, particularly
for apartment listings and entertainment, proving stiff competition
to more mainstream papers whose rates were higher. In retaliation,
in some municipalities mainstream papers with paid circulation lob-
bied to have free papers made illegal by supporting antilittering and
antihandbill ordinances. Though the Supreme Court declared in 1939
that such ordinances were unconstitutional, they have continued to
emerge wherever newspapers exercise significant control over local
town councils.[74]

Community Newspapers Redefined: CNHI

Beginning in the late 1970s and early 1980s, as many mainstream
newspapers began to merge or fold and many local alternative papers
went out of business, interest in weekly community newspapers in-
tensified, and they, improbably, have become the most lucrative
newspaper properties in the country. Community weeklies are typically located outside major urban areas in monopoly markets and
operate with skeleton staffs on high advertising-to-editorial ratios. As
a result, their profit margins are large, and they have attracted the
notice of investors outside the realm of the newspaper industry. Because of their large profits, with some as high as 50 percent margins,
these properties have become much sought after. The increased demand has raised the sale price of the papers, and it has also increased
the rate at which they changed hands. Changes in the capital gains
tax laws in the 1980s also made selling the family newspaper business
more enticing, since sellers got to keep more of their asking price.

There were approximately 856 newspapers sold in the 1990s, twice as
many as in the previous decade.[75] This represents about 40 percent of
the country's small newspapers, and many of them were sold more
than once.[76] The overwhelming majority of sales, 85 percent, were newspaper chains selling to other newspaper chains.[77] Most of these sales

were made in order to further consolidate geographical concentrations, or clusters, so that several newspapers in one area have one owner and thus can share advertisers, editorial content and a printing press:

> Stimulated by new opportunities for cutting costs and building revenues, and encouraged by tax laws and changing trends in retail advertising, such established companies as Thomson, Knight Ridder, Cox, Media General, Hollinger, Gannett, Donrey and MediaNews are swapping properties like baseball cards, unloading papers that don't fit their geographic strategies and acquiring ones that do.[78]

The frequent turnover in owners has left many such papers unsure of who their owners are at any given time, but when new owners take over the routine is often the same: they raise rates, cut the newsroom budget, cut personnel, merge editions with neighboring papers, and cluster printing at a common centralized plant.[79] Such community weeklies are typically small operations whose labor force is not organized, and salaries are kept low, often not much above minimum wage. Employees often do not share in benefits given to workers at companies of comparable size to their new parent.

Community weeklies were once indispensable sources for coverage of local events which no other news outlet would cover: town council meetings, school board decisions, youth sports, picnics, parades, family reunions, and all the assorted activities of local citizens. Coverage of surrounding areas was sent in by an army of stringers, people who wrote about their communities or neighborhoods in exchange for a nominal fee or a free subscription. The owners of such newspapers have historically been residents of the places where the newspapers were printed and had vested interests in the health of the communities where they operated. Now it is much more likely that local papers are owned by a chain headquartered in another state, which may have little knowledge or interest in the community, just as the community may have little knowledge of the chain. In many cases the name of the chain is nowhere to be found in the pages of the paper. The chains' distance from the community protects them from the backlash from local businesses when advertising and circulation rates are raised.

Today the largest newspaper chains are companies that have materialized within the last ten years. They are chains that are produced out of leveraged buy-outs, and their main stakeholders are investment banks. The companies are at times so leveraged that the pressure to realize consistent quarterly profit is constant. One of the first companies to overextend into the newspaper industry was led by Ralph

Ingersoll, who was funded by junk-bond dealer Michael Milkin and the venture capital firm Warburg Pincus. In the late 1980s, Ingersoll bought over 180 weeklies and sixty dailies in less than four years.[80] The strategy for increasing profit at each newspaper was to increase pricing, exploit the advantages of monopoly markets, rationalize the workforce, and modernize the printing operations.[81] His company, which became known as the Journal Register Company, operated papers all over the country, with many located in New England and Pennsylvania and a concentration surrounding St. Louis, with as many as thirty-eight different papers clustered around the city. With the Pulitzer-owned *St. Louis Post-Dispatch* hemmed in on all sides, the suburban chain was sold to Pulitzer for $306 million in 2000, eliminating all competition in the area. At one point, Ingersoll was the highest-paid executive in the newspaper industry.[82]

When Thomson Newspapers and Hollinger International divested themselves of most of their American newspapers in the 1990s, most of the papers that became available were purchased by two groups, Liberty Group Newspapers, which had the backing of buy-out specialist Leonard Green Partners, and Community Newspaper Holdings Incorporated (CNHI). Thomson sold ninety daily papers over the decade, and Hollinger's American Publishing sold 130. Of these, fifty-six went to Liberty, and twenty-seven went to CNHI.[83]

Presently the largest of these companies is CNHI, based in Birmingham, Alabama, and financed by the Retirement Systems of Alabama, the state pension fund. CNHI is representative of the latest shift in newspapering, in which "community" has come to be defined as any location small enough not to have competition from other media and in which local news has been reduced to local advertising. The formula and format of its papers is repeated throughout thousands of nearly identical properties, and the owners are scarcely able to name all of the company's holdings. CNHI was formed in 1997, and in its first three years it purchased 107 newspapers and sold sixteen.[84] The company's strategy is to

> seek out newspapers in smaller markets with growth potential. A premium has been placed on purchasing newspapers in geographic proximity, for operational efficiency and in order to provide additional services to readers.[85]

The *Hazard Herald*

Among the most lucrative weekly newspapers in the CNHI chain is the *Hazard Herald* in Hazard, Kentucky. With a circulation of only

Hazard, Kentucky, home of the *Hazard Herald*. Photo by Francis Miller/
Time Life Pictures/Getty Images.

4,859, the *Herald* has over forty percent profit margins. Despite CNHI's
strategy to seek out papers in markets with growth potential, the city
of Hazard is actually shrinking; its population has been diminishing
steadily since the 1960s. The average resident's income and education
are well below the national average. In 1999, President Bill Clinton, the
first sitting president ever to visit Hazard, began his antipoverty tour
there, noting that it was a community that had been untouched by the
boom times of the 1990s. Located in the Eastern Kentucky valley surrounded by the Appalachians, Hazard is an isolated, small community
of fewer than five thousand residents. Founded in 1821, Hazard is the
county seat of Perry County. The town and its county were named for
Oliver Hazard Perry, a commodore in the U.S. Navy during the War of
1812, who was famous for saying "We have met the enemy and they are
ours." In the early 1920s Hazard was a prosperous coal-mining town, but
it was hit hard by the Depression when the price of coal plummeted. It
experienced another boom in the 1950s, was hit by a general strike in
the 1960s, and bounced back slightly in the 1970s when the oil crisis
revived the price of coal. Hazard's population is now half of what it was

in the 1950s, and suffers from chronic unemployment.[86] The valley falls prey to frequent flooding from the Kentucky River, and the desperate local economy has generated spurts of crime and mayhem worse than those in any inner city. Moonshine wars, wildfires, coal miners' strikes, and rampant poverty have filled the pages of the weekly newspaper, the *Hazard Herald*, since the paper began in 1911.

In the 1930s, the paper was run by Bailey P. Wootton, a school-teacher who over the course of his career would become a banker, a power company executive, and a member of the Hazard Board of Education. He served as president of the chamber of commerce, vice president of the Rotary Club, vice president of the Appalachian Way Association, delegate to the Southern Agricultural Congress in 1913, and delegate to the Good Roads Association in 1923. He served as Kentucky's attorney general from 1932 to 1935, after which he was a Democratic candidate for governor and chairman of the Democratic state central committee. He was unequivocally a community leader and builder. Running the local newspaper was one of many of the things he did to shape the direction of Hazard.[87] He sold the paper in 1946 to Ed Scripps.

The Scripps League of Newspapers

Grandson of E. W. Scripps, who founded the first large American newspaper chain, Ed Scripps took over a small group of papers from his mother, who had been written out of E. W.'s will. Over the course of his presidency, which began in 1931, Scripps expanded the chain from eight newspapers to fifty-one. Rather than compete in large markets in second or third place, he decided to seek smaller markets where he could achieve dominance. This would have the added benefit of further differentiating the two Scripps chains, as Scripps-Howard was increasingly investing in larger markets—seen in its purchases that resulted in the merger of the *World Telegram* and *Sun* (later the *World Journal Tribune*) in New York. The Scripps League looked to markets at the other end of the spectrum, not just to growing postwar suburbs, but also to small towns that were far from big-city centers, in communities of less than a hundred thousand people.

Ed and his wife Betty Scripps began a string of acquisitions on behalf of the League in the early 1950s. *The Dalles Chronicle* in Oregon had been added to the League in 1949, emblematic of the small-market direction of the chain. The Scripps League approached each prospective acquisition cautiously. Ed and Betty Scripps traveled to each town to study its local conditions firsthand. They inspected supermarket parking lots, noting the county names on license plates to gauge the distance people had traveled, to expand the advertiser base. The Scrippses looked for towns with steady church attendance, good schools, and stable industry where the local newspaper had a monopoly.

When Ed and Betty Scripps bought a newspaper, they typically left the local editors and reporters in place. Throughout the chain, Ed Scripps streamlined management techniques, added new technology for printing and layout, and improved distribution systems. He was early among his industry peers to bring computers into the newsroom. By 1970 the Scripps League had in many ways surpassed its rival, Scripps-Howard, in company value. Among the Scripps League's holdings were several California papers, the *Argus Courier* in Petaluma, the *Daily Midway Driller* in Taft, the *Record Gazette* in Banning, the *Hanford Sentinel*, the *Napa Valley Register*, the *Novato Advance*, and the *Santa Maria Times*. In Oregon it owned *The Dalles Chronicle* in The Dalles and the *World* in Coos Bay. The rest of its holdings were scattered around the country: the *Arizona Daily Sun* in Flagstaff, Arizona; the *Daily Chronicle* in De Kalb, Illinois; the *Daily Herald* in Provo, Utah; the *Daily Journal* in Flat River, Missouri; the *Daily News* in Rhineland, Wisconsin; the *Garden Island* in Kauai, Hawaii; the *Haverhill Gazette* in Haverhill, Massachusetts; the *Newport Daily Express* in Newport, Vermont; the *Ravalli Republic* in Hamilton, Montana; and the *Hazard Herald* in Hazard, Kentucky.[88]

The Scripps League did not, however, remain a good newspaper steward to all the papers under its purview. In 1993, citing recession cutbacks, the League closed down four newspapers, including the *Santa Paula Chronicle* in California and weeklies in Rohnert Park, California; Georgetown, Kentucky; and Crestview, Florida.[89] In 1996, the remaining Scripps League newspapers were sold to the Pulitzer Company, publishers of the *St. Louis Post-Dispatch* and the *Arizona Daily Star,* for $214 million.[90] The deal gave Pulitzer Newspapers a total of twelve daily and more than sixty-five weekly newspapers, shoppers, and other targeted publications, and through Suburban Journals of Greater St. Louis, purchased from Ralph Ingersoll, another group of thirty-seven weekly papers.

A year after acquiring the Scripps League papers, Pulitzer completed a newspaper swap with the Hollinger International subsidiary American Publishing. Pulitzer received two papers in Montana, the *Daily Press Leader* in Farmington, and the *Democrat News* in Fredericktown, and American got the *Newport Daily Express* in Vermont, the *Midway Driller* in Taft, California, and the *Hazard Herald* in Kentucky.[91]

One year later, in 1998, Hollinger sold forty-five of its newspapers to CNHI for $475 million. The papers were located in fourteen states, but most were in Alabama, Kentucky, Oklahoma, and Texas. These rapid turnovers of ownership meant that in three years the *Hazard*

Herald changed hands three times, and not once had it been sold on its own. When CNHI took over, it created a merged Sunday edition called the "Sunday Edition of the *Times Herald*" with the nearby *Floyd County Times*, which it also owned, in order to add another edition for local advertisers. CNHI also merged all of its free weekly shoppers in the area. The acquisition made CNHI the single largest owner of newspapers in Kentucky and the largest newspaper owner in the United States. By consistently cutting costs and raising rates, the *Hazard Herald* continues to be one of the chain's most profitable operations, despite its location in an economically depressed area.

A 2003 deal to sell the *Hazard Herald* along with twenty-two other papers to Brown Publishing of Ohio fell through, but an April 2004 deal to sell to Heartland Publications did not. Heartland, a company created for the acquisition, was funded the way many emerging newspaper companies are, by venture capitalists and private equity firms. In this case, the investment money was provided by Wachovia Capital Partners and the Wicks Group of Companies. The purchase included a string of CNHI papers in Thomaston, Georgia; Harlan, Hazard, Leitchfield, Middlesboro, Prestonsburg, and Russellville, Kentucky; Apex, Clinton, Elizabethtown, Fuquay-Varina, Garner, and Lumberton, North Carolina; Gallipolis, Pomeroy, and Portsmouth, Ohio; Altus, Durant, and Frederick, Oklahoma; Lafayette and Tazewell, Tennessee; and Point Pleasant, West Virginia. The sale left CNHI with 87 daily newspapers, 49 nondaily newspapers, and 155 specialty publications in 20 states.[92] The sale also left the *Hazard Herald* with yet another absentee owner whose only goal is to increase an already sizable profit margin.

The example of the *Hazard Herald* is illustrative of hundreds of other small community newspapers in the United States. They are valued primarily for their locations in monopoly markets and their proximity to surrounding papers whose operations can be shared. Short-term profits are realized when new ownership makes staff cutbacks so that there are fewer people contributing to the news-making process. The result is that the news of each local community comes to resemble that of every other community, and the reduced coverage is not specific to any particular place.

As this shift has taken place in mainstream local newspapers, the remaining press left with the charge of speaking for the community, the alternative media, has seen similar consolidation. The *Village Voice*, once fiercely independent, locally owned and anticorporate, is now itself part of a chain of alternative papers. Since 1971, the *Voice* has had five different owners. From Carter Burden it was sold to Clay Felker of *New York Magazine*, who briefly merged its operations with the glossy society magazine and fired the founders Ed Wolf and Dan Fancher. These properties were sold to Rupert Murdoch, who then sold to Leonard Stern in 1985 for approximately $50 million. Stern had amassed his fortune in land speculation and pet care products, and he added other alternative papers to his holdings, including papers in Cleveland, Minneapolis–St. Paul, Seattle, and Los Angeles and Orange County, California. This group of papers was purchased from Stern in 2000 in a leveraged buy-out by a group that included the firm Weiss, Peck, and Greer and the *Voice* editor, David Schneiderman. The new company, called Village Voice Media, kept the *Voice* from being taken over by another growing alternative media company, NT Media, the chain which operates eleven *New Times* papers. This rivalry, however, appeared more friendly than not, when in 2002 NT Media closed its Cleveland paper in exchange for the *Voice* closing its Los Angeles paper, leaving each with a monopoly in those markets.[93] The deal caused many in the industry to wonder if there was any reason to believe that alternative newspapers were still an alternative to mainstream papers.

In fact, the lines between alternative and mainstream papers have become considerably blurred. With high profit margins and readers whom advertisers are eager to capture, alternatives have been prone to the same kinds of operational strategies that are found in the rest of the industry. The mainstream press has also begun to get involved in the alternative sector, notably in the case of the Times Mirror Company, whose subsidiary New Mass Media bought the *Hartford Courant* and its competing alternative, the *Hartford Advocate*, along with three other alternative weeklies.[94] Other chains, including Gannett, Tribune, Knight Ridder, and Cox have begun to invest in alternative weeklies as well. Large and small, mainstream or alternative, the consolidation in the newspaper industry that has taken place over the last twenty years has resulted in far fewer newspapers, and at those that remain, there is less substantive coverage of local politics and complex issues and increased coverage of weather and entertainment-related stories.[95] Quality journalism has been left in the hands of a shrinking number of top-tier newspapers with an increasingly national focus.

Notes

1. Donna Lloyd Ellis, "The Underground Press in America: 1955–1970," *Journal of Popular Culture* V(1971) 102–104.

2. Morris Dickstein, *Gates of Eden: American Culture in the Sixties* (New York: Basic Books, 1977), 132.

3. Kevin McAuliffe, *The Great American Newspaper: The Rise and Fall of the Village Voice* (New York: Charles Scribner's Sons, 1978), 41.

4. McAuliffe, *Great American*, 25.

5. McAuliffe, *Great American*, 38.

6. McAuliffe, *Great American*, 141.

7. *Village Voice*, 23 February 1961.

8. "Greenwich Village in 1956," *Village Voice*, 2 January 1957.

9. "Greenwich Village in 1956," *Village Voice*, 2 January 1957.

10. "Boldness," *Village Voice*, 1 May 1957.

11. "Take Slum Sign Off Village, Group Urges City Planners," *Village Voice*, 13 March 1957.

12. Mindy Fullilove, *Root Shock: How Tearing Up City Neighborhoods Hurts America, and What We Can Do About It* (New York: Ballantine, 2004).

13. "Villagers Bus to City Hall in Relays to Save Homes," *Village Voice*, 30 March 1961.

14. Mary Perot Nichols, "City Official Blasts West Village Groups," *Village Voice*, 23 November 1961.

15. McAuliffe, *Great American*, 92.

16. "Roadway Through Square Inevitable, Villagers Hear," *Village Voice*, 30 January 1957.

17. "Pressure Mounts to Close Off Park," *Village Voice*, 5 June 1957.

18. "Villagers Win Major Victory in Hearing," *Village Voice*, 24 September 1958.

19. "The Rape of the Square," *Village Voice*, 1 May 1957.

20. "Forum on Greenwich Village," *Village Voice*, 2 January 1957.

21. Jane Jacobs, "Reason, Emotion, Pressure: There is No Other Recipe," *Village Voice*, 22 May 1957.

22. Mary Perot Nichols, "Village Wins Major Victory; City Plans Trial Closing of Washington Square to Traffic," *Village Voice*, 29 October 1958.

23. "The Battle of Washington Square: 1958," *Village Voice*, 31 December 1958.

24. McAuliffe, *Great American*, 75.

25. "Keep it Safe for Buses!" *Village Voice*, 13 April 1961.

26. McAuliffe, *Great American*, 132.

27. McAuliffe, *Great American*, 134.

28. A. Kent McDougall, "Greenwich Village Paper Gains Stature and Four-Letter Words," *Wall Street Journal*, 20 November 1967.

29. Ibid., *Wall Street Journal*, 20 November 1967.

30. Ibid., *Wall Street Journal*, 20 November 1967.

31. Ibid., *Wall Street Journal*, 20 November 1967.

32. McAuliffe, *Great American*, 250.

33. McAuliffe, *Great American*, 261.

34. Michael Emery, Edwin Emery, and Nancy L. Roberts, *The Press and America: An Interpretive History of the Mass Media*. 6th Edition. (Englewood Cliffs, NJ: Prentice-Hall, Inc., 1988), 421.

35. McAuliffe, *Great American*, 347–351.

36. Peter Bart, "Bohemian Newspapers Spread Across the Country," *New York Times*, 1 August 1966.

37. "Vietnamese Crosstown," *East Village Other*, 15 July 1966.

38. Allan Katzman, "Does an East Village Exist?" *East Village Other*, 15 February 1966.

39. D. A. Latimer, "No, I Will Not Go," *East Village Other*, 14 February 1969.

40. Ibid., *East Village Other*, 14 February 1969.

41. John Green, "Action + Anxiety = Chaos: Notes on the New Bohemia," *East Village Other*, 1 August 1966.

42. John Chamberlain, "The Hippies Can't Have Thoreau," *Washington Post*, 17 July 1967.

43. "Cyanara," *East Village Other*, 15 April 1967.

44. "East Village Survival Bulletin," *East Village Other*, 28 May 1969.

45. Richard R. Lingeman, "Offerings at the Psychedelicatessen," *New York Times*, 10 July 1966.

46. Nan Robertson, "Senators Urged to Take LSD Trip," *New York Times*, 16 June 1966.

47. Soloman Prometheus, "In the Garden," *East Village Other*, 15 April 1967.

48. Robertson, "LSD Trip."

49. A. Kent McDougall, "Greenwich Village Paper Gains Stature and Four-Letter Words," *Wall Street Journal*, 20 November 1967.

50. "Business Bulletin," *Wall Street Journal*, 25 May 1967.

51. Abe Peck, *Uncovering the Sixties: The Life and Times of the Underground Press* (New York: Citadel, 1991), 183.

52. Peck, *Uncovering*, 50.

53. "Chicago Fashion Through the Years," *Chicago Sun-Times*, 1 May 2000.

54. Al Podgorski, "2 Developments Further Boost Wells Street," *Chicago Sun-Times*, 6 March 1994.

55. Peck, *Uncovering*, 109.

56. Peck, *Uncovering*, 263, 251.

57. Abbie Hoffman, *Steal This Book* (New York: Four Walls Eight Windows, 1996), 255.

58. Peck, *Uncovering*, 109.

59. Peck, *Uncovering*, 112.

60. *Seed* 2, no. 13 (1968).

61. *Seed* 3, no. 2 (1968).

62. Peck, *Uncovering*, 260.

63. Podgorski, "Wells Street."

64. Peck, *Uncovering*, 67.

65. *Seed* 4, no. 1 (1969).

66. Peck, *Uncovering*, 225.

67. Ellen Gruber Garvey, "Out of the Mainstream and Into the Streets," in *Perspectives on American Book History*, ed. Scott E. Casper, Joanne D. Chaison, and Jeffrey D. Groves (Amherst: University of Massachusetts Press, 2002), 395.

68. Peck, *Uncovering*, xv.

69. Peck, *Uncovering*, 231.

70. Beth Bailey and David Farber, *The Columbia Guide to America in the 1960s* (Columbia University Press, 2001), 252.

71. Garvey, "Out of the Mainstream," 394.

72. Peck, *Uncovering*, 75–77.

73. Peck, *Uncovering*, 183, 267.

74. Victor Jose, *The Free Paper in America: Struggle for Survival* (Richmond, IN: Graphic Press, 2000), 131.

75. *Presstime*, February 2000.

76. Mary Walton, "The Selling of Small-Town America," *American Journalism Review* 21 (May 1999): 58–73.

77. "A Decade of Deals: Dailies Changed Hands 856 Times in the '90s,"*Presstime*, February 2000, 33–34.

78. Jack Bass, "Newspaper Monopoly," *American Journalism Review*, 21 (July 1999): 64–77.

79. Loren Ghiglione, ed., *The Buying and Selling of American Newspapers*. (Indianapolis: R. J. Berg, 1984).

80. Nicholas Coleridge, *Paper Tigers: The Latest Greatest Newspaper Tycoons and How They Won the World* (London, UK: Heinemann Ltd., 1993), 106–107.

81. Coleridge, *Paper Tigers*, 108.

82. Coleridge, *Paper Tigers*, 117.

83. Mary Walton, "The Selling of Small-Town America," *American Journalism Review* 21 (May 1999): 58–73.

84. "A Decade of Deals: Dailies Changed Hands 856 Times in the '90s,"*Presstime*, February 2000, 33–34.

85. Community Newspaper Holdings, Inc., (date), <http://www.cnhi.com/ourcompany/>, (date accessed).

86. Penny M. Miller, *Kentucky Politics and Government: Do We Stand United?* (Lincoln, NE: University of Nebraska Press, 1994), 17.

87. *The Daily Messenger*, Madisonville, Kentucky, May 1935; *New York Times*, 17 April 1949.

88. Jack Casserly, *Scripps: The Divided Dynasty* (New York: Fine, 1993), 142–143.

89. "Scripps League Closes One Daily, Two Weeklies," *Editor & Publisher*, 16 January 1993.

90. "Pulitzer Acquires Scripps League," *New York Times*, 5 July 1996.

91. Tony Case, "Hefty Haul in Third Quarter," *Editor and Publisher*, 13 December 1997, 16–22.

92. Michael Clinebell, "Florida Publisher to Buy 3 North Carolina Newspapers," *Knight Ridder Tribune Business News*, 6 April 2004, 1.

93. Lucia Moses, "Alternative Approaches," *Editor & Publisher*, 2 December 2002, 14.

94. Carly Berwick, "The New Harmonics in Hartford," *Columbia Journalism Review*, July/August 1999.

95. *Media Professionals and Their Industry*, Lauer Research, Inc. Report, 20 July 2004.

7

NATIONAL NEWS AND THE NATION

The *New York Times*, the *Washington Post*,
the *Wall Street Journal*,
and *USA Today*

By the 1970s, the state of American newspapers had become a concern for all in the industry. Readership was down, the number of newspapers was declining rapidly, and one-newspaper towns were becoming the norm. It was becoming more and more difficult to capture an increasingly fragmented audience divided by geographic location, age, and political orientation. The postwar economy had made workers more mobile, and Americans moved more often and further away from their hometowns than ever before. High-rise living made urban delivery of newspapers more challenging, and longer car commutes cut into the time people had available in the morning to read. Newspaper readers claimed they wanted more in-depth coverage but shorter stories that they could read in less time. They wanted more lifestyle news, more news that was relevant to their personal lives, news about their immediate neighborhoods, and news that was concrete rather than abstract. These were the findings of a study conducted by Ruth Clark in 1979 on behalf of the Yankelovich research firm, which culminated in the report "Changing Needs of Changing Readers." The study became a guide to newspaper research, encouraging more and more papers of all sizes to undertake reader surveys in order to tailor the news more specifically to their markets.

In many ways, the new market-research approach to making news was an impossible paradox. How were papers to become more comprehensive, more relevant, and more useful in shorter stories with fewer resources? How could they cover the news, politics, sports, and all of the traditional categories of news, as well as the personal health, finance, real estate, and advice columns people seemed to want in such a small space? And how could they do this and satisfy advertisers at the same time? In addition to these challenges, mainstream papers faced a new threat from alternative weeklies, whose in-depth and provocative investigative journalism was drawing new readers just as television was providing information in formats that were brief, colorful, and personality-driven. Both threats led top-tier newspapers to become more focused and more analytical, while trying to serve an ever-elusive and finicky audience.

Until the 1980s, there was no American paper that could be considered a national paper. Not, perhaps, since Horace Greeley's *New York Tribune*, which in the nineteenth century had a subscriber base that spanned the country through the postal system. As a result of satellite transmission, the *New York Times*, the *Wall Street Journal*, and the *Washington Post* are now all distributed nationally. As television news bites got smaller, a niche was opened for extensive, lengthy coverage in these newspapers, which took the nation as their focus, even though each was located and named for its specific location. With correspondents and bureaus all over the country and with a mission to cover the federal government and the nation's politics and economics, these papers more than others set the news agenda over the twentieth century. By setting policy, establishing important legal precedents for the press, and blanketing the nation in their coverage, these papers shaped not only their immediate local environment, but also the country as a whole. It is through them that the nation itself was shaped.

The *New York Times* Becomes the Paper of Record

One of the oldest continuously published newspapers in the United States, the *New York Times* is at the top of the elite tier of newspapers. Over the twentieth century it garnered the title "the newspaper of record" by publishing the full text of speeches, announcements, treaties, and all manner of public discourse. It has distinguished itself through extensive coverage of both World Wars, all manner of foreign and domestic policy, and one of the most important Washington bureaus in the world.

The *New-York Daily Times*, as it was called in its first incarnation, began in New York in 1851. Its competition was a growing field of cheap penny-press papers, like the *New York Sun*, the *New York Herald*, and the *New York Tribune*, that were sold on the streets. As competition mounted among these papers, they sought new ways to draw readers through expanding coverage of the city's police, criminal courts, and political scandals. While the *Herald* published the grisly details of prostitute Helen Jewett's murder for weeks at a time, the new *New-York Daily Times* oriented its coverage toward factual, noncrusading business news. It focused on commercial transactions, publishing ship's manifests of arriving goods, and aimed to be an indispensable tool for the merchant class.

The founders of the first *New-York Daily Times*, Henry Jarvis Raymond and George Jones, both formerly of the *New York Tribune*, were eager to expand their purview beyond New York and within a year had initiated a California edition of the paper to be delivered by ship. When local California papers emerged, the *Times* could no longer compete and closed down its long-distance operation. It would be another century before the paper would have a California edition again.

The *Times* started its Sunday issue in 1861 to serve the demand for increased Civil War news. That year the paper also published its first illustration, taking aim at the publisher of the *New York Herald*, James Gordon Bennett, who was pictured "inflating his Well-Known First-Class, A No. 1 Wind-Bag, *Herald*."[1] But Bennett was not the paper's only target. By going after corrupt government officials, most notably the Tweed ring in City Hall, the *Times* provoked many of the wrong people and made itself vulnerable to attack and boycott. When Raymond died, the paper was left to George Jones. Under Jones, the paper struck out on its own against the Grant administration and moved away from the Republican Party to back Democrat Grover Cleveland for President in 1884.

These controversial positions left the paper on shaky ground even before the death of George Jones left it without a publisher. The cover price of the paper was raised to three cents to help pay for a prestigious office renovation by architect George B. Post, which saw the height of the building go from five stories to thirteen. The hubris surrounding the new building, however, was not matched by the fortunes of the paper, and as a result of its price increase daily circulation dropped. The board was mismanaged, and Jones's heirs did not have the wherewithal to carry the paper forward.

It was in this compromised state that Adolph Ochs, publisher of the *Chattanooga Times*, became the owner of the *New-York Daily Times* in 1896. With borrowed money and working against local sentiment that no small-town Tennessean stood a chance in the big city, Ochs took on the fledgling *Times*, circulation nine thousand. The hyphen was dropped in December, 1896 and the paper became the *New York Times*.[2] Earlier in the year, Ochs ran a contest soliciting suggestions for a slogan to signal the direction of the paper. The winning entry was "All the World's News, But Not a School for Scandal," but Ochs decided that he preferred his own slogan, "All the News That's Fit To Print," which took its place on the upper left hand corner of the front page starting in February, 1897.[3] This would be the guiding motto for decency against the prevailing race to the gutter that competing papers, Pulitzer's *World* and Hearst's *Journal*, were engaged in. These new "yellow papers" had pushed the envelope of Bennett's *Herald* a step further; the moral war of the 1840s newspapers was now a gloves-off, by-any-means-necessary circulation war, complete with gossip, slander, sleaze, and violence. By contrast, the slogan found at the bottom of the Times Company stationery read, "In many thousands of the best homes in New York City and Brooklyn, THE NEW YORK TIMES is the only morning newspaper admitted."[4]

Where Ochs did compete with his yellow paper rivals was in price, and he found in 1898 that by cutting the cover price to one penny he could triple circulation. It was a calculated, albeit counterintuitive, risk—to have mass appeal through pricing but not through content. Although the price cut did not bring readers from the *World* or the *Journal*, it did impact the *Sun, Herald,* and *Tribune,* the paper's real competitors.[5] The *Times* readers were already distinguishing themselves as a class separate from those of the other one-cent papers, drawn to Ochs's expanded literary and cultural coverage in the new Saturday *Review of Books and Art.* With this came more publisher advertising and other business ventures as well. In Ochs's first year he initiated the "Arrival of Buyers" section, announcing who was in town and in what market.[6] Later a hotel beat was added, which reported on important people visiting from out of town. The *Times* soon had more advertising than any competing daily in New York, despite the fact that it did not accept several categories of advertising, including risky money ventures, questionable medicines, and other dubious schemes that were the mainstay of his competition's ad pages.

After the turn of the century, the *New York Times* began to take its self-appointed role as the standard-bearer of news more seriously. It signaled its new position of strength with an extravagant move into a tall Gothic tower at the intersection of Forty-Second Street, Broadway, and Seventh Avenue. It was further uptown than any newspaper had ever ventured, anticipating the population shift to midtown that would soon occur. Built on top of what would become the largest subway station in the New York system, the intersection known as Longacre Square was renamed in honor of the newspaper. The ball drop from the top of the paper's new building on New Year's Eve in 1906 would become an annual event witnessed by millions of people and would solidify the central place of the *New York Times* in the city and at the center of world events.

In addition to this public role as timekeeper, the *Times* was also becoming an accomplished archivist and historian. From this new location at Times Square, the paper began to archive its own stories to be used as a reference file of historical events. This clippings file, which became standard in newsrooms everywhere as "the morgue," would serve as an index for journalists and historians alike and would

make the *New York Times Index* an authoritative resource for information. As the official record-keeper of the nation, the *Times* established the precedent of printing any official document that was
relevant to the citizenry, regardless of its length. The *Times* provided
comprehensive coverage of the sinking of the *Titanic*, including the
first radio dispatches—amounting to a world exclusive—printing a
full passenger list, and surrounding the story with histories of the
ship, similar ships, and extensive nautical background and context.
On July 4, 1918, the *Times* printed the full Declaration of Independence in its pages, and continued to do so every subsequent Independence Day.[7] It was also from this new location at Times Square, on
January 1, 1905, that the *Times* began its tradition of running poetry
on the editorial page, where it appeared until 1973.[8]

The New York Times *at War*

It was during wartime that the *New York Times* distinguished itself
most, and during World War I its reputation of trust and service was
honored with its first Pulitzer Prize in recognition of having published
in full "so many official reports, documents, and speeches by European statesmen relating to the progress and conduct of the war."
Government White Papers from all sides leading up to the war found
space in the *Times*, as did argument and debate by readers and reporters alike.[9] To withstand claims of Allied partisanship, the *Times*
published military accounts by former German officers and sent an
army of foreign correspondents to the front to cover each maneuver.
Such comprehensive coverage necessitated creative layout strategies
to accommodate all of the news within wartime paper restrictions:

> The amount of news received by the *Times*, by cable and wireless, from
> its own correspondents, on a number of days in the latter part of the war
> surpassed in the total number of words the dispatches of the largest
> news associations, and often exceeded all the special dispatches to all
> other American newspapers combined. The handling of this mass of
> news in the office naturally involved problems unexampled in magni-
> tude if not new in kind, and in the delicate technical question of make-
> up, the arrangement of news with due consideration of its relative
> importance, as well as of the appearance of the page on which it is
> printed, the *Times* in the course of the war developed a general style to
> which many of its competitors paid the compliment of imitation. It was
> impossible, in the war period, to get all the big news on the front page,
> but the *Times* usually got more of it there than other papers, and in an
> arrangement which was at once pleasing to the eye and calculated to

make it easy for the reader to see at once what had happened, as well as to give him some idea of the importance of the various dispatches.[10]

The resulting layout, with the most important story positioned in the upper right-hand corner, became standard across many other papers following its institutionalization at the *Times*. The *Times's* coverage was rewarded with readership; the circulation went from 250,000 before the war to 390,000 after.[11] In peace, the *Times* was the only paper to print the full text of the Treaty of Versailles, on June 10, 1919.

Because of the *Times's* location in New York, it was particularly important for the paper to serve the local audience well with substantive foreign news. With a large and growing population, many of whom were newly arrived immigrants from Europe, readers were more demanding of complete coverage of events back home and monitored the *Times* coverage closely.[12] What made this task especially challenging was serving the varying political allegiances of the readers and finding correspondents with insider knowledge equal to or better than that of the paper's readers. Locally, the "About New York" column was initiated in 1939 and saw a host of writers at its helm, including Meyer Berger, Gay Talese, Anna Quindlen, and Francis X. Clines. According to Ivan Viet, the paper's promotions manager, this column was an attempt to rectify the fact that "local New York news is a category in which we have not made our best impression."[13]

When Adolph Ochs died in 1935, the paper was left to his son-in-law Arthur Hays Sulzberger—who was married to Ochs's daughter Iphigene—and to his nephew Julius Ochs Adler. Sulzberger, who ran the paper until 1961, was made the publisher, largely in charge of the editorial side, while Julius was in charge of the business side, including advertising, circulation, and promotion. Sulzberger led the paper through some of its most significant periods, including the Depression and World War II. In addition to the *New York Times*, the pair was also left with the responsibility of the *Chattanooga Times*, a circumstance Sulzberger was strictly against, not wanting to be in control of more than one newspaper at a time or to have one paper determine the editorial policy of another. That the *Times* in New York would set the agenda for *Chattanooga* should have been the least of their concerns, as over the twentieth century the *New York Times* would come to set the agenda for most other newspapers in the country.

This did not mean that the *Times* covered every world event in perfect proportion with its significance. There were several occasions during which the *Times's* position as the agenda setter has done more harm than good, as its avoidance of a story can help guarantee its obscurity in other papers. Such was the case in the coverage of Nazi concentration camps during World War II, which the *Times* mentioned only in brief, back-page stories. Speculation was that the family did not want to wear its Jewish ethnicity on its sleeve by prioritizing or showing favor to Jewish causes. The paper's policy also encouraged Jewish writers to use initials in their bylines to disguise first names such as Abraham.[14] But this did not help to explain the editorial treatment of *Brown v. Board of Education* in the *Times*. In an editorial called "All God's Chillun," published following the decision, the *Times* found the case most useful as ammunition against communists:

> When some hostile propagandist rises in Moscow or Peiping to accuse us of being a class society we can if we wish recite the courageous words of yesterday's opinion.[15]

It is and was testament to the significance of the *New York Times* that readers and historians alike have traced and documented its flaws—from news oversights to mistakes in the crossword puzzle—finding errors in its pages more egregious than those found in other papers.

On August 14, 1945, the bulletin on the zipper of the *New York Times* building read: "Official: Truman Announces Japanese Surrender." The crowds once again converged on the square as they had done on May 7, V-E Day, with noisemakers, ticker tape, and strangers embracing strangers.[16] The *Times* had become the official source of authoritative news, and its office building the official site of celebration. The crowds would also gather regularly on election nights to watch the returns as they scrolled around the front of the marquee.

Perhaps the most significant report in the *Times* during World War II was one that very few of the staff knew about until it reached the front page. William L. Laurence, the first person to ever occupy the post of full-time science reporter, translated physics and natural science into language the newspaper audience could understand. He interviewed Albert Einstein, and he had the ability to make complex concepts palatable to a wide audience. For these skills he was chosen by the government to be the only journalist to cover the Manhattan Project. Working secretly, Laurence followed the development of the atomic bomb through its development in Oak Ridge, Tennessee, and its testing in New Mexico, filing his stories in a government safe until they could be revealed. Though he was not aboard the *Enola Gay* for the bombing of Hiroshima, he instructed a crew member to take notes for him, and three days later he was aboard the *Great Artiste*, the surveillance plane that accompanied the mission to bomb Nagasaki. His reports appeared in a ten-part series in the *Times* in September and October of 1945.[17]

After the war Sulzberger determined to make coverage in the *Times* more comprehensive, with better layout, more bureaus, and more photography.[18] The photos of Mussolini's hanging and the B-25 bomber crash into the Empire State Building in 1945 distinguished *Times* photography in a field dominated by tabloids. *Times* writers were dispatched to cities across the nation, many of which had never had bureaus before, to capture the conversion to a domestic economy. Boston, San Francisco, Akron, and Detroit all became regular beats. And despite the paper's location in New York, at least one-fifth of the coverage in the *New York Times* came from Washington, rivaling the coverage of the wire services and the local Washington papers for political news.[19]

With its legion of correspondents in the farthest-flung areas of the world, the reputation of the paper was known worldwide. Its elite status as a world journal allowed its staff to gain entry into the upper echelons of leadership, not only at home but also abroad. Since the days of Raymond, *Times* leadership has enjoyed a close relationship with American presidents, and the influence of this relationship has been a point of contention since the beginning of the paper, one which becomes particularly acute in times of crisis and war. As Ochs wrote to President Franklin D. Roosevelt, "It is the fixed policy of the *New York Times* to aid the Government in every way possible and not willingly to embarrass it," although this did not translate into easy endorsements or support of any particular administration.[20] During World War I, the *Times* enacted "voluntary censorship" in order to withhold information that was deemed threatening to national security. During World War II, the paper's staff was often used to send messages to diplomats from various countries. As James Reston, who was the head of the Washington bureau, wrote, "Nothing gave us more trouble during my years on [the paper] than the conflict with the government over what should and should not be published during periods of war or threats of war."[21]

The *Times* again would come under fire for knowing more than it printed in its pages. Although Reston himself had learned that the Soviets had armed Cuba with missiles and that an invasion at the Bay of Pigs was "imminent," the *Times* withheld the story at the request of President Kennedy, who did not want Americans distracted from a speech he was planning to give on the subject. In the end, a hundred people were killed who might not have been had the report appeared, and even President Kennedy regretted the decision.[22]

Arthur Ochs Sulzberger's Reign

When Arthur (Punch) Ochs Sulzberger took over in 1963 the paper changed dramatically in form and content. The pages were made more readable when eight columns became six and there was more white space. The four sections of the paper became standardized and new sections were added. New technology converted the paper from hot-metal type to "cold" computer typesetting.[23] The content of the *Times*, and every other newspaper from that day forward, would also be changed by a landmark libel decision in the *Times*'s favor in 1964, when the Supreme Court overturned the decision of a lower court that had given a libel award to a Montgomery, Alabama, official. The Supreme Court found that the case did not qualify as libel because no "actual malice" had occurred; only if a falsehood was printed knowingly or recklessly could damages be awarded. In the absence of malice, libel could not be charged. This changed the burden of proof to the person charging libel, who had to show that journalists knew that what they were writing was untrue. The case, *New York Times v. Sullivan*, also cleared the way for the press to become more aggressive toward public figures and policy and laid the foundation for the era of investigative reporting to come.

By 1964, the changing tide in journalism was felt at the *Times*, whose readers were now also often reading papers such as the *Village Voice* and in-depth weekly newsmagazines. The response was to recruit more aggressively from Ivy League schools for more highly educated writers, to infuse stories with more color and analysis, and to blur the separation between "hard" and "soft" news, as editor Clifton Daniel wrote in a memo:

> What we should be doing, in my opinion, is getting more good stuff into the main body of all stories. And by "good stuff" I mean illuminating flashes of color, description and background that can be obtained only by first-hand original reporting and skillful writing.[24]

Such reporting would find its way into the *Times* with uncommon regularity in the 1960s and 1970s. Correspondent Harrison Salisbury wrote from North Vietnam in 1966 that nonmilitary targets were being bombed by American warplanes, despite official government statements to the contrary. Salisbury, who had been awarded a Pulitzer Prize in 1955 for international reporting from Russia, met with severe resistance from the Defense Department for his Saigon reporting, and his work ultimately helped to sway public opinion against the war.

The blatant disregard for the wishes of a presidential administration reached new heights following the decision to publish the Pentagon Papers. When reporters came into possession of a massive, forty-seven-volume, three-thousand-page document entitled "History of U.S. Decision-Making Process on Vietnam Policy," a clear indictment of

American foreign policy that incriminated the government back to the Truman administration, it was a journalistic coup. The documents were acquired by the *Times* in April 1971, and a team of journalists devoured them, ensconced in a hotel room taking copious notes. It was far from certain, however, whether what they wrote would ever be published.

The risks included having an accurate judgment on whether or not the papers were even authentic, given how damning they appeared to be. But there were also significant legal questions relating to their publication. Some lawyers who were consulted refused to counsel on the matter, not wanting to be involved with what they deemed to be stolen property. Ignoring that advice, Sulzberger authorized the publication of a series on what came to be known as the Pentagon Papers beginning on June 13, 1971. In Neil Sheehan's lead paragraph of the page-one story, he wrote that

> a massive study of how the United States went to war in Indochina, conducted by the Pentagon three years ago, demonstrates that four administrations progressively developed a sense of commitment to a non-Communist Vietnam, a readiness to fight the North to protect the South, and an ultimate frustration with this effort—to a much greater extent than their public statements acknowledged at the time.[25]

Two days later, the Attorney General in Nixon's cabinet, John Mitchell (who the following year would become the head of the Committee for the Re-Election of the President), requested that the *Times* cease publication on national security grounds. Ruling that the Nixon administration could not stop the publication of the Pentagon Papers, Judge Murray Gurfein wrote, "A cantankerous press, an obstinate press, a ubiquitous press, must be suffered by those in authority in order to preserve the even greater values of freedom of expression and the right of the people to know."[26] With that blessing, the press was free to publish what they wanted of the documents in the name of the public's right to know.

By the time Daniel Ellsberg, who had leaked the papers, was put on trial in 1973, his case was overshadowed by the events of the Watergate scandal in Washington, which secured a place for the *Washington Post* in the top tier of newspapers. In their decisions to publish what they had found, both the *Times* and the *Post* would change the political and media landscape of the United States.

The *Washington Post* Makes National News

The *Washington Post* began publishing on December 6, 1877. It was first owned by a Democrat but was bought by a Republican and a Democrat in

1889, one a cabinet member and the other a former Congressman. The *Post* was sold to the owner of the *Cincinnati Enquirer* in 1905, who was a Democrat, but when his son took over after his death, the paper again favored the Republicans. Finally in 1933 the financially struggling paper went into receivership and was sold at auction to Republican Eugene Meyer, a financier from California, who intended to keep the paper independent. He inaugurated his purchase with these words:

> The first mission of a newspaper is to tell the truth as nearly as the truth may be ascertained. The newspaper shall tell ALL the truth so far as it can learn it, concerning the important affairs of America and the world. As a disseminator of news, the paper shall observe the decencies that are obligatory upon a private gentleman. What it prints shall be fit reading for the young as well as for the old. The newspaper's duty is to its readers and to the public at large, and not to the private interests of its owner. In the pursuit of truth, the newspaper shall be prepared to make sacrifice of its material fortunes, if such course be necessary for the public good. The newspaper shall not be the ally of any special interest, but shall be fair and free and wholesome in its outlook on public affairs and public men.[27]

Meyer had worked in the Wilson administration in the War Finance Corporation until 1925 and later served on the Federal Reserve Board in a financial post. He had made millions in railroads, oil, and copper as a capital investor in Allied Chemical Company and Anaconda Copper.[28] Eugene's wife Agnes, who had been a reporter at the *New York Sun*, also became a significant influence in Washington, working to ameliorate overcrowding in the schools, racial discrimination, and community health and welfare by trying to establish a Department of Health, Education, and Welfare. As President Truman noted, "There's hardly a day I don't get a letter from that Meyer woman or from Eleanor Roosevelt telling me how to run this job."[29]

At the time, the paper was running fifth in a field that included the *Washington Herald* and the *Times*, both owned by Hearst, and the *Evening Star* and the *Daily News*. Even in last place, however, the *Washington Post* had been a desirable property for various factions and was considered a useful political power tool. Not being affiliated with any party in a city dominated by politics gave the paper a certain leverage, although Meyer or any publisher of his stature could never be completely outside politics. In 1946 President Truman appointed Meyer to be the first president of the International Bank for Reconstruction and Development.[30] Meyer also worked to get Eisenhower to run on the GOP ticket after being impressed with his wartime record by using, among other things, the Gallup Poll to do advance opinion polling on the candidate and publishing the results in the paper.[31]

When Eleanor (Cissy) Patterson, of the *Chicago Tribune* and *Daily News* Pattersons, bought and merged the *Times* and the *Herald*, she turned their fortunes around; but after she died in 1948, the merged paper was vulnerable to a takeover. Though it took many years, the *Times-Herald* eventually fell to the *Post* under the direction of Philip Graham, Meyer's son-in-law, who took over in 1946 at the age of thirty. Graham closed the rival paper and appropriated some of its more popular features, including comic strips and sports coverage, so as not to lose all of its readers.[32] The growing success of the paper was seen in a new $6 million plant that Graham commissioned at 1515 L Street NW and his purchase in 1950 of the CBS affiliate television station in Washington, WTOP-TV.[33] The circulation of the *Washington Post* after it annexed the most valuable parts of the *Times-Herald* was 380,000 in 1954. From this vaunted post, Graham became part of the inner circle of elite journalists in Washington, and like Meyer before him, he would engineer similar political maneuvers and polling to get Lyndon B. Johnson on Senator John F. Kennedy's ticket.

Not all of the *Washington Post*'s importance was at the highest levels of electoral politics, however. It also exerted significant influence on the social and physical shape of the nation's capital. The social register of Washington was unlike any other in the country. It was dominated not by aristocracy as in Europe or by financiers as in New York, but by politicians and would-be politicians. The population was also very fluid, with representatives coming from their home states to live in the area while Congress was in session, sometimes with their families and sometimes without. All of this movement necessitated a structure of organization, so that people were made aware of who was who and who they needed to know. The *Washington Post* would emerge to fill this gap in its highly lauded "Style" section.

In 1963, after Philip Graham succumbed to depression and finally suicide, his wife Katharine Graham, daughter of Eugene and Agnes, took over the paper. She had been working in journalism since she graduated from the University of Chicago but had never been groomed to lead a company. She put together a team of executive advisors including Ben Bradlee, former Washington bureau chief of *Newsweek* magazine, which was owned by the Washington Post Company. Reflecting on her new responsibility at the paper, she commented, "The power is to set the agenda. What we print and what we don't print matter a lot. What leads the paper or the magazine impacts on events and people's awareness."[34] This was never more evident than in her two biggest decisions at the paper, to support the publication of the Pentagon Papers and to dispatch a full-time investigative team to a story about a break-in at the Democratic National headquarters.

Katharine Graham, publisher of the *Washington Post*, and Ben Bradlee, executive editor of the *Washington Post*, leave U.S. District Court in Washington, D.C., on June 21, 1971. Courtesy of AP/Wide World Photos.

The *Washington Post* was the top paper in the city when Katharine Graham took over, but it was rivaled by the *New York Times* both in national and in local coverage. The *Times* had more Washington correspondents than did the *Post*,[35] but the two companies eventually cooperated in the joint ownership of the *International Herald Tribune*, a significant international source to which both papers contributed stories. The rivalry with the *Times*, however, was not abated by such business deals, and in 1971, after the *Times* was restrained from publishing any further material from the Pentagon Papers, Katharine Graham made a decision to ignore the injunction and publish them in her own paper. Fearing the same legal quagmire facing the *Times*, and not wanting to jeopardize the stock price of a company that had only three days earlier gone public, most decision makers at the *Post* were reluctant to get involved in the *Times*'s drama. But on Graham's orders, the day after the *Times* first published its exposé, the *Washington Post* began printing its own excerpts. In a June 17, 1971 editorial, the *Post* wrote,

> those of us who believe that the reader, which is to say the public, always gains from the maximum possible comprehension of what the government is doing and how it all works (particularly when it works badly) can only applaud the Times' enterprise; it is hard for us to think of an argument for withholding such material once it was in hand.[36]

When the Supreme Court sided with the newspapers, both the *Post* and the *Times* were lauded for their actions.

A year after the Pentagon Papers victory was chalked up on the *Post*'s side, what was called by many at the time "a third-rate burglary" found its way onto the front page of the *Washington Post*. Either because it was an election year or because the details of the case showed slightly more sophisticated methods than an average break-in, the *Post* highlighted the story and followed it relentlessly. The first story, by staff writer Alfred E. Lewis, was headlined "5 Held in Plot to Bug Democrats' Office Here," published on Sunday, June 18, 1972.

Once it became clear that there was more to the story than a simple burglary, two reporters were assigned to work full-time together to track down leads that would connect the burglars to the highest levels of the Nixon administration. They were Bob Woodward, an eager Republican from Illinois, and Carl Bernstein, a native Washingtonian with leftist activist parents. The advantage the *Post* had over other papers in this story was a deep bench of metro reporters with good local contacts—such as Bernstein's friends at the phone company who would give him any number he asked for—that the wire services and the *Times* simply did not have.

The *Washington Post* ran the Watergate story on June 18 as its second lead. Most papers and other media did not highlight the story initially, but the investigation at the *Post* was certainly implicated in the resignation of President Nixon on August 9, 1974. Throughout the investigation the *Post* was threatened and bullied by various branches of the federal government, including the Federal Communications Commission, which made renewing television licenses difficult.

After Watergate, the press was driven to unravel the secrets and scandals of both public officials and institutions. A surge of interest in journalism, which had been building for several years, followed, strengthened by a renewed faith in the role of the press in public service. National magazines and television news magazines began to seek out their own Watergates. The mainstream media's relationship to the elected officials became much more antagonistic than it had ever been prior to the Nixon administration.

Washington Post writers Carl Bernstein, left, and Bob Woodward,
lead Watergate reporters. May 7, 1973. Courtesy of AP/Wide
World Photos.

In 1976 Graham's son Donald Graham was made vice president
and general manager of the *Washington Post*. He had served at the
paper in a number of different positions, including both editorial and
production. But perhaps his most useful training ground for the job
was the two years he spent on the Washington police force, giving
him insight into local affairs that few writers at the Washington bureaus of other newspapers could draw on. Under Donald, the *Post* also
started a financial section called *Washington Business*, a weekly that
appeared in the Monday edition starting April 14, 1980. The forty-
eight-page tabloid insert was designed to

> report on business activities in Washington and the region. It will
> publish expanded tables on 100 major Washington area stocks, supply
> in-depth reports on economic trends, and provide additional informa-
> tion on major business news and the people who make the news.
>
> Regular columns on consumer affairs, on the legal profession, and on
> personal finance also will appear in Washington Business.[37]

Significantly timed to coincide with the boom of the 1980s, major stories emphasized the turn toward luxury goods and lifestyles, intended to attract a wealthier demographic to the paper including "the area's executives, government officials, investors and money-minded consumers." The features included a story about taking the Concorde to and from Dulles airport and the first of a weekly series of charts measuring the economic activity of the area "by combining indicators that measure employment, personal income, retail sales, telephone use, energy output and other industry data."[38] In the inaugural issue, business advertisers proclaimed aggressive attitudes for the "No Guts, No Glory" 1980s (so called by marketer Earle Palmer Brown). Century 21 Realtors announced that "We Have Decided Not to Join the Recession!" and Dupont Circle Condominiums declared that "It's Hard to Smile When You Don't Own." Business-to-business advertising for legal and clerical services was interspersed with ads for Porsche, Mercedes Benz, and Audi, all in anticipation of a Reagan-era economy of deregulation and boundless wealth for capital investors.

A feature called "Washington's Top 60" profiled the leading businesses in every industry in the region, and the Washington Post Company itself was listed first in the "Communications, Publishing" category. In this digest of the company's earnings and profits, readers learned that

> big ticket items on the spending side of the ledger this year will include an expected $8 million reduction of pre-tax earnings due to start-up costs for Inside Sports, a new monthly now on newsstands, plus $5 million of expenses for the *Post*'s new $65 million satellite printing plant in Springfield, due to open next fall. A new management team is seeking to build circulation and advertising revenues at the Trenton newspaper, which has been a weak performer. In broadcasting, Post-Newsweek stations are inaugurating a test of satellite distribution for syndicated programs and has opened a Los Angeles office to develop new TV programming.[39]

That the *Washington Post* found 1980 an appropriate time to begin an all-business section and a sports magazine supplement was indicative of the shift in the 1980s toward niche publications in general and business- and luxury-targeted publications in particular. What had been primarily a political newspaper, known for strong investigative reporting and local coverage of Washington, fell prey to the same lure as other papers: celebrating the deregulated 1980s and congratulating its beneficiaries. In fact the business beat was being strengthened at all newspapers claiming a national focus by this time, all of them working to secure some of the success enjoyed by the *Wall Street Journal*.

From Main Street to the *Wall Street Journal*

The *Wall Street Journal*, on the other hand, was from the start a financial services company with a newspaper, originally a "flimsy," on the side. The hand-carboned newssheet announcing the day's stock trades was delivered by messenger to brokerage houses along Wall Street and Broad Street in New York beginning in 1889. The *Journal* offices themselves were on Broad, not Wall, as the paper's name might have been thought to indicate.

While the *New York Times* and the *Washington Post* might be considered the country's political papers of record, the *Journal* serves as the economic paper of record. It does not cover crime, except of the financial sort, and its form defies all modern typographical strategies of sensationalism. It lacks bright graphics and photographs and still looks very much as it did sixty years ago.

The *Wall Street Journal* both is and is not a family-owned company. From the first it was owned by Charles Dow and Edward Jones, who started the financial sheet of notably small proportions at the end of the nineteenth century. But after Dow's death, the paper and service were purchased by Clarence Barron, or more specifically Barron's wife—Barron did not have the money at the time to cover the cost. Barron had been performing a similar stock-tracking service in Boston and Philadelphia, and he acted as the Boston correspondent to the *Wall Street Journal*. When ownership transferred to Barron's daughter Jane, she became the matriarch of Dow Jones and Company, staying out of the trouble and the spotlight that such a prestige position often brings. She never meddled by putting her own family members in positions of power at the paper, and few people would have known she was the owner at all.

In the early days it was the news ticker that was most important to Dow Jones and Company. Thirty-second scoops on financial news over other services made or broke the business. It was an industry revolutionized by the new technologies of mass communication, particularly the telegraph and the telephone, which afforded split-second advantages to companies in close competition. *Wall Street Journal* reporters were often stationed outside company annual meetings and raced on foot to a telephone to get the news back to the paper as quickly as they could. They devised numerous schemes, signaling prearranged hand gestures to colleagues nearest the telephone, tying up the lines against rivals, and relaying messages across town, all in an effort to be first with a dividend report.

By 1928, the circulation of the *Journal* had reached 52,000 copies a day, but its own probusiness, antiregulation stance led the paper to vastly underestimate the scope and magnitude of the stock exchange crash of October 1929.[40] The *Journal*, reluctant to believe that stocks would not bounce back, took investors' financial ruin rather lightly. Clarence Barron, who died in 1928, did not witness the most devastating stock plummet ever to hit Wall Street, and thus never had to amend his own boundless optimism for growth. On October 30, the day after Black Tuesday, the paper celebrated the low price of stocks: "Stocks are off 25, 50, 100 and in some cases 200 points. Many have shrunk 50% or more. All of which means that bargain days are near, and bargain days do not come along very often."[41] The *Journal*'s page-one story was headlined, "Pressure Continues," but found reason for optimism: "A number of favorable factors were in evidence, and strong support appeared to stem the decline in pivotal issues."[42] The *New York Times*, on the other hand, led the day with a multi-decked headline of alarm:

CLOSING RALLY VIGOROUS; Leading Issues Regain From 4 to 14 Points in 15 Minutes. INVESTMENT TRUSTS BUY Large Blocks Thrown on Market at Opening Start Third Break of Week. BIG TRADERS HARDEST HIT Bankers Believe Liquidation Now Has Run Its Course and Advise Purchases. Two Extra Dividends Declared. Change Is Expected Today. Bank and Trust Stock Prices Crumble in Record Trading Third Day of Collapse. Three Factors in Market. Bids Provided Where Needed. Huge Blocks Offered at Opening. Brokerage Offices Crowded. Ticker Finishes at 5:32. Record of the Day's Volume. Table of Declines. Losses on Curb Market. Peaks Reached in September.[43]

1929 was also the year that the *Wall Street Journal Pacific Coast Edition* was started, a poor cousin to the original but significant for its attempt to reach beyond the insular world of Wall Street. The West Coast version contained news relevant to California-based companies and indicated the company's desire to become a more national newspaper. Bernard Kilgore, who became managing editor of the *Journal* in 1941, was responsible for making the paper truly national, beyond its money-losing Pacific Coast edition. Just as Al Neuharth would do years later, Kilgore imagined a paper that the whole country would read at the same time but wondered how to design a format that would appeal to everyone equally. Reasoning that sports were of greater regional importance than national, he fell back on the one topic that he thought was of interest to all Americans, everywhere: the economy.[44] He would broaden the scope of the paper beyond the reporting of stock prices to consider all manner of financial news: wages, prices of goods, and companies expanding and closing, so that even noninvestors would find it useful.

Part of the rationale for this broadened scope had to do with the skepticism that many Americans had about Wall Street following the 1929 crash. The insider world of stock trading, impenetrable to most, was seen as a dubious and secret scam by people who lost their life savings and believed that the *Wall Street Journal* had been complicit in the hoodwinking. Using jargon that few could understand, and vastly understating the severity of the crash, the *Journal* weathered the Depression largely in a state of denial. In order to expand readership, it had to take on subjects of wider interest and use more-accessible vocabulary. Furthermore, according to Kilgore, there was good reason to suspect that even though most people read the *Journal* as their second paper, some newsworthy items beyond the world of finance would not be out of order in its pages. Against the tradition of the paper, Kilgore added the front-page summary "What's News" box, bridging the political and economic activities of the nation and the world.[45]

As Kilgore's management post coincided closely with America's entry into World War II, the difference in coverage was seen in how the war was followed not with foreign correspondents but with reporters stationed in the industrial cities at home. The war was covered not as a series of advances and retreats, but as a complicated intersection of production, factories, prices, shortages, and rations. It was largely a story about the domestic economy, and the paper's Washington bureau was of substantial size, just slightly smaller than that of the *New York Times*.

The front page of the *Journal* was also the laboratory for a new style of news writing, one that diverged notably from the Journalism 101 dictate that a story's lead should answer the questions "who, what, when, where, and why." Instead, the *Journal*'s stories were presented in argument form, first one side of an issue and then the other, the argument and the counterargument, so that readers could choose—or more likely see the implicit rightness of—one side over the other. Even with this radical break in newswriting style, however, the paper's appearance did not become any more inviting in its layout. It remained mostly a dull black and white, with narrow columns, no photographs, and very few bylines.[46] The decision not to include photos was a practical one. In most business news, visuals hardly added to the story's impact, since financial deals are significantly less visually stimulating than most news stories. The lack of photographs also helped to speed up the transmission of the paper over the wires, which was a much more important priority.[47]

In 1945, Bernard Kilgore was named president and chief executive of Dow Jones, and the circulation of the *Journal*, which had suffered significant losses during the Depression, had climbed up to 70,982.[48]

Four years later, the company's largest stockholder, Clarence Barron's daughter Jane Waldron Bancroft, died, leaving her interest in the company to her daughters, Jessie Bancroft Cox and Jane Bancroft Cook. Their ownership was secured in family trusts that prevented the company from falling into anyone else's hands, but the daughters maintained the same hands-off approach to the *Wall Street Journal* that had been initiated by their mother.[49]

The newspaper continued to prosper under their watch, largely as a result of Kilgore's prescience in marketing the *Wall Street Journal* brand as an exclusive and crucial source of financial news. The paper's ad rates were relatively low when compared to other newspapers at the time, but because of the small readership, the cost-per-reader was actually quite high. The sales director, Robert Feemster, turned this negative into a positive with advertisers by arguing the quality of the small readership, in effect selling a "niche demographic" well in advance of the emergence of such terminology in marketing. A belief in their own "desirable readership" led the ad department to increase rates even further, to be commensurate with such glossy financial publications as *Fortune* and *Business Week*, despite not being inclined to print in color.[50]

The other trend that the *Journal* was able to capitalize on in the postwar era was that of mobility. Improvements in transportation and communication led many businesses to relocate and open up branch offices where local conditions were most favorable, rather than only where the largest markets were. Having gotten used to the idea of traveling during the war, veterans were also less averse to the idea of picking up their families and moving to new towns and cities across the country in order to follow the best job opportunities. Thus a paper that could keep readers, and most importantly, strivers, abreast of where the next opportunity lay was bound to achieve some success. To reach this audience and keep them hooked, the *Journal* began listing real estate ads to help the increasingly mobile workforce find their new homes and sell their old ones, often in different states. The *Journal* was helping to create a community, not bound by town or city limits, but of national scope and with a foundation rooted in the economy.[51] This new community was beckoned by the paper's longstanding advertising slogan, "Everywhere, Men Who Get Ahead in Business Read the *Wall Street Journal*."[52]

The circulation of the *Journal* went from half a million in 1957 to more than a million by 1966,[53] as the paper began more coverage of issues outside the strict parameters of financial news, including social issues, education, and science. It also continued its tradition, begun in 1941, of printing quirky page-one, center-column stories of general, if not esoteric, interest written with humor. A story announcing the stunning success of the *Reader's Digest* franchise was headlined: "Bible's Runner-up—Reader's Digest Posts Top Publishing Success Since the Scriptures—Spiritual Guidance, Self-Help, 'Square' Sex Articles Sell 27 Million Copies a Month—'A Vat of Warm Maple Syrup.'"[54] As often as not, these page-one stories were inspired by the peculiar animal-human dynamic of twentieth-century America. Bizarre animal stories included one that provided edification on the elusive cricket industry in a story headlined: "The Cricket Industry: It's Small and Noisy But Fairly Important—Demand for Crickets, by Frogs and Fishermen, Increases."[55] Another warned, "The Komodo Dragon, Big, Mean and Hungry, Is Eager for Visitors; Carnivorous Prehistoric Lizard Is the Featured Attraction Of a Tour Drawing No One."[56] These oddball front-page stories served to lighten the tone of the bland newssheet and to attract readers not typically drawn to the financial daily.

The particular and "distinguished" readership of the *Wall Street Journal*, according to management, was distinct in another way too: they did not seem to mind the frequent price increases of the *Wall Street Journal*, which kept it more expensive than any other newspaper. The higher price seemed to confer value on the content that readers were happy to pay for.[57] Indeed, the wealthier its readers became, the more the *Wall Street Journal*'s own usefulness seemed to be confirmed.

The orientation of the *Wall Street Journal* has remained, despite its frequent forays into the eclectic, steadfastly financial, and corporate. It preaches a "life, liberty, and pursuit of happiness" approach to the market economy, which it prefers to be unfettered by government regulation. Its editorial policy has remained simply: "free people, free markets." Although Kilgore once considered moving the paper to Chicago to be more geographically central in the United States,[58] it has remained, importantly, located in the financial district of lower Manhattan.

In his desire to expand readership even further, Bernard Kilgore began again to imagine a more national paper with a broader mandate that would attract the younger generation. His *National Observer* debuted on February 4, 1962. In *Wall Street Journal* ads for the new news weekly, the *Observer* was called, "America's most surprising newspaper." It was to contain

surprises galore in each and every issue...provocative and friendly reading that is full of varied and often unexpected observations about the quality of life on this fast-paced globe of ours...compelling news stories that zero in on the trends and get to the heart of national and world-wide events by examining their impact on *you*, your family and your life. National Observer...a journal of living America that helps you discover and enjoy the riches of life itself.[59]

Had it been more successful or lasted longer, Kilgore's plan for the *National Observer* would have been a more obvious blueprint for the later emergence of *USA Today*. It marked a trend toward personalized and lifestyle features in newspapers—"news you can use"—that was about the issues people cared about most. It was also to be a reporterless paper, constructed entirely by rewrite men working from wire stories. When this plan failed to produce interesting news, reporters were hired, money was spent, and the *National Observer* became a well-written paper. It was about twenty pages long, with large pictures and three feature articles on the front page. Based in White Oak, Maryland, it was produced close to its intended suburban readership, and it shared presses with the *Wall Street Journal*. It emphasized stories about Vietnam, education, and civil rights, but it found few advertisers and only lasted until July 4, 1977.[60]

A New Economic Agenda

The demise of the *Observer* overlapped with a new direction at the *Wall Street Journal,* which saw it expand into electronic publishing and community newspapers. The company also expanded beyond the United States with the *Asian Wall Street Journal* in 1976, a second section to its U.S. edition in 1980, and a European edition in 1983. By then, the *Wall Street Journal* had achieved new status as the bible of Reaganomics, espousing supply-side economics in editorials before anyone else had ever heard the term. This was largely due to the influence of Arthur Laffer, an economist in the Nixon administration who had developed a new model of economic forecasting that struck most observers at the time as ridiculous. Jude Wanniski at the *National Observer*, however, found it intriguing, and when Robert Bartley was put in charge of the editorial page of the *Wall Street Journal* in the early 1970s, he chose Wanniski to accompany him.[61] Wanniski and Laffer had long debated economic policy, although Laffer's ideas had fallen so out of favor that he lost his post at the University of Chicago's Department of Economics. The idea was that inflation could be curbed not by tax increases, but by tax cuts, which put more money in people's hands to purchase goods, which would in turn promote more production. It went against the grain of tight monetary policy at the *Journal,* which followed traditional Keynesian economics. In one early explanatory article, economist Paul Craig Roberts wrote, when tax rates are reduced, the after tax rewards to saving, investing, and taxable income rise. People switch into these activities out of leisure, consumption, tax shelters, and working for nontaxable income. The incentive effects cause an increase in the market supply of goods and services—thus the name, "supply-side economics."[62]

The theory was taken up by Republican Congressman Jack Kemp and California Governor Ronald Reagan. It was an economic program almost entirely devised and elaborated in the pages of the *Wall Street Journal*, and one that was largely ignored by other newspapers.[63] By 1980, Roberts could look back on the 1970s as the dark days of economic thinking before supply-side:

> At the time there were only a handful of supply-siders. Supply-side economics wasn't a subject taught in textbooks or discussed by professors at conferences. The prestigious proprietors of the Chase, DRI and Wharton economic models didn't know a thing about it, and the Treasury, the Office of Management and Budget, and the Congressional Budget Office were more or less sure that the subject was unimportant. . . .
>
> Today all this is changing. Supply-side economics is rapidly gaining ground and picking up new adherents even from the ranks of leading Keynesians.[64]

Following the election of Ronald Reagan to the presidency, an article called "Supply-Side Economics and How it Grew from a Theory to a Presidential Program" in the *Journal* quoted economist and future under-secretary of the Treasury for Tax and Economic Affairs Norman Ture on the remarkable shift in economic thinking that had just taken place: "It's one of the most dramatic, revolutionary developments I have ever seen, I don't know the like of it."[65]

And so it was that a newspaper, the *Wall Street Journal*, engineered a shift in economic policy so powerfully that it set the political and economic agenda of the country for the next eight years and beyond. With the support of the *Journal*, Reagan's cabinet appointees espoused supply-side economics, and the administration was distinguished by dramatic tax cuts, fewer government regulations, and increased military spending. Fervent supply-sider and *Wall Street Journal* editorial writer Paul Craig Roberts became assistant treasury secretary for economic policy.[66] He and other appointees were determined to leave the allocation of resources to the market, give the wealthy more disposable income with which to stimulate the economy, and hope that this would provide the necessary incentives to the poor to work harder. In the end, the political economy of the 1980s in America was shaped largely through the efforts of a newspaper based in lower Manhattan.

The once narrowly focused stock sheet had grown in stature and circulation to become one of the most-read newspapers in the country, and boasting one of the wealthiest reader demographics of any daily newspaper, estimated to have an average annual income of $200,000.[67] The *Wall Street Journal* is also one of the few newspapers whose paid online subscription service is profitable, charging even print subscribers a fee to access online content. This has enlarged the sphere of the newspaper's reach beyond its paper-copy points of sale and helped it to become not only a widely accessible national paper, but an international one as well. In this reach, the *Journal* is not alone. The *New York Times* has also expanded its purview, and after several failed attempts at a West Coast edition, in 1980 it launched a national edition, transmitted by satellite and printed in a multitude of locations around the country. Its average weekday circulation is almost as high outside the New York area as it is inside, and on Sundays, the national edition sells a hundred thousand more copies than the local edition.[68]

Among these three top newspapers, there is some degree of collaboration. None is responsible for shaping the national character of the United States on its own. Although the *New York Times* and the *Washington Post* no longer coproduce the *International Herald Tribune*—it was sold to the *Times* in 2003—the international edition of the *Wall Street Journal* carries some *Washington Post* content.[69] Together, the three papers are largely responsible for setting the political, social, and economic agenda of the country, but they no longer lead the country in circulation. The circulation of the *Wall Street Journal*, 1.8 million copies a day, is surpassed by one newspaper, a paper one hundred fewer years in operation than the *Washington Post*, the *New York Times,* or the *Wall Street Journal.*

Gannett Newspapers and *USA Today*

The Gannett Company has been the largest newspaper chain in the United States since 1979, when, with eighty-one daily newspapers, it overtook Knight-Ridder in circulation, printing 3.2 million copies a day. The company was formed by Frank Gannett, who began his news career at the *Ithaca Daily News*, a newspaper at Cornell University, in 1900. From there he bought half of the *Elmira Gazette* and later the *Elmira Star*, merging them into the *Star-Gazette*. Focusing on upstate New York, he bought papers in Utica and Rochester, where he built the headquarters of his company and merged four papers into two. The resulting papers were the *Rochester Democrat and Chronicle* and the *Times Union.*[70]

After building up a small, regional chain of newspapers and radio and television stations, Frank Gannett died in 1957, and Paul Miller, a Washington correspondent for the Associated Press, was made president and chief executive officer. While at Gannett, he became chairman of the Associated Press and was consequently one of the best-connected and nationally focused newspaper executives in the country. Miller's most significant decision as head of the company was to recruit Al Neuharth from Knight Newspapers, where he had worked at both the *Miami Herald* and the *Detroit Free Press*. Neuharth reasoned that with no family heirs to take over the Gannett company, his chances for advancement would be better at Gannett than at Knight. He was made general manager of the Rochester newspapers in 1963.[71]

Neuharth, like Gannett, had been in newspapers since high school, and after college had produced a statewide sports paper in South Dakota called *SoDak Sports*. It covered every game in every town in the state, including high school, college, and professional games. Neuharth and his partner would drive around collecting scores, trying to use the time difference inside the state line to their advantage while on the road. *SoDak Sports* was a critical success, but it had trouble finding advertisers. It went out of business in 1954, but not before Neuharth established the reputation and the experience of someone who could start a newspaper out of nothing.

While in Miami, Neuharth paid particular attention to the sleepy Cocoa Beach resort up the coast that was becoming the new center of the space race following the launch of Sputnik by the Russians in 1957. The Cape Canaveral area would soon see a population explosion that was being underserved by the area's local newspapers. Though his superiors at Knight Newspapers did not support the idea, Neuharth was determined to launch a paper in the place that was about to become famous for its launches. At Gannett, he had the resources and support to revisit his idea of a Florida newspaper. On behalf of Gannett, he purchased the *Cocoa Tribune* in 1965.

Rather than reengineering the *Tribune*, Neuharth converted its presses to create a brand-new newspaper. After a thorough and clandestine readership study, he designed a seven-and-a-half-column broadsheet with a thin news index down the left side, organized into three sections, "News," "Business," and "Sports," with exhaustive weather coverage. The new paper brought color to the front page and an intense focus on new technology, science, and space. Its staff was culled from across the Gannett chain, many of whom were happy to have a furlough in Florida during winter months. The first issue went out to the public on March 21, 1966, as *Today*, "Florida's Space Age Newspaper," with a planetary-orbit graphic around the O.[72] The publicity campaign surrounding the launch took over every billboard in the county, and though home delivery throughout the county was a constant problem, it had a circulation of 33,000 in just ten weeks.[73] The paper emphasized "one voice": a single, unitary identity for the people of Brevard County, expressed through *Today*. The paper was in every way the culmination of Neuharth's background and the prototype for the new national paper he would soon develop, and its success helped to take the company public in 1967. Having convinced Wall Street bankers of the high rates of return to be had in the newspaper industry, Gannett was listed on the New York Stock Exchange in 1969.

When Gannett bought Combined Communications in 1979, it brought the *Cincinnati Enquirer* and the *Oakland Tribune* under the company umbrella, and the total number of newspapers grew to eighty.[74] Gannett could be considered a national newspaper chain, although it had none of the prestige papers in its stable that Knight Ridder had, nor any of the top-tier papers in the northeast. Reasoning that "when you look at a map of the United States, you will find that Gannett has production and distribution facilities within two hours of at least forty very big markets,"[75] Neuharth initiated "Project NN," a secret research and development initiative to investigate the possibility of producing a national newspaper.[76]

At the same time as the *New York Times*, the *Wall Street Journal,* and the *Washington Post* were all contemplating going national, Neuharth began to survey the country's habits, tastes, and preferences. Two years of market research and audience analysis went into determining whether or not a new paper was viable. Despite competition from the top-tier newspapers, Gannett's real challenge came from television and the new twenty-four-hour news channels that were filling up the cable spectrum. When CNN went on the air in 1980, it extended the terms of news production and reception beyond the morning newspaper and the national news broadcasts at 6 p.m. and 11 p.m. News had become a constant stream of headlines scrolling along the bottom of a television screen, with datelines from around the world. News items were short, plentiful, and available any time of day or night, often when viewers were away from home and in transit, airports, and hotels. Neuharth's research showed that in 1979, 28 million Americans—750,000 a day—traveled by air, 1.5 million people stayed in hotels and motels each night, and 100 million people had moved in the past ten years.[77] *USA Today* could be a little piece of home on the road.

Research also indicated that the new paper had to be in color. It would have to compete not only with television but also with the national newsmagazines. Advertising for top national brands demanded high production values for the display of their goods. The color problem, however, was an enormous logistical hurdle, since the paper would

The *USA Today* newsroom: newspaper and television working together.
Photo by John Neubauer. Courtesy of Time-Life Pictures/Getty Images,
1987.

have to be printed at sixty-four local presses Gannett already owned, and
each one had a different system, using different quality papers, different
inks, and different water. To satisfy advertisers and readers, every single
issue of the paper had to be exactly the same from coast to coast. This
consistency and predictability was only one of the reasons the new
paper was easily compared with a McDonald's Big Mac.

The other reason was the writing. Al Neuharth's introduction on
the front page of the first issue set up what would become the formula
for *USA Today* style: short, bulleted, and alliterative declarations,
written in the first person plural. Most importantly, it aimed to
construct a single, unambiguously American perspective:

> Welcome to *USA Today*. This country's first nationwide, satellite-
> delivered, general interest daily newspaper is published by Gannett,
> the nationwide diversified information company.
>
> *USA Today* is designed and edited to be
>
> 1. enlightening and enjoyable to the nation's readers
> 2. informative and impelling to the nation's leaders
> 3. challenging and competitive to the nation's journalists
> 4. refreshing and rewarding to the nation's advertisers
>
> *USA Today* begins its reach across the USA with a commitment to
> serve as a clear and true mirror that reflects all of our nation's images,

inspects all of our problems, projects all of our opportunities and respects all of our people.

USA Today hopes to serve as a forum for better understanding and unity to make the USA truly one nation.

We hope you will enjoy starting your day with *USA Today* every day.[78]

USA Today was designed to compete with television news. Its stories are short and its color images are plentiful. Even its street-corner vending machines were deliberately designed to look like television sets, with the paper tilted back slightly to reduce overhead glare and the change slot occupying the right-hand side where the dial would be. The blue globe on the white background, taken from the paper's logo, is reminiscent of the image of the world often found in the opening credits of the nightly news. When these boxes appeared on the street next to other newspapers', they encouraged readers to see the front page of the paper as a screen. And like weather and sports, television is a national pastime that competes for prominent position in the pages of *USA Today*.

USA Today box with other news boxes in Coral Gables, Florida, October 16, 1995. AP Photo/Rick Bowmer.

The paper's four sections reflected the new logic of newspaper content, which emphasized lifestyle information, celebrity publicity, and a glossy envelope in which to insert luxury goods advertising: "News," "Money," "Sports," and "Life," in that order. It was also a close companion to the new era of Reaganomics heralded by the *Wall Street Journal*, and the official launch party of the paper on the Washington Mall boasted invited guests such as Reagan himself, the Speaker of the House of Representatives Tip O'Neill, and the Senate majority leader Howard Baker Jr.

The most significant aspect of *USA Today*'s design and focus is the way it represents and constructs the nation. News briefs are printed from all fifty states, and all fifty states are graphically depicted every day. A map of the United States is found in the detailed full-color weather map that distinguishes every issue, but it is found elsewhere in the pages of the paper as well. The map serves to bind the country together even as its daily shadings reflect voting trends, age distribution, income levels, and all manner of polling and census data that might otherwise appear divisive. By reflecting its geographic entirety as a single entity rather than fractured by region or state, the United States are presented as an indivisible whole by the paper. The use of the first person plural also helps to smooth over the separations. Traditional journalistic impartiality is replaced with news of what "we" are doing and what is happening to "us." A Sports section headline urged, "Say it, sports fans: We're not going to take it any more,"[79] while a Money section headline warned, "Don't be market-shy: We're here to help."[80] A Life story announced that "we're hard-wired to be hooked by horror,"[81] while another informed us of "the writers we're reading."[82] News in the front section has been that "we're far less exposed to dangers of dioxin,"[83] "we're having bacon and eggs for breakfast—again,"[84] "we're so complacent, it's almost scary,"[85] and "we're eating more garlic."[86] One particularly self-reflexive headline noted that "we're obsessed with trivia."[87]

Graphically *USA Today* makes abundant use of pie charts, tables, bar graphs, and any other available means to display, with as few words as possible, a trend in one direction or the other. Every section of the paper contains "USA Snapshots," featuring a simple trend, graphically displayed, relating to one of the four news areas. The average distance traveled on summer vacation, for example, is displayed with an icon of a car climbing up a bar graph made of asphalt. "Voices Across the USA" shows reader photographs next to their answers to the question of the day, the range of possible opinions reduced to a handful of people from the paper's database.[88] The editorial page is typically centered on a single issue, determined by the paper's editorial board, with two sides represented, simplifying the top issues of the day into easily digestible "pro" or "con" positions. The research firm Louis Harris and Associates, acquired by Gannett in 1975 to undertake readership surveys to help guide the direction of the paper, provides a constant supply of data about Americans from which to construct news stories. Unlike other newspapers with a national focus and distribution, the newspaper does not set the news agenda so much as reflect what it imagines Americans are already thinking.

The paper was originally designed to be read in twenty-five minutes, and it was written at a level that a fifteen-year-old could grasp, although the average age of readers is forty-five.[89] The initial twenty-five-cent cover price was below that of other major papers, and although *USA Today* took five years to show a profit, the circulation of the paper, which was at first based mainly on single-copy newsstand sales, rose steadily. In 1986 it overtook the *Wall Street Journal*, with research that claimed *USA Today* had 4.7 million daily readers buying 1.5 million papers. Circulation hit 2 million in 1987.[90] By this time, the paper was also available in more than fifty other countries, widely distributed in the world's hotel rooms and airports, just like its precursor, CNN.

The format of *USA Today* has been widely emulated by other newspapers, particularly in the use of color and maps. The *New York Times* began using full color in its book review section in 1993, followed by other Sunday sections including Travel, Arts and Leisure, and Real Estate. The front-page photograph appeared in color for the first time in 1996, and a full-page weather map was added. Similar changes have taken place at smaller newspapers around the country.

With twenty-four-hour news channels in most markets, all-news radio, and the Internet, the newspaper faces more competition now than ever before. For the most part, the industry's response to this competition has been to consolidate, cut back, and crop. With some notable exceptions— the *New York Times*, the *Wall Street Journal,* and the *Washington Post* included—less money is devoted to newsgathering, and coverage of local news has disappeared. The success of the *New York Times* and other elite papers rests on the targeting of elite readers, just as the success of all contemporary newspapers rests largely on their ability to create new audiences rather than creating new papers or more comprehensive coverage. *USA Today* and Gannett are more typical of contemporary newspapers in their brevity and scope of news. In a multimedia environment, the printed news page must struggle for survival.

Notes

1. Richard Shepard, *The Paper's Papers: A Reporter's Journey Through the Archives of the* New York Times (New York: Random House, 1996), 131.

2. Susan E. Tifft and Alex S. Jones. *The Trust: The Private and Powerful Family Behind the* New York Times (Boston: Little, Brown, and Co., 1999), 52.

3. Tifft and Jones, 46.

4. Shepard, *Paper's Papers,* 68.

5. Shepard, *Paper's Papers,* 55.

6. Shepard, *Paper's Papers,* 113.

7. Tifft and Jones, *The Trust,* 56.

8. Elmer Davis, *The History of the* New York Times, 1851–1921 (New York: New York Times Co., 1921), 339.

9. Davis, *History,* 363.

10. Clyde Haberman, "Banner Headlines and Comic Strips," *New York Times,* 14 November 2001.

11. Davis, *History,* 331.

12. Tifft and Jones, *The Trust,* 120.

13. Shepard, *Paper's Papers,* 236.

14. Tifft and Jones, *The Trust,* 95–97.

15. *New York Times,* 18 May 1954.

16. Arthur Gelb, *City Room* (New York: Putnam, 2003), 104.

17. Gelb, *City Room,* 102–103.

18. Gelb, *City Room,* 76.

19. Gelb, *City Room,* 77.

20. Shepard, *Paper's Papers,* 215.

21. James Reston, *Deadline: A Memoir* (New York: Random House, 1991).

22. Neil Hickey, "The Cost of Not Publishing: The *New York Times* Decided Not to Print What It Knew about the Bay of Pigs Invasion. Later, There Were Some Regrets," *Columbia Journalism Review* 40, no. 4 (2001): 50.

23. Shepard, *Paper's Papers,* 83.

24. Shepard, *Paper's Papers,* 102.

25. Neil Sheehan, "Vietnam Archive: Pentagon Study Traces 3 Decades of Growing US Involvement," *New York Times,* 13 June 1971.

26. Anthony Lewis, *Written Into History: Pulitzer Prize Winning Reporting of the Twentieth Century from the* New York Times (New York: Times Books, 2001), xiii.

27. W. Parkman Rankin, *The Practice of Newspaper Management* (New York: Praeger, 1986), 103.

28. Howard Bray, *The Pillars of the Post: The Making of a News Empire in Washington* (New York: Norton, 1984), 5.

29. Maurine Beasley and Sheila Gibbons, *Taking Their Place: A Documentary History of Women and Journalism* (Washington, D.C.: American University Press, 1993), 161.

30. Rankin, *Newspaper Management,* 106.

31. Bray, *Pillars of the Post,* 9.

32. Bray, *Pillars of the Post,* 16.

33. Rankin, *Newspaper Management,* 107.

34. Bray, *Pillars of the Post,* 2.

35. Bray, *Pillars of the Post,* 25.

36. "Vietnam: The Public's Need to Know," *Washington Post,* 17 June 1971.

37. "New Financial Section Starts," *Washington Post,* 14 April 1980.

38. "Washington Business Regional and Economic Index," *Washington Post,* 14 April 1980.

39. "Washington's Top 60," *Washington Post,* 14 April 1980.

40. Edward E. Scharff, *Worldly Power: The Making of the Wall Street Journal* (New York, Beaufort, 1986), 43.

41. "Broad Street Gossip; Watch for Bargains," *Wall Street Journal,* 30 October 1929.

42. "Pressure Continues: Stocks Sink Lower Under Record Volume of Liquidation," *Wall Street Journal,* 30 October 1929.

43. "Closing Rally Vigorous," *New York Times,* 30 October 1929.

44. Scharff, *Worldly Power,* 57.

45. Scharff, *Worldly Power,* 58–63.

46. Scharff, *Worldly Power,* 64–66.

47. Scharff, *Worldly Power,* 79.

48. Scharff, *Worldly Power,* 88.

49. Scharff, *Worldly Power,* 90.

50. Scharff, *Worldly Power,* 100.

51. Scharff, *Worldly Power,* 102–103.

52. Scharff, *Worldly Power,* 105.

53. Scharff, *Worldly Power,* 154.

54. A. Kent McDougall, "Bible's Runner-Up," *Wall Street Journal,* 17 March 1966.

55. Jim Hyatt, "The Cricket Industry: It's Small and Noisy But Fairly Important," *Wall Street Journal,* 28 May 1970.

56. W. Stewart Pinkerton, "The Komodo Dragon, Big, Mean and Hungry, Is Eager for Visitors," *Wall Street Journal,* 7 October 1971.

57. Scharff, *Worldly Power,* 110.

58. Scharff, *Worldly Power,* 157.

59. "America's Most Surprising Newspaper," *Wall Street Journal* display ad, 30 March 1977.

60. Deirdre Carmody, "Dow Jones Gives Up on *National Observer*; Will Cease Publication," *New York Times,* 1 July 1977.

61. Scharff, *Worldly Power,* 255.

62. Paul Craig Roberts, "The Economic Case for Kemp-Roth," *Wall Street Journal,* 1 August 1978.

63. David S. Broder, *Behind the Front Page: A Candid Look at How the News Is Made* (New York: Simon and Schuster, 1987), 123–124.

64. Paul Craig Roberts, "Political Economy," *Wall Street Journal,* 28 February 1980.

65. Robert W. Merry and Kenneth H. Bacon, "Supply Side Economics," *Wall Street Journal,* 18 February 1981.

66. "Supply Side Economics."

67. Ken Auletta, "Family Business," *New Yorker,* 3 November 2003.

68. Audit Bureau of Circulation's Fast Fax Reader Profile Study for the six-month period ended 31 March 2004.

69. Auletta, "Family Business," 56.

70. Ellis Cose, *The Press: Inside America's Most Powerful Newspaper Empires—From the Newsrooms to the Boardrooms* (New York: William Morrow and Co., 1989), 287.

71. Peter Prichard, *The Making of McPaper: The Inside Story of USA Today* (Kansas City and New York: Andrews McMeel & Parker, 1987), 53–54.

72. Prichard, *McPaper*, 59–61.

73. Prichard, *McPaper*, 68.

74. Prichard, *McPaper*, 77.

75. Prichard, *McPaper*, 88.

76. Prichard, *McPaper*, 83.

77. William H. Jones, "Gannett Airs 2 Prototypes for New Daily," *Washington Post*, 25 June 1981.

78. *USA Today*, 15 September 1982.

79. "Say It, Sports Fans," *USA Today*, 4 September 2002.

80. Susan Scherreik, "Don't Be Market Shy, We're Here to Help," *USA Today*, 3 April 2002.

81. Cathy Lynn Grossman, "We're Hard-Wired to be Hooked by Horror," *USA Today*, 17 May 2004.

82. "The Writers We're Reading," *USA Today*, 18 December 2001.

83. Elizabeth Weise, "We're Far Less Exposed to Dangers of Dioxin," *USA Today*, 2 July 2003.

84. Nanci Hellmich, "We're Having Bacon and Eggs for Breakfast—Again," *USA Today*, 26 September 2002.

85. Walter Shapiro, "We're So Complacent, It's Almost Scary," *USA Today*, 15 May 2002.

86. "We're Eating More Garlic," *USA Today*, 19 June 2000.

87. Patrick Cox, "We're Obsessed with Trivia," *USA Today*, 5 October 1994.

88. Prichard, *McPaper*, 124.

89. *"USA Today's* Tomorrow," *Economist*, 25 November 1989; Mediamark Research, Inc., Spring 2004.

90. Prichard, *McPaper*, 341–342.

Conclusion

Over the course of the twentieth century, American newspapers have gone from being the primary source of news and information to being one among many. Radio, television, cable, and the Internet have all cut into the popularity of the printed page. For the first half of the century the newspaper maintained its pride of place, but by the second half television began to challenge the dominance of the newspaper and the ritual of reading afternoon and evening editions. News radio provided instantaneous bulletins around the clock in a way that the newspaper could not match, and cable news soon provided video feed from the furthest reaches of the globe. The Internet blended customized content, accessibility, graphics, unlimited sources, and seemingly endless points of view. As these newer media compete for the attention of newspaper readers, the industry has suffered declines in circulation, budget cutbacks, and ongoing challenges to its perceived relevance. For all that newspapers have achieved in the last century, one does not have to listen too carefully for pronouncements of the death of print.

As the population has shifted from rural to urban to suburban, the task of keeping up with the community in order to support it has become ever more difficult. But the local paper can, and does, do things that no other medium has yet been able to achieve. It provides regular, in-depth coverage of events near and far, in sections organized by topic, and delivered in the same package to everyone. When newspapers are successful, they give readers a daily snapshot of the world they live in that makes that world more comprehensible. For its cost, it is a remarkably affordable delivery mechanism for the information needed to conduct one's daily life. Newspapers are central to a democratic society, but they have other functions as well. They keep readers informed, but they are also an engine behind the construction and maintenance of strong communities locally and nationally. When they falter, we must ask what else will suffer as a result.

The newspaper is a place where communities are formed. To have one's name in the paper is a sign of participation in social life. In his survey of local weeklies, Morris Janowitz found that the newspaper functioned to democratize prestige, that people read the paper to see people they knew—and even those they didn't—mentioned. The newspaper was an extension of their real life social networks.[1] It is on the editorial pages of the local newspaper that the community communicates with itself. It sees what others think and responds in kind. Those pages stand as a testament to the times of that place, and they are available to all who want to be involved. Over the century, reporters, editors, publishers, and owners have believed this to be true. They have used their newspapers to campaign for what they thought their communities needed, to expose wrongdoing, to celebrate causes big and small, to announce what had happened and what was about to happen, and to document the everyday, every day.

As the newspaper industry gained its own prestige over the century, the number of papers rose and their circulations skyrocketed, from over 27 million in 1920 to over 62 million in 1970.[2] Since the 1970s, however, both the number of newspapers in operation and their readership have declined. In the 1920s, more than five hundred cities had competing dailies, while it is estimated that 98 percent of American cities now have only one daily newspaper.[3] Larger and larger chains have concentrated the industry into fewer hands, with independently owned newspapers now few and far between. By the 1990s, 80 percent of daily papers in the United States were owned by a chain. As chain ownership grows, newspapers across the country have come to look and sound the same, sharing content across the vast geography of the nation. This makes them less able to speak to, and for, the local reader. When staff writers are cut to achieve economies of scale across a chain, one voice is heard on a subject—on sports, news, or the latest movie—instead of many.

The papers that have survived are more beholden to the bottom line and driven by the pressure to achieve wider profit margins. As a result, they have grown increasingly dependent on advertising for support, with news content tailored to wrap around ads for luxury goods targeted to the most affluent segments of the population. New sections have sprung up to encase consumer goods advertising: Wheels, Homes, Styles, and Technology now nest among the news, sports and entertainment sections.

Not all that has befallen the newspaper industry has been self-induced. The shift toward concentration of ownership has mirrored the growth patterns of other industries, including those that were once reliable local advertisers. When local department stores, hardware stores, and pharmacies were replaced by national chains, newspapers lost an important source of ad revenue. National chains no longer have to advertise individual products for sale as much as they have to construct brand identities, and for this, television is well suited. Advertisers have also turned to newer media, where they can target more specific audiences. The loss of classified advertising to online sites has been a direct blow to newspapers, a source of revenue that was once the cornerstone of newspaper profits.[4]

The audience for newspapers continues to get older, while younger readers increasingly seek their news online. In an attempt to capture the younger market, newspapers have tried to become more like the Internet in their presentation: shorter stories with brighter graphics, and news cycles that are sped up on twenty-four-hour schedules. The space devoted to serious news coverage has shrunk and gossip, celebrity publicity, lifestyle, and "infotainment" occupy more and more column inches. For journalists, this means there is less time to get stories from the event to the page, less space to fit them in, and less of the detail that once distinguished the newspaper from other forms of mass media.[5]

The news website has offered some relief to news corporations fearful of losing readers. Most major newspapers now offer an online version, and news companies have begun to buy other content delivery sites as well. The New York Times Company has purchased the online encyclopedia About.com, and the Washington Post Company now owns the arts and culture site Slate.com. Three of the largest newspaper companies, Gannett, Knight Ridder, and the Tribune Company have joined together in Topix.net, an online company that sorts and tracks Internet news.[6] Of these moves one thing is certain: newspapers are hedging their bets against who their readers will be in the future.

These two developments describe the current state of the news: corporate ownership on one hand, putting out papers in chains that sound the same across the country; and on the other hand, smaller, customized news delivered via websites that track the age, location, and income level of each reader. In neither case is the fate of the locale entirely secure. Who will mount the grand campaigns of the 21st century for new hospitals, roads, bridges, and schools? Who will advocate for the less fortunate reader and make sure their voice is heard? And how will people hear of this news?

The question of newspaper readership has become ever more in doubt as the industry endures new challenges in circulation. The summer of 2004 saw the revelation of a number of newspaper circulation scandals by the Audit Bureau of Circulation: several papers were artificially inflating the number of paid subscriptions and newsstand sales. At *Newsday* this resulted in a legal case brought forward by the paper's advertisers, who claimed that the rates they had paid to advertise were consequently too high.[7] It was also discovered that at many of the country's largest and most admired newspapers, including the *New York Times*, the *Miami Herald*, the *Wall Street Journal*, and the *Boston Globe*, large numbers of subscriptions were in fact being paid for by sponsors, rather than readers. Adding to these pressures faced by mainstream newspapers has been the proliferation of free dailies in cities such as New York, Washington, Philadelphia, Boston, and Chicago, which increasingly draw readers and advertisers away from traditional papers with cover prices, particularly among commuters.[8] These new developments have begun to cast serious doubt on whether the mainstream media's claims to a robust and solid audience base can be taken for granted, and whether or not that audience can be counted on to pay for content in the future.

With thousands of individual investigators networked together sharing pieces of information, weblogs, or "blogs," now provide 24-hour scrutiny on mainstream reporting. The outcomes of this new dynamic have already been significant. Top tier news organizations, including the *New York Times* and *USA Today*, have, in the last several years, suffered damage to their credibility on charges of plagiarism. The spate of recent scandals has refueled the debate about journalistic ethics, including discussions about mechanisms to achieve transparency in sources, fact-checking, and procedure.

The move online might signal something of a return to the 19th century news world, when personal journalism was the hallmark of the industry. Before notions of "objectivity" were aspired to, readers followed papers run by outgoing personalities like Pulitzer and Hearst. But personal journalism existed in an environment of vibrant readership, when people were likely to read more than one different newspaper per day. In order to maximize their audience, newspaper owners, over time, grew less partisan in their approach, and the sharp edges were flattened out to appeal more widely. This was a decision motivated as much by profit as anything else, but readers responded to it. The difference between that era and this one is that when something appeared in the newspaper, a critical mass of readers would see it, whereas the personal journalism of online reporting now reaches a splintered audience. There are online communities, but they do not have to exist in a specific geographic location and they do not have to be accountable to a particular place. For the job of constructing and maintaining communities, towns, cities, and states, the newspaper is a uniquely suited medium.

Notes

1. Morris Janowitz, *The Community Press in an Urban Setting* (Chicago: University of Chicago Press, 1952).

2. Historical Statistics of the United States: Colonial Times to 1970. Washington: U.S. Dept. of Commerce, Bureau of the Census, Series R 224–231, 809.

3. Doris Graber, *Mass Media and American Politics* (Washington, DC: CQ Press, 1997).

4. Leo Bogart, "Newspapers: Figure Out How to Give Readers a Choice and Take Your Eye off the Quarterly Earnings Report," *Media Studies Journal* (spring/summer 1999): 60–68.

5. John Pavlik, "The Impact of Technology on Journalism," *Journalism Studies* 1, no. 2 (2000): 229–237.

6. Katharine Q. Seelye, "Newspaper Giants Buy Web News Monitor," *New York Times*, 23 March 2005, C14.

7. James Madore, "Advertisers Accepting Rebates; Nearly Half of More Than 40,000 Parties Are Settling, Including Seven of Newspaper's 10 Largest Ad Buyers," *Newsday*, 29 October 2004, A64.

8. Piet Bakker, "Free Daily Newspapers–Business Models and Strategies," *The International Journal on Media Management* 4, no. 3 (2002): 180–187.

Bibliography

Agran, Edward Gale. *Too Good a Town: William Allen White, Community, and the Emerging Rhetoric of Middle America.* Fayetteville: University of Arkansas Press, 1999.

Akin, Edward. *Flagler: Rockefeller Partner and Florida Baron.* Gainesville: University Press of Florida, 1992.

Allen, Frederick Lewis. *Only Yesterday: An Informal History of the 1920s.* New York: Harper and Row, 1931.

Aucoin, James L. "The Re-emergence of American Investigative Journalism, 1960–1975," *Journalism History* 21, no.1 (1995): 3–15.

Auletta, Ken. "Family Business." *New Yorker,* November 3, 2003, 54–67.

Bailey, Beth and David Farber. *The Columbia Guide to America in the 1960s.* New York: Columbia University Press, 2001.

Bakker, Piet. "Free Daily Newspapers—Business Models and Strategies." *The International Journal on Media Management* 4, no. 3 (2002): 180–187.

Baldasty, Gerald. *E. W. Scripps and the Business of Newspapers.* Urbana and Chicago: University of Illinois Press, 1999.

Ballinger, J. Kenneth. *Miami Millions: the Dance of the Dollars in the Great Florida Land Boom of 1925.* New York: Franklin Press, Inc., 1936.

Bass, Jack. "Newspaper Monopoly." *American Journalism Review* 21 (July 1999).

Baxandall, Rosalyn and Elizabeth Ewen. *Picture Windows: How the Suburbs Happened.* New York: Basic Books, 2001.

Beasley, Maurine and Sheila Gibbons. *Taking Their Place: A Documentary History of Women and Journalism.* Washington, D.C.: American University Press, 1993.

Benjaminson, Peter. *Death in the Afternoon: America's Newspaper Giants Struggle for Survival.* Kansas City, MO: Andrews McMeel & Parker, 1984.

Berges, Marshall. *The Life and Times of Los Angeles.* New York: Atheneum, 1984.

Bogart, Leo. "Newspapers: Figure out How to Give Readers a Choice and Take your Eye off the Quarterly Earnings Report," *Media Studies Journal* (spring/ summer 1999): 60–68.

Bradlee, Ben. *A Good Life: Newspapering and Other Adventures*. New York: Touchstone, 1996.

Bray, Howard. *The Pillars of the Post: The Making of a News Empire in Washington*. New York: Norton, 1984.

Brendon, Piers. *The Life and Death of the Press Barons*. London: Atheneum, 1983.

Broder, David S. *Behind the Front Page: A Candid Look at How the News Is Made*. New York: Simon and Schuster, 1987.

Buni, Andrew. *Robert L. Vann of the Pittsburgh Courier: Politics and Black Journalism*. Pittsburgh: University of Pittsburgh Press, 1974.

Canaan, Gareth. "Part of the Loaf: Economic Conditions of Chicago's African-American Working Class During the 1920s," *Journal of Social History* 35, no. 1 (2001): 147–74.

Casserly, Jack. *Scripps: The Divided Dynasty*. New York: Donald I. Fine, Inc., 1993.

Cavanaugh, Darien. *Huelga! Labor Activism and Unrest in Ybor City: 1886 to 1950*. Tampa, FL: Ybor City Museum Exhibit Catalogue, 2002.

Chandler, David Leon. *Henry Flagler: The Astonishing Life and Times of the Visionary Robber Baron Who Founded Florida*. New York: Macmillan, 1986.

Chapman, John. *Tell it to Sweeney: An Informal History of the New York Daily News*. Garden City, NY: Doubleday, 1961.

Claiborne, Jack. *The Charlotte Observer: Its Time and Place 1869–1986*. Chapel Hill: University of North Carolina Press, 1986.

Claussen, Dane. "The Myths and Realities of Newspaper Acquisition Costs: Fiduciary Responsibilities, Fungibility of Assets, Winners' Penalties and Excess Cash 'Problems'." Paper delivered at AEJMC Convention, New Orleans, LA, August 4–7, 1999.

Cleghorn, Reese. "Florida's Newspaper Set a Fast Pace." *American Journalism Review* 18 (November 1996).

Coleridge, Nicholas. *Paper Tigers: The Latest Greatest Newspaper Tycoons and How They Won the World*. London: Heinemann Ltd., 1993.

Cooper, Caryl A. "The Chicago *Defender*: Filling in the Gaps for the Office of Civilian Defense, 1941–1945," *The Western Journal of Black Studies* 23, no. 1 (1999): 111–118.

Cose, Ellis. *The Press: Inside America's Most Powerful Newspaper Empires—From the Newsrooms to the Boardrooms*. New York: William Morrow and Co., 1989.

Cox, James M. *Journey Through My Years*. New York: Simon and Schuster, 1946.

Cranberg, Gilbert, Randall Bezanson, and John Soloski. *Taking Stock: Journalism and the Publicly Traded Newspaper Company*. Ames, IA: Iowa State University Press, 2001.

Davis, Elmer. *The History of the New York Times, 1851–1921*. New York: New York Times Co., 1921.

Demers, David. *The Menace of the Corporate Newspaper: Fact or Fiction?* Ames: Iowa State University Press, 1996.

DeSantis, Alan D. "A Forgotten Leader: Robert S. Abbott and the Chicago *Defender* from 1910–1920," *Journalism History* 23, no. 2 (1997): 63–71.

Dickstein, Morris. *Gates of Eden: American Culture in the Sixties*. New York: Basic Books, 1977.

Domke, David. "The Black Press in the 'Nadir' of African Americans," *Journalism History* 20, nos. 3–4 (1994): 131–138.

Downie, Leonard Jr. and Robert G. Kaiser. *The News about the News*. New York: Vintage, 2003.

Emery, Michael, Edwin Emery, and Nancy L. Roberts. *The Press and America: An Interpretive History of the Mass Media,* 9th ed. Pearson Allyn and Bacon, 1999.

Fellig, Arthur. *Weegee By Weegee: An Autobiography*. New York: Ziff-Davis, 1961.

Farrar, Hayward. *The Baltimore Afro-American, 1892–1950*. Westport, CT: Greenwood Press, 1998.

Felsenthal, Carol. *Power, Privilege and the Post: The Katharine Graham Story*. New York: Seven Stories, 1999.

Finkle, Lee. *Forum for Protest: The Black Press During World War II*. Cranbury, New Jersey: Associated University Presses, Inc., 1975.

Fogelson, Robert M. *Fragmented Metropolis: Los Angeles, 1850–1930*. Berkeley: University of California Press, 1993.

Frazer, William and John J. Guthrie Jr. *The Florida Land Boom: Speculation, Money, and the Banks*. Westport, CT: Quorum Books, 1995.

Friedricks, William B. *Covering Iowa: The History of the Des Moines Register and Tribune Company, 1849–1985*. Ames: Iowa State University Press, 2000.

Friedricks, William B. *Henry E. Huntington and the Creation of Southern California*. Columbus, OH: Ohio State University, 1992.

Fullilove, Mindy. *Root Shock: How Tearing Up City Neighborhoods Hurts America, and What We Can Do About It*. New York: Ballantine, 2004.

Gabler, Neal. *Walter Winchell: Gossip, Power and the Culture of Celebrity*. New York: Alfred A. Knopf, 1994.

Gans, Herbert. *Deciding What's News*. New York: Vintage Books, 1979.

Gauvreau, Emile. *The Scandal Monger*. New York: Macaulay, 1932.

Gelb, Arthur. *City Room*. New York: Putnam, 2003.

Ghiglione, Loren, ed. *The Buying and Selling of America's Newspapers*. Indianapolis: R. J. Berg, 1984.

Glessing, Robert. *The Underground Press in America*. Indianapolis: Indiana University Press, 1970.

Goulden, Joseph C. *Fit to Print: A.M. Rosenthal and His Times*. Secaucus, NJ: Lyle Stewart, 1988.

Graber, Doris. *Mass Media and American Politics*. Washington, DC: CQ Press, 1997.

Griffith, Sally Foreman. *Home Town News: William Allen White and the Emporia Gazette*. New York: Oxford University Press, 1989.

Grossman, James R. *Land of Hope: Chicago, Black Southerners, and the Great Migration*. Chicago: University of Chicago Press, 1989.

Gruber Garvey, Ellen. "Out of the Mainstream and Into the Streets." In *Perspectives on American Book History,* edited by Scott E. Casper, Joanne D. Chaison, and Jeffrey D. Groves. Amherst: University of Massachusetts Press, 2002.

Gruen, John. *The New Bohemia: Art, Music, Drama, Sex, Film, Dance in New York's East Village*. New York: Grosset and Dunlap, 1966.

Guimond, James. *American Photography and the American Dream*. Chapel Hill: University of North Carolina Press, 1991.

Halberstam, David. *The Powers That Be*. New York: Knopf, 1979.

Hannigan, William. *New York Noir*. New York: Rizzoli, 1999.

Harrison, S. L. *Cavalcade of Journalists, 1900–2000*. Miami: Wolf Den Books, 2002.

Hart, Jack. *The Information Empire: The Rise of the Los Angeles Times and the Times Mirror Corporation*. Washington DC: University Press of America, 1981.

Heimer, Mel. *The Long Count: The Legendary Battle for the Heavyweight Championship*. New York: Atheneum, 1969.

Hickey, Neil. "The Cost of Not Publishing: The *New York Times* Decided Not to Print What It Knew about the Bay of Pigs Invasion. Later, There Were Some Regrets," *Columbia Journalism Review* 40, no. 4 (2001).

Historical Statistics of the United States: Colonial Times to 1970. Washington: U.S. Dept. of Commerce, Bureau of the Census, Series R 224–231.

Hohenberg, John. *The Pulitzer Prize Story: News Stories, Editorials, Cartoons, and Pictures from the Pulitzer Prize Collection at Columbia University*. New York: Columbia University Press, 1959.

Janowitz, Morris. *The Community Press in an Urban Setting*. Glencoe, IL: Free Press, 1952.

Jefferson, Robert F. "African Americans in the U.S. Army During World War II." In *A Historic Context for the African American Military Experience*, edited by Steven D. Smith and James A. Ziegler. U.S. Army Construction Engineering Research Laboratories (USACERL), 1998.

Johnson, Michael L. *The New Journalism: The Underground Press, the Artists of Nonfiction, and Changes in the Established Media*. Lawrence: University Press of Kansas, 1971.

Johnson, Walter. *William Allen White's America*. New York: Henry Holt and Co., 1947.

Jordan, William G. *Black Newspapers and America's War For Democracy, 1914–1920*. Chapel Hill: University of North Carolina Press, 2001.

Jose, Victor. *The Free Paper in America: Struggle for Survival*. Richmond, IN: Graphic Press, 2000.

Keeler, Robert. *Newsday: A Candid History of the Respectable Tabloid*. New York: William Morrow, 1990.

Kessler, Lauren. *The Dissident Press: Alternative Journalism in American History*. Beverley Hills, CA: Sage Publications, 1984.

Kornweibel, Theodore, Jr. "The Most Dangerous of all Negro Journals: Federal Efforts to Suppress the Chicago Defender During World War I." *American Journalism* 11, no. 2 (1994): 154–168.

Lauer Research, Inc. *Media Professionals and Their Industry*. Report. July 20, 2004.

Lee, Alfred McClung. *The Daily Newspaper in America*. New York: Macmillan Co., 1937.

Lendt, David L. *Ding: The Life of Jay Norwood Darling*. Ames: Iowa State University Press, 1989.

Leuchtenberg, William. *The Perils of Prosperity, 1914–1932*. 2nd ed. Chicago: University of Chicago Press, 1958.

Lewis, Anthony. *Written Into History: Pulitzer Prize Winning Reporting of the Twentieth Century from the New York Times.* New York: Times Books, 2001.

Lippman, Walter. *Public Opinion.* New York: Macmillan, 1922.

Lutz, William W. *The News of Detroit: How a Newspaper and a City Grew Together.* Boston and Toronto: Little, Brown and Co., 1973.

Martin, Shannon. *Newspapers of Record in a Digital Age: From Hot Type to Hot Link.* Westport, CT: Praeger, 1998

Marzolf, Marion. *Up From the Footnote: A History of Women Journalists.* New York: Hastings House, 1977.

McAuliffe, Kevin. *The Great American Newspaper: The Rise and Fall of the Village Voice.* New York: Charles Scribner's Sons, 1978.

McDougal, Dennis. *Privileged Son: Otis Chandler and the Rise and Fall of the L.A. Times Dynasty.* Perseus, 2001.

McGivena, Leo E. *The News: The First Fifty Years of New York's Picture Newspaper.* New York: News Syndicate Company, 1969.

Meyer, Philip. "The Influence Model and Newspaper Business." *Newspaper Research Journal* 25, no. 1 (2004): 66–83.

Miller, Penny M. *Kentucky Politics and Government: Do We Stand United?* Lincoln: University of Nebraska Press, 1994.

Mills, George. *Harvey Ingham and Gardner Cowles, Sr: Things Don't Just Happen.* Ames: Iowa State University Press, 1977.

Moore, Samuel T. "Those Terrible Tabloids," *The Independent,* March 6, 1926, 264.

Morison, Bradley L. *Sunlight on Your Doorstep: The Minneapolis Tribune's First Hundred Years.* Minneapolis: Ross & Hayes, 1966.

Mott, Frank Luther. *American Journalism: A History of Newspapers in the United States Through 250 Years, 1690 to 1940.* New York and London: Routledge, 2000.

Myrdal, Gunnar. *An American Dilemma: The Negro Problem and Modern Democracy.* New York: Harper, 1944.

Nasaw, David. *The Chief: The Life of William Randolph Hearst.* Boston and New York: Houghton Mifflin Company, 2000.

Newton, Virgil M. Jr. *Crusade for Democracy.* Ames: Iowa State University Press, 1961.

Nolan, David. *Fifty Feet in Paradise: The Booming of Florida.* New York: Harcourt Brace, 1984.

Ogden, Christopher. *Legacy: A Biography of Moses and Walter Annenberg.* Boston: Little, Brown and Company, 1999.

O'Hagan, John. Director. *Wonderland.* 1997. Film.

Olmsted, Kathryn, "An American Conspiracy': The Post-Watergate Press and the CIA," *Journalism History* 19, no. 2 (summer 1993): 51–58.

Orrick, Bentley and Harry Crumpacker. *The Tampa Tribune: A Century of Florida Journalism.* Tampa: University of Tampa Press, 1998.

Pavlik, John. "The Impact of Technology on Journalism," *Journalism Studies* 1, no. 2 (2000): 229–237.

Peck, Abe. *Uncovering the Sixties: The Life and Times of the Underground Press.* New York: Citadel, 1991.

Pierce, Robert. *A Sacred Trust: Nelson Poynter and the St. Petersburg Times.* Gainesville, FL: University of Florida Press, 1993.

Pleasants, Julian. *Orange Journalism: Voices From Florida Newspapers.* Gainesville: University Press of Florida, 2003.

Plummer, Brenda Gayle. *Rising Wind: Black Americans and U.S. Foreign Affairs, 1935–1960.* Chapel Hill: University of North Carolina Press, 1996.

Pozzetta, George E. *Immigrants on the Land: Agriculture, Rural Life, and Small Towns.* London: Taylor and Francis, 1991.

Pratte, Alfred. *Gods Within the Machine: A History of the American Society of Newspaper Editors, 1923–1993.* Westport, CT: Praeger, 1995.

Prichard, Peter. *The Making of McPaper: The Inside Story of USA Today.* Kansas City and New York: Andrews McMeel & Parker, 1987.

Pride, Armistead S. and Clint C. Wilson II. *A History of the Black Press.* Washington, DC: Howard University Press, 1997.

Rankin, W. Parkman. *The Practice of Newspaper Management.* New York: Praeger, 1986.

Reston, James. *Deadline: A Memoir.* New York: Random House, 1991.

Risser, James V. "Endangered Species," *American Journalism Review* 20 (June 1998).

Roberts, Chalmers M. *In the Shadow of Power: The Story of the Washington Post.* Washington, DC: Seven Locks Press, 1989.

Roberts, Gene, Thomas Kunkel, and Charles Layton, eds. *Leaving Readers Behind: The Age of Corporate Newspapering.* Fayetteville: U of Arkansas Press, 2001.

Rosenberg, Jerry. *Inside the Wall Street Journal: The History and the Power of Dow Jones and Company and America's Most Influential Newspaper.* New York: MacMillan, 1982.

Rudenstine, David. *The Day the Presses Stopped: A History of the Pentagon Papers Case.* Berkeley, CA: University of California Press, 1996.

Runyon. Damon. *Trials and Tribulations.* London: Xanadu Publications, 1946.

Ruth, David E. *Inventing the Public Enemy: The Gangster in American Culture, 1918–1934.* Chicago and London: University of Chicago Press, 1996.

Sachsman, David and Warren Sloat. *The Press and the Suburbs: The Daily Newspapers of New Jersey.* New Brunswick, NJ: Center for Urban Policy Research, 1985.

Scharff, Edward E. *Worldly Power: The Making of the Wall Street Journal.* New York: Beaufort, 1986.

Schaub, Diana. "The Spirit of a Free Man." *Public Interest* (summer 2000).

Schroth, Raymond A. *The Eagle and Brooklyn: A Community Newspaper, 1841–1955.* Westport, CT: Greenwood Press, 1974.

Schudson, Michael. *Discovering the News: A Social History of American Newspapers.* New York: Basic Books, 1978.

Schuyler, George Samuel. *Fifty Years of Progress in Negro Journalism.* Pittsburgh: Pittsburgh Courier, 1950.

Scott, Emmett J. *Negro Migration During the War.* New York: Oxford University Press, 1920.

Shepard, Richard. *The Paper's Papers: A Reporter's Journey Through the Archives of The New York Times.* New York: Random House, 1996.

Sloan, William David. *The Media in America: A History*. 5th ed. Northport, AL: Vision Press, 2002.

Smiley, Nixon. *Knights of the Fourth Estate: The Story of the Miami Herald*. Miami: E.A. Seeman, 1974.

Spellman, Charles G. "The Black Press: Setting the Political Agenda During World War II," *Negro History Bulletin* 51 (December 1993).

Stamm, Keith. *Newspaper Use and Community Ties: Toward a Dynamic Theory*. Norwood, NJ: Ablex, 1985.

Starr, Kevin. *Embattled Dreams: California in War and Peace, 1940–1950*. New York and London: Oxford University Press, 2002.

Starr, Kevin. *Material Dreams: Southern California Through the 1920s*. New York and London: Oxford University Press, 1991.

Steinberg, Theodore. *Acts of God: The Unnatural History of Natural Disaster in America*. New York and London: Oxford University Press, 2000.

Stevens, John D. "From the Back of the Foxhole: Black Correspondents in World War II," *Journalism Monographs* 27 (February 1973).

Streitmatter, Rodger. *Mightier Than the Sword: How the News Media Have Shaped American History*. Boulder, CO: Westview Press, 1997.

Sylvie, George. *Time, Change, and the American Newspaper*. Mahwah, NJ: Lawrence Erlbaum Associates, 2002.

Tebbel, John. *The Compact History of the American Newspaper*. New York: Hawthorn Books, 1963.

Theoharis, Athan. "The FBI, the Roosevelt Administration, and the 'Subversive' Press," *Journalism History* 19, no.1 (1993): 3–10.

Thomas, Dana. *The Media Moguls: From Joseph Pulitzer to William S. Paley, Their Lives and Boisterous Times*. New York: G.P. Putnam's Sons, 1981.

Tifft, Susan E. and Alex S. Jones. *The Trust: The Private and Powerful Family Behind the New York Times*. Boston: Little, Brown and Co., 1999.

Villard, Oswald Garrison. *Some Newspapers and Newspaper-men*. New York: Knopf, 1923.

Villard, Oswald Garrison. *The Disappearing Daily: Chapters in American Newspaper Evolution*. New York: Knopf, 1944.

Wachsberger, Ken, ed. *Voices from the Underground: Insider Histories of the Vietnam-Era Underground Press*. Tempe, AZ.: Mica Press, 1993.

Wagner, Rob Leicester. *Red Ink, White Lies: The Rise and Fall of Los Angeles Newspapers, 1920–1962*. Upland, CA: Dragonflyer Press, 2000.

Walker, Juliet E.K. "The Promised Land: The *Chicago Defender* and the Black Press in Illinois: 1862–1970." In *The Black Press in the Middle West, 1865–1985*, edited by Henry Louis Suggs. Westport, CT: Greenwood Press, 1996.

Walker, Stanley. *City Editor*. Baltimore: Johns Hopkins University Press, 1999.

Walton, Mary. "The Selling of Small-Town America," *American Journalism Review* 21 (1999).

Wang, Karissa S. "Tampa's Media Barn: New Complex Unites WFLA-TV, Tampa Tribune and TBO.com," *Electronic Media*, 27 March 2000.

Washburn, Patrick S. "The *Pittsburgh Courier's* Double V Campaign in 1942," *American Journalism* 3, no. 2 (1986): 73–86.

Washburn, Patrick S. *A Question of Sedition: The Federal Government's Investigation of the Black Press During World War II*. New York: Oxford University Press, 1986.

Wells, Ken. *Floating Off the Page: The Best Stories from the Wall Street Journal's "Middle Column."* New York: Wall Street Journal Book, 2003.

Wendt, Lloyd. *Chicago Tribune: The Rise of a Great American Newspaper*. Chicago: Rand McNally and Co., 1979.

Wendt, Lloyd. *The Wall Street Journal: The Story of Dow Jones and the Nation's Business Newspaper*. Chicago: Rand McNally and Co., 1982.

White, William Allen. *The Autobiography of William Allen White*. New York: MacMillan, 1946.

White, William Allen. "Blood of the Conquerors." *Collier's*, 10 March 1923.

Whited, Charles. *Knight: A Publisher in the Tumultuous Century*. New York: Dutton, 1988.

Willey, M. McDonald and Stuart A. Rice. *Communication Agencies and Social Life*. New York and London: McGraw-Hill, 1933.

Williams, Carol and Irwin Touster. *The Washington Post: Views from the Inside*. New York: Prentice-Hall, 1976.

Wolf, Daniel and Edwin Fancher, eds. *The Village Voice Reader*. Garden City, NY: Doubleday & Company, 1962.

Wolseley, Roland E. *The Black Press, U.S.A.* Ames: Iowa State University Press, 1990.

Wyand, Charles. *The Economics of Consumption*. New York: MacMillan Company, 1937.

Wynn, Neil A. *The Afro-American and the Second World War*. New York: Holmes & Meier, 1976.

Index

About the Author

AURORA WALLACE is Assistant Professor in the Department of Culture and Communications at New York University. She received a Ph.D. in Communications from McGill University in Montreal and was a visiting Fulbright Scholar at Columbia University. Her research looks at media, architecture and urban space, 19th and 20th century newspaper and journalism history, and crime in the media.